4

Device Driver Interface / Driver-Kernel Interface Reference Manual

Intel Processors

Published by Prentice-Hall, Inc.
A Division of Simon & Schuster
Englewood Cliffs, New Jersey 07632

IMPORTANT NOTE TO USERS

TRADEMARKS

10 9 8 7 6 5 4 3 2

ISBN 0-13-879529-0

UNIX
PRESS
A Prentice Hall Title

P R E N T I C E   H A L L

ORDERING INFORMATION

UNIX® SYSTEM V RELEASE 4 DOCUMENTATION

To order single copies of UNIX® SYSTEM V Release 4 documentation, please call (201) 767-5937.

ATTENTION DOCUMENTATION MANAGERS AND TRAINING DIRECTORS:

For bulk purchases in excess of 30 copies, please write to:

Corporate Sales
Prentice Hall
Englewood Cliffs, N.J. 07632

Or call: (201) 461-8441.

ATTENTION GOVERNMENT CUSTOMERS:

For GSA and other pricing information, please call (201) 767-5994.

Prentice-Hall International (UK) Limited, *London*
Prentice-Hall of Australia Pty. Limited, *Sydney*
Prentice-Hall Canada Inc., *Toronto*
Prentice-Hall Hispanoamericana, S.A., *Mexico*
Prentice-Hall of India Private Limited, *New Delhi*
Prentice-Hall of Japan, Inc., *Tokyo*
Simon & Schuster Asia Pte. Ltd., *Singapore*
Editora Prentice-Hall do Brasil, Ltda., *Rio de Janeiro*

Introduction

The *Device Driver Interface/Driver–Kernel Interface Reference Manual* provides
reference information needed to write device drivers for UNIX System V Release
4 Multi-Processor for Intel Processors. It describes two device driver interface
specifications: the Device Driver Interface (DDI) and the Driver–Kernel Interface
(DKI). Drivers written to conform to one or both of these interfaces are more
likely to be portable to other environments. DDI and DKI address different
aspects of the compatibility problem, as summarized in Figure 1.

Figure 1: Scope of DDI and DKI

```
processor          DDI
specific           only
routines           (DxD)

processor          DDI          DKI
independent        and          only
routines           DKI          (DxK)
                   (DxDK)

                   supported    supported
                   after        through
                   SVR4 MP      SVR4 MP
```

Each box in Figure 1 represents a different set of interfaces. The "DDI only" set
(indicated throughout this manual with the D*x*D or D*x*X cross-reference code)
are processor-specific and are intended to be supported beyond the current
release. In addition, the D*x*X manual pages are platform-specific. The DDI
described in this manual is specific to UNIX System V for Intel processors. The
"DKI only" set (D*x*K cross-reference code) are processor-independent, but are
not guaranteed to be supported in the next release. As interfaces are removed
from the DDI/DKI, they will be retained in the operating system for at least one
future release to provide compatibility with drivers written to use them.

Any driver interfaces not documented in this manual are specifically not part of
the DDI or DKI. For example, the **poll** entry point, documented in the
Integrated Software Development Guide, is not part of the DDI or DKI, and hence is
not documented in this guide.

Most of the routines, functions, and structures described in this manual are part of both the DDI and the DKI (cross-referenced by DxDK). As Figure 1 shows, drivers written to conform to both interfaces are portable to all computers supporting UNIX System V Release 4 Multi-Processor for Intel Processors, and they will be compatible through and beyond Release 4 Multi-Processor.

NOTE	Note that drivers written to conform with this version of the DDI/DKI may not run on systems running UNIX System V Release 4 or Release 4.1 Enhanced Security, as those releases do not implement the new multiprocessor interfaces.

However, a driver written to conform to both interfaces is not guaranteed to be *binary* compatible with future releases of the operating system. Binary compatibility requires more than just interface definition. It also requires that values for **#define**'s be standardized, for example. The DDI/DKI is a source code interface. Following it is a necessary, but not sufficient, condition for binary compatibility. To understand more completely what is meant by "portable" and "compatible" for the DDI and DKI, the scope of each interface must be more thoroughly explained.

Porting

Software is usually considered portable if it can be adapted to run in a different environment at a lower cost than if one were to rewrite it. The new environment may include a different processor, operating system, and even the language in which the program is written, if a language translator is available. More often, however, software is ported between environments that share an operating system, processor, and source language. The source code is modified to accommodate the differences in compilers, processors, or releases of the operating system.

In the past, device drivers did not port easily for one or more of the following reasons:

■ To enhance functionality, members had been added to kernel data structures accessed by drivers, or the sizes of existing members had been redefined.

- The calling or return syntax of kernel functions had changed.

- Driver developers did not use existing kernel functions where available, or relied on undocumented side effects that were not maintained in the next release.

- Processor-specific code had been scattered throughout the driver when it could have been isolated.

- The proper interfaces and rules for their use had never been clearly documented.

Operating systems are periodically reissued to customers as a way to improve performance, fix bugs, and add new features. This is probably the most common threat to compatibility encountered by developers responsible for maintaining software. Another common problem is upgrading hardware. As new hardware is developed, customers occasionally decide to upgrade to faster, more capable computers of the same family. Although they may run the same operating system as those being replaced, processor-specific code may prevent the software from porting.

Scope of Interfaces

Although application programs have all of the porting problems mentioned, developers attempting to port device drivers have special challenges.

Device drivers are kernel modules that control data transferred to and received from peripheral devices. Although drivers are configured into the UNIX system as part of the kernel, they can be developed independently from the rest of the kernel. If the goal of achieving complete freedom in modifying the kernel is to be reconciled with the goal of compatibility with existing drivers, the interaction between drivers and the kernel must be rigorously regulated. This driver/kernel service interface is one of the three distinguishable interfaces for a driver, summarized as follows:

- Driver–Kernel. I/O System calls result in calls to driver entry point routines. These make up the kernel-to-driver part of the service interface, described in Section 2 of this manual. Drivers may call any of the functions described in Section 3. These are the driver-to-kernel part of the interface.

- Driver–Hardware. Most hardware drivers include an interrupt handling entry point, and may also perform direct memory access (DMA). These and other hardware-specific interactions make up the driver/hardware interface.

- Driver–Boot/Configuration Software. At boot time, the existence of a driver is made known to the system through information in system files, enabling the system to include the driver. The interaction between the driver and the boot and configuration software is the third interface affecting drivers. Refer to the sections on Installable Drivers (ID) in Chapter 3 of the *Integrated Software Development Guide* for more information on this.

Scope of the Device Driver Interface (DDI)

The primary goal of DDI is to facilitate both source and binary portability across successive releases of UNIX System V on a particular machine. Implicit in this goal is an important fact. Although there is only one DKI, each processor product has its own DDI. Therefore, if a driver is ever to be ported to different hardware, special attention must be paid to the machine-specific routines that make up the "DDI only" part of a driver. These include, but are not confined to, the driver/hardware interface (as described in the previous section). Some processor-specific functionality also may belong to the driver/kernel interface, and may not be easy to locate.

To achieve the goal of source and binary compatibility, the functions, routines, and structures specified in the DDI must be used according to these rules.

- Drivers cannot access system state structures (for example, **u** and **sysinfo**) directly.

- For structures external to the driver that may be accessed directly, only the utility functions provided in Section 3 of this manual should be used. More generally, these functions should be used wherever possible.

- The header file **ddi.h** must be included at the end of the list of system header files. This header file "undefines" several macros that are reimplemented as functions. Device driver-specific include files should be listed after **ddi.h** to insure only the DDI/DKI interface is used by the driver.

Scope of the Driver–Kernel Interface (DKI)

As its name implies, the DKI (Driver–Kernel Interface) is a defined service interface for the entry point routines and utility functions specified for communication between the driver and kernel. It does not encompass the driver/hardware or the driver/boot software interface.

Information is exchanged between the driver and kernel in the form of data structures. The DKI specifies the contents of these structures as well as the calling and return syntax of the entry points and utility functions.

The intent of the DKI is to promote source portability across implementations of UNIX System V on different machines, and applies only to System V Release 4 Multi-Processor for Intel Processors. Because the DKI applies only to the driver/kernel interface, it must be understood that the sections of driver code affecting the hardware and boot/configuration interfaces may need to be rewritten, and should be isolated in subroutines as much as possible.

NOTE | Certain interfaces documented in the DKI are not part of the DDI. Driver writers should be aware that the use of these interfaces is not guaranteed to be supported beyond System V Release 4 Multi-Processor.

Uniprocessor vs. Multiprocessor Considerations

This document applies to both uniprocessor and multiprocessor hardware environments. Drivers that are written in such a way that their code may be safely executed on multiple processors concurrently are said to be multithreaded (or multiprocessor-safe). Drivers which are not written in this way are said to be single-threaded. Although the DKI includes interfaces that permit the development of multithreaded drivers, drivers are not required to be multithreaded in order to benefit from conformance to the DDI/DKI. The source portability of DDI/DKI conforming drivers across both uniprocessor and multiprocessor hardware platforms can be summarized as follows:

- Multithreaded drivers which conform to the DDI/DKI will be portable across both uniprocessor and multiprocessor implementations which support the DDI/DKI.

- Single-threaded drivers which conform to the DDI/DKI will be portable across uniprocessor implementations which support the DDI/DKI.

- Multiprocessor implementations which support the DDI/DKI are not required to support single-threaded drivers that conform to the DDI/DKI, although some multiprocessor implementations may choose to support such drivers by preventing concurrent execution of code within a given single-threaded driver.

Driver writers are encouraged to write multithreaded rather than single-threaded drivers, as these will be more widely portable and can benefit from the parallelism inherent on a multiprocessor. Writing a multithreaded driver requires that shared data within the driver be protected against certain forms of concurrent access. This is done by using appropriate locking primitives to prevent concurrent execution of code which accesses a given piece of shared data. This document defines interfaces to several types of locking and synchronization primitives, namely basic locks, read/write locks, sleep locks and synchronization variables. Basic locks and read/write locks are intended for use within multithreaded drivers, while sleep locks and synchronization variables are useful in both single-threaded and multithreaded drivers. The characteristics of the various locking and synchronization primitives are described on the relevant manual pages in Section 3.

Audience

This manual is for experienced C programmers responsible for creating, modifying, or maintaining drivers that run on UNIX System V Release 4 Multi-Processor for Intel Processors and beyond. It assumes that the reader is familiar with UNIX system internals and the advanced capabilities of the C Programming Language. In addition, programmers writing multithreaded drivers are assumed to be familiar with the fundamentals of concurrent programming and the appropriate use of locking primitives to protect shared data.

How to Use This Manual

This manual is organized as follows:

- "Introduction" introduces the DDI, DKI, and other driver interfaces, lists the notational conventions used in this manual, and lists related documents.

- Section 1, "Driver Data," contains reference pages for all driver-defined data needed by the system.

- Section 2, "Driver Entry Point Routines," contains reference pages for all driver entry point routines.

- Section 3, "Kernel Utility Routines," contains reference pages for all kernel functions used in DDI/DKI drivers.

- Section 4, "Data Structures," contains reference pages for structures used in DDI/DKI drivers.

- Section 5, "Kernel Defines," contains reference pages for kernel **#define**'s used in DDI/DKI drivers.

- Appendix A, "Migration from Release 3.2 to Release 4 Multi-Processor," describes the changes to DDI/DKI between Release 3.2 and Release 4 Multi-Processor of System V.

- Appendix B, "Migration from Release 4 to Release 4 Multi-Processor," describes the changes to the Release 4 DDI/DKI to support multiprocessing.

- Appendix C, "Multibus Extensions," contains reference pages for the extensions to the DDI to support Multibus II.

Organization of Driver Reference Manual

Driver reference manual pages are similar to those in the *Programmer's Reference Manual*, with the page name followed by a section number in parentheses. All driver reference manual section numbers begin with a "D" to distinguish them as driver reference pages.

The manual contains five sections:

D1   driver data definitions

D2   driver entry points

D3   kernel functions used by drivers

D4   kernel data structures accessed by drivers

D5   kernel **#define**'s used by drivers

Each section number is suffixed with a letter indicating the interfaces covered. The suffixes used are:

D   Device Driver Interface only (DDI)

K   Driver–Kernel Interface only (DKI)

DK   both DDI and DKI

X   DDI-only Platform-specific Interface

For example, **open**(D2DK) refers to the **open** entry point routine for a driver, not to the **open**(2) system call documented in the *Programmer's Reference Manual*. For clarity, the platform-specific manual pages have been put in an appendix, separate from the rest of the DDI/DKI manual pages.

Reference pages contain the following headings, where applicable:

- NAME gives the routine's name and a short summary of its purpose.
- SYNOPSIS summarizes the routine's calling and return syntax.
- ARGUMENTS describes each of the routine's arguments.
- DESCRIPTION provides general information about the routine.
- STRUCTURE MEMBERS describes all accessible data structure members.
- RETURN VALUE summarizes the return value from the function.
- LEVEL gives an indication of when the routine can be used.
- NOTES provides restrictions on use and cautionary information.
- SEE ALSO gives sources for further information.
- EXAMPLE provides an example of common usage.

Conventions Used in This Manual

Table 1 lists the textual conventions used in this manual.

Table 1: Textual Conventions Used in This Manual

Item	Style	Example
C Reserved Words	Constant Width	typedef
C typedef Declarations	Constant Width	caddr_t
Driver Routines	Constant Width	open routine
File Names	Constant Width	sys/conf.h
Flag Names	Constant Width	B_WRITE
Kernel Macros	Constant Width	minor
Kernel Functions	Constant Width	kmem_alloc
Kernel Function Arguments	*Italics*	*bp*
Structure Members	Constant Width	b_addr
Structure Names	Constant Width	buf structure
Symbolic Constants	Constant Width	NULL
System Calls	Constant Width	ioctl(2)
C Library Calls	Constant Width	printf(3S)
Shell Commands	Constant Width	layers(1)
User-Defined Variable	*Italics*	*prefix*close

Related Documentation

Several UNIX System V Release 4 documents are useful for device driver development. They are listed below.

Driver Development and Packaging

The *Integrated Software Development Guide* discusses driver development concepts, debugging, performance, installation, and other related driver topics for UNIX System V Release 4 Multi-Processor for Intel Processors. In addition, the document describes how to write the scripts necessary to install a driver (or other software) under the System Administration utility.

STREAMS

The *Programmer's Guide: STREAMS* tells how to write drivers and access devices that use the STREAMS driver interface for character access.

The *Programmer's Guide: Networking Interfaces* provides detailed information, with examples, on the Section 3N library that comprises the UNIX system Transport Level Interface (TLI).

The *Programmer's Guide: ANSI C and Programming Support Tools* includes instructions on using a number of UNIX utilities, including **make** and SCCS.

Operating Systems

The UNIX System V reference manuals are the standard reference materials for the UNIX operating system. This information is organized into three manuals, published separately for each system:

- The *User's Reference Manual/System Administrator's Reference Manual* includes information on UNIX system user-level commands (Section 1) and administrative commands (Section 1M).

- The *Programmer's Reference Manual: Operating System API* includes information on UNIX system calls (Section 2) and C language library routines (Section 3).

- The *System Files and Devices Reference Manual* includes information on UNIX system file formats (Section 4), miscellaneous facilities (Section 5), and special device files (Section 7).

Table of Contents

D1. Driver Data

D2. Driver Entry Point Routines

D3. Kernel Utility Routines

Table of Contents _____

Table of Contents

D4. Data Structures

D5. Kernel Defines

Appendix A: Migration from Release 3.2 to Release 4 Multi-Processor

Appendix B: Migration from Release 4 to Release 4 Multi-Processor

DDI/DKI Reference Manual

Appendix C: Multibus II DDI Extensions

Table of Contents _____

Permuted Index

PERMUTED INDEX

read a 16 bit short word from a 16 | bit I/O port inw .... inw(D3DK)
outb write a byte to an 8 | bit I/O port .... outb(D3DK)
write a 32 bit long word to a 32 | bit I/O port outl .... outl(D3DK)
write a 16 bit short word to a 16 | bit I/O port outw .... outw(D3DK)
outl write a 32 | bit long word to a 32 bit I/O port .... outl(D3DK)
port inw read a 16 | bit short word from a 16 bit I/O .... inw(D3DK)
outw write a 16 | bit short word to a 16 bit I/O port .... outw(D3DK)
inl read a 32 | bit word from a 32 bit I/O port .... inl(D3DK)
port repoutsd write 32 | bit words from buffer to an I/O .... repoutsd(D3DK)
port repoutsw write 16 | bit words from buffer to an I/O .... repoutsw(D3DK)
repinsd read 32 | bit words from I/O port to buffer .... repinsd(D3DK)
repinsw read 16 | bit words from I/O port to buffer .... repinsw(D3DK)
allocb allocate a message | block .... allocb(D3DK)
copyb copy a message | block .... copyb(D3DK)
size return size of logical | block device .... size(D2DK)
a previously allocated DMA command | block dma_free_cb free .... dma_free_cb(D3X)
dma_get_cb allocate a DMA command | block .... dma_get_cb(D3X)
dupb duplicate a message | block .... dupb(D3DK)
freeb free a message | block .... freeb(D3DK)
rmvb remove a message | block from a message .... rmvb(D3DK)
unlinkb remove a message | block from the head of a message .... unlinkb(D3DK)
biodone release buffer after | block I/O and wakeup processes .... biodone(D3DK)
processes pending completion of | block I/O biowait suspend .... biowait(D3DK)
buf | block I/O data transfer structure .... buf(D4DK)
strategy perform | block I/O .... strategy(D2DK)
datab STREAMS data | block structure .... datab(D4DK)
dma_cb DMA command | block structure .... dma_cb(D4X)
msgb STREAMS message | block structure .... msgb(D4DK)
buffer esballoc allocate a message | block using an externally-supplied .... esballoc(D3DK)
processor spl | block/allow interrupts on a .... spl(D3DK)
linkb concatenate two message | blocks .... linkb(D3DK)
the interconnect register of the | board in the specified slot /reads .... ics_find(D3DK)
the interconnect register of the | board in the specified slot /reads .... ics_read(D3DK)
into the specified register of the | board in the specified slot /value .... ics_write(D3DK)
ics_agent_cmp checks for certain | board types in the designated slot .... ics_agent_cmp(D3DK)
field of the HOST ID record in this | board's interconnect space /host id .... ics_hostid(D3DK)
space for buffer page list | bp_mapin allocate virtual address .... bp_mapin(D3DK)
address space for buffer page list | bp_mapout deallocate virtual .... bp_mapout(D3DK)
manageable units dma_pageio | break up an I/O request into .... dma_pageio(D3DK)
system's free list | brelse return a buffer to the .... brelse(D3DK)
mps_mk_brdcst constructs a | broadcast message to be sent .... mps_mk_brdcst(D3DK)
in pages (round down) | btop convert size in bytes to size .... btop(D3DK)
in pages (round up) | btopr convert size in bytes to size .... btopr(D3DK)
structure | buf block I/O data transfer .... buf(D4DK)
buffer becomes available | bufcall call a function when a .... bufcall(D3DK)
unbufcall cancel a pending | bufcall request .... unbufcall(D3DK)
processes biodone release | buffer after block I/O and wakeup .... biodone(D3DK)

DDI/DKI Reference Manual

determine whether credentials are	privileged drv_priv	drv_priv(D3DK)
put call a put	procedure	put(D3DK)
intr	process a device interrupt	intr(D2DK)
number of clock ticks delay delay	process execution for a specified	delay(D3DK)
proc_ref obtain a reference to a	process for signaling	proc_ref(D3DK)
proc_signal send a signal to a	process	proc_signal(D3DK)
proc_unref release a reference to a	process	proc_unref(D3DK)
SV_SIGNAL wake up one	process sleeping on a/	SV_SIGNAL(D3DK)
buffer after block I/O and wakeup	processes biodone release	biodone(D3DK)
block I/O biowait suspend	processes pending completion of	biowait(D3DK)
SV_BROADCAST wake up all	processes sleeping on a/	SV_BROADCAST(D3DK)
occurred pollwakeup inform polling	processes that an event has	pollwakeup(D3DK)
/execute a function on a specified	processor, after a specified length/	dtimeout(D3DK)
spl block/allow interrupts on a	processor	spl(D3DK)
process for signaling	proc_ref obtain a reference to a	proc_ref(D3DK)
process	proc_signal send a signal to a	proc_signal(D3DK)
process	proc_unref release a reference to a	proc_unref(D3DK)
subsequent hardware/ dma_prog	program a DMA operation for a	dma_prog(D3X)
subsequent software/ dma_swsetup	program a DMA operation for a	dma_swsetup(D3X)
in bytes	ptob convert size in pages to size	ptob(D3DK)
putq	put a message on a queue	putq(D3DK)
qprocsoff disable	put and service routines	qprocsoff(D3DK)
qprocson enable	put and service routines	qprocson(D3DK)
put call a	put call a put procedure	put(D3DK)
	put procedure	put(D3DK)
put call a	put receive messages from the	put(D2DK)
preceding queue	putbq place a message at the head	putbq(D3DK)
of a queue	putctl send a control message to a	putctl(D3DK)
queue	putctl1 send a control message with	putctl(D3DK)
a one-byte parameter to a queue	putnext send a message to the next	putnext(D3DK)
queue	putnextctl send a control message	putnextctl(D3DK)
to a queue	putnextctl1 send a control message	putnextctl(D3DK)
with a one byte parameter to a/	putq put a message on a queue	putq(D3DK)
memory pool mps_free_msgbuf	puts a buffer back into the free	mps_free_msgbuf(D3DK)
routine to be run	qenable schedule a queue's service	qenable(D3DK)
structure	qinit STREAMS queue initialization	qinit(D4DK)
routines	qprocsoff disable put and service	qprocsoff(D3DK)
routines	qprocson enable put and service	qprocson(D3DK)
opposite direction in a stream	qreply send a message in the	qreply(D3DK)
on a queue	qsize find the number of messages	qsize(D3DK)
available SLEEP_LOCKAVAIL	query whether a sleep lock is	SLEEP_LOCKAVAIL(D3DK)
by the caller SLEEP_LOCKOWNED	query whether a sleep lock is held	SLEEP_LOCKOWNED(D3DK)
canput test for room in a message	queue	canput(D3DK)
flushq flush messages on a	queue	flushq(D3DK)
noenable prevent a	queue from being scheduled	noenable(D3DK)

DDI/DKI Reference Manual

qprocson enable put and	service routines	qprocson(D3DK)
enableok allow a queue to be	serviced	enableok(D3DK)
drv_setparm	set kernel state information	drv_setparm(D3DK)
of/ /messages for transmission and	sets up table entries for reception	
		mps_AMPsend_rsvp(D3DK)
inw read a 16 bit	short word from a 16 bit I/O port	inw(D3DK)
outw write a 16 bit	short word to a 16 bit I/O port	outw(D3DK)
system shuts down halt	shut down the driver when the	halt(D2DK)
down the driver when the system	shuts down halt shut	halt(D2DK)
signals	signal numbers	signals(D5DK)
proc_signal send a	signal to a process	proc_signal(D3DK)
obtain a reference to a process for	signaling proc_ref	proc_ref(D3DK)
	signals signal numbers	signals(D5DK)
ptob convert size in pages to	size in bytes	ptob(D3DK)
(round down) btop convert	size in bytes to size in pages	btop(D3DK)
(round up) btopr convert	size in bytes to size in pages	btopr(D3DK)
btop convert size in bytes to	size in pages (round down)	btop(D3DK)
btopr convert size in bytes to	size in pages (round up)	btopr(D3DK)
ptob convert	size in pages to size in bytes	ptob(D3DK)
an empty buffer of the specified	size ngeteblk get	ngeteblk(D3DK)
size return	size of logical block device	size(D2DK)
device	size return size of logical block	size(D2DK)
SLEEP_LOCKAVAIL query whether a	sleep lock is available	SLEEP_LOCKAVAIL(D3DK)
SLEEP_LOCKOWNED query whether a	sleep lock is held by the caller	
		SLEEP_LOCKOWNED(D3DK)
allocate and initialize a	sleep lock SLEEP_ALLOC	SLEEP_ALLOC(D3DK)
deallocate an instance of a	sleep lock SLEEP_DEALLOC	SLEEP_DEALLOC(D3DK)
SLEEP_LOCK acquire a	sleep lock	SLEEP_LOCK(D3DK)
SLEEP_LOCK_SIG acquire a	sleep lock	SLEEP_LOCK_SIG(D3DK)
SLEEP_TRYLOCK try to acquire a	sleep lock	SLEEP_TRYLOCK(D3DK)
SLEEP_UNLOCK release a	sleep lock	SLEEP_UNLOCK(D3DK)
SV_WAIT	sleep on a synchronization variable	SV_WAIT(D3DK)
SV_WAIT_SIG	sleep on a synchronization variable	
		SV_WAIT_SIG(D3DK)
a sleep lock	SLEEP_ALLOC allocate and initialize	
		SLEEP_ALLOC(D3DK)
instance of a sleep lock	SLEEP_DEALLOC deallocate an	
		SLEEP_DEALLOC(D3DK)
SV_BROADCAST wake up all processes	sleeping on a synchronization/	SV_BROADCAST(D3DK)
SV_SIGNAL wake up one process	sleeping on a synchronization/	SV_SIGNAL(D3DK)
	SLEEP_LOCK acquire a sleep lock	SLEEP_LOCK(D3DK)
sleep lock is available	SLEEP_LOCKAVAIL query whether a	
		SLEEP_LOCKAVAIL(D3DK)
sleep lock is held by the caller	SLEEP_LOCKOWNED query whether a	
		SLEEP_LOCKOWNED(D3DK)

NAME

intro – introduction to driver data

SYNOPSIS

```
#include <sys/types.h>
#include <sys/ddi.h>
```

DESCRIPTION

This section describes the data definitions a developer needs to include in a device driver. The system finds this information in an implementation-specific manner, usually tied to the way system configuration is handled.

Each driver is uniquely identified by a prefix string specified in its configuration file. The name of all the driver-supplied routines and global variables should begin with this prefix. This will reduce the chance of a symbol collision with another driver. Any private routines defined by a driver that are not entry point routines should be declared as **static**. Also, any global variables that are private to the driver should be declared as **static**.

DRIVER DATA (D1)

NAME

    devflag – driver flags

SYNOPSIS

    `#include <sys/conf.h>`

    `int` *prefix*`devflag = 0;`

DESCRIPTION

    Every driver must define a global integer containing a bitmask of flags that indicate its characteristics to the system. The valid flags that may be set are:

    `D_DMA`   The driver does DMA (Direct Memory Access).

    `D_TAPE`   The driver controls a tape device (mount read-only).

    `D_NOBRKUP` The driver understands the `B_PAGEIO` flag in the buffer header (the I/O job is not broken up along page boundaries into multiple jobs by the kernel).

    `D_MP`   The driver is multithreaded (it handles its own locking and serialization).

    If no flags are set for the driver, then *prefix*`devflag` should be set to 0.

SEE ALSO

    Integrated Software Development Guide

DRIVER DATA (D1)

NAME

info – STREAMS driver and module information

SYNOPSIS

```
#include <sys/stream.h>

struct streamtab prefixinfo = { ... };
```

DESCRIPTION

Every STREAMS driver and module must define a global **streamtab**(D4DK) structure so that the system can identify the entry points and interface parameters.

SEE ALSO

Programmer's Guide: STREAMS

streamtab(D4DK)

NAME

    `prefix` – driver prefix

SYNOPSIS

    int *prefix*`close();`
    int *prefix*`open();`
      ...

DESCRIPTION

    Every driver must define a unique prefix, whose maximum length is implementation-defined. The prefix is usually specified in a configuration file. Driver entry points names are created by concatenating the driver prefix with the name for the entry point. This enables driver entry points to be identified by configuration software and decreases the possibility of global symbol collisions in the kernel.

SEE ALSO

    `devflag`(D1D), `info`(D1D), `chpoll`(D2DK), `close`(D2DK), `halt`(D2D), `init`(D2D), `intr`(D2D), `ioctl`(D2DK), `mmap`(D2DK), `open`(D2DK), `print`(D2DK), `put`(D2DK), `read`(D2DK), `size`(D2DK), `srv`(D2DK), `start`(D2DK), `strategy`(D2DK), `write`(D2DK)

EXAMPLE

    An ETHERNET driver might use a driver prefix of "**en.**" It would define the following entry points: `enclose`, `eninit`, `enintr`, `enopen`, `enwput`, `enrsrv`, and `enwsrv`. It would also define the data symbols `endevflag` and `eninfo`.

NAME

intro – introduction to driver entry point routines

SYNOPSIS

```
#include <sys/types.h>
#include <sys/ddi.h>
```

DESCRIPTION

This section describes the routines a developer needs to include in a device driver. These routines are called "entry point routines" because they provide the interfaces that the kernel needs from drivers. The kernel calls them when needed. Some are called at well-defined times, such as system start up and system shut down. Others are called as a result of I/O-related system calls or external events, such as interrupts from peripheral devices.

Each driver is organized into two logical parts: the base level and the interrupt level. The base level interacts with the kernel and the device on behalf of processes performing I/O operations. The interrupt level interacts with the device and the kernel as a result of an event such as data arrival, and usually cannot be associated with any particular process.

Each driver is uniquely identified by a prefix string specified in its configuration file. The name of all the driver-supplied routines and global variables should begin with this prefix. This will reduce the chance of a symbol collision with another driver. Any private routines defined by a driver that are not entry point routines should be declared as **static**. Also, any global variables that are private to the driver should be declared as **static**.

In general, any number of instances of the same driver entry point routine can be running concurrently. It is the responsibility of the driver or module to synchronize access to its private data structures.

Drivers do not have to worry about making kernel buffers addressable to their DMA controllers. The kernel will make sure that any kernel buffer addresses passed to a driver entry point will be addressable by the driver's hardware.

DRIVER ENTRY POINT ROUTINES (D2)

DRIVER ENTRY POINT ROUTINES (D2)

NAME

chpoll – poll entry point for a non-STREAMS character driver

SYNOPSIS

```
#include <sys/poll.h>
```

int *prefix*chpoll(dev_t *dev*, short *events*, int *anyyet*, short *reventsp*,
　　　struct pollhead **phpp*);

ARGUMENTS

dev　　　　The device number for the device to be polled.

events　　Mask (bit-wise **OR**) indicating the events being polled. Valid events
　　　　　　are:

POLLIN	Data are available to be read (either normal or out-of-band).
POLLOUT	Data may be written without blocking.
POLLPRI	High priority data are available to be read.
POLLHUP	A device hangup.
POLLERR	A device error.
POLLRDNORM	Normal data are available to be read.
POLLWRNORM	Normal data may be written without blocking (same as **POLLOUT**).
POLLRDBAND	Out-of-band data are available to be read.
POLLWRBAND	Out-of-band data may be written without blocking.

anyyet　　A flag that indicates whether the driver should return a pointer to its
　　　　　　pollhead structure to the caller.

reventsp　A pointer to a bitmask of the returned events satisfied.

phpp　　　A pointer to a pointer to a **pollhead** structure (defined in
　　　　　　sys/poll.h.)

DESCRIPTION

The **chpoll** entry point indicates whether certain I/O events have occurred on a given device. It must be provided by any non-STREAMS character device driver that wishes to support polling [see **poll**(2)].

A driver that supports polling must provide a **pollhead** structure for each minor device supported by the driver. The driver must use **phalloc**(D3DK) to allocate the **pollhead** structure. It can be freed later, if necessary, with **phfree**(D3DK). The definition of the **pollhead** structure is not included in the DDI/DKI, and can change across releases. It should be treated as a "black box" by the driver; none of its fields may be referenced. Drivers should not depend on the size of the **pollhead** structure.

The driver must implement the polling discipline itself. Each time the driver detects a pollable event, it should call **pollwakeup**(D3DK), passing to it the event that occurred and the address of the **pollhead** structure associated with the device. Note that **pollwakeup** should be called with only one event at a time.

When the driver's **chpoll** entry point is called, the driver should check if any of the events requested in *events* have occurred. The driver should store the mask, consisting of the subset of **events** that are pending, in the **short** pointed to by *reventsp*. Note that this mask may be 0 if none of the events are pending. In this case, the driver should check the *anyyet* flag and, if it is zero, store the address of the device's **pollhead** structure in the pointer pointed at by **phpp**. The canonical **chpoll** algorithm is:

```
if (events_are_satisfied_now) {
    *reventsp = events & mask_of_satisfied_events;
} else {
    *reventsp = 0;
    if (!anyyet)
        *phpp = my_local_pollhead_pointer;
}
return (0);
```

NOTES

This entry point is optional.

The **chpoll** routine may not call any function that sleeps.

The **chpoll** routine has user context.

RETURN VALUE

The **chpoll** routine should return 0 for success, or the appropriate error number.

SEE ALSO

phalloc(D3DK), **phfree**(D3DK), **pollwakeup**(D3DK)

poll(2) in the *Programmer's Reference Manual*

NAME

close – relinquish access to a device

SYNOPSIS   [Block and Character]

```
#include <sys/types.h>
#include <sys/file.h>
#include <sys/errno.h>
#include <sys/open.h>
#include <sys/cred.h>
#include <sys/ddi.h>
```

int *prefix*close(dev_t *dev*, int *flag,* int *otyp,* cred_t **crp*);

ARGUMENTS

dev   Device number.

flag   File status flag. Possible flag values and their definitions can be found in open(D2DK).

otyp   Parameter supplied so that the driver can determine how many times a device was opened and for what reasons. The values are mutually exclusive.

OTYP_BLK   Close was through block interface for the device.

OTYP_CHR   Close was through the raw/character interface for the device.

OTYP_LYR   Close a layered device. This flag is used when one driver calls another driver's **close** routine.

crp   Pointer to the user credential structure.

SYNOPSIS   [STREAMS]

```
#include <sys/types.h>
#include <sys/stream.h>
#include <sys/file.h>
#include <sys/errno.h>
#include <sys/cred.h>
#include <sys/ddi.h>
```

int *prefix*close(queue_t **q,* int *flag,* cred_t **crp*);

ARGUMENTS

q   Pointer to queue used to reference the read side of the driver.

flag   File status flag.

crp   Pointer to the user credential structure.

DESCRIPTION

The **close** routine ends the connection between the user process and the device, and prepares the device (hardware and software) so that it is ready to be opened again.

For **OTYP_BLK** and **OTYP_CHR**, a device may be opened simultaneously by multiple processes and the driver **open** routine is called for each open, but the kernel will only call the **close** routine when the last process using the device issues a **close**(2) system call or exits.

There is one exception to this rule. If a device is opened through both its character and its block interfaces, then there will be one close per interface. For example, if the same device is opened twice through its block interface and three times through its character interface, then there will be two calls to the driver's close routine; one when the block interface is finished being used, and one when the character interface is finished being used.

For **OTYP_LYR**, there will be one such close for every corresponding open. Here, the driver should count each open and close based on the *otyp* parameter to determine when the device should really be closed.

A **close** routine could perform any of the following general functions, depending on the type of device and the service provided:

disable interrupts

hang up phone lines

rewind a tape

deallocate buffers from a private buffering scheme

unlock an unsharable device (that was locked in the **open** routine)

flush buffers

notify a device of the close

cancel any pending timeout or bufcall routines that access data that are de-initialized or deallocated during close

deallocate any resources allocated on open

If the **FNDELAY** or **FNONBLOCK** flags are specified in the *flag* argument, the driver should try to avoid sleeping, if possible, during close processing.

The **close** routines of STREAMS drivers and modules are called when a stream is dismantled or a module popped. The steps for dismantling a stream are performed in the following order. First, any non-persistent multiplexor links present are unlinked and the lower streams are closed. Next, the following steps are performed for each module or driver on the stream, starting at the head and working toward the tail:

1. The write queue is given a chance to drain.

2. The **close** routine is called.

3. The module or driver is removed from the stream.

4. Any remaining messages on the queues are freed.

NOTES

This entry point is required in all drivers.

The **close** routine has user context and can sleep.

STREAMS drivers and modules must call **qprocsoff**(D3DK) to disable their **put**(D2DK) and service [**srv**(D2DK)] routines before returning from the **close** routine.

RETURN VALUE

The **close** routine should return 0 for success, or the appropriate error number. Refer to **errnos**(D5DK) for a list of DDI/DKI error numbers. Return errors rarely occur, but if a failure is detected, the driver should still close the device and then decide whether the severity of the problem warrants displaying a message on the console.

SEE ALSO

open(D2DK), **drv_priv**(D3DK), **qprocsoff**(D3DK), **unbufcall**(D3DK), **untimeout**(D3DK), **queue**(D4DK), **errnos**(D5DK)

NAME

halt – shut down the driver when the system shuts down

SYNOPSIS

void *prefix*halt();

DESCRIPTION

The **halt** routine if present, is called when the system is shut down. The device driver shouldn't assume that the interrupts are enabled. The driver should make sure that no interrupts are pending from its device, and inform the device that no more interrupts should be generated. After the **halt** routine is called, no more calls will be made to the driver entry points.

NOTES

This entry point is optional.

User context is not available, so the driver's **halt** routine should not sleep.

RETURN VALUE

None.

NAME

init – initialize a device

SYNOPSIS

void *prefix*init ( );

DESCRIPTION

init and start(D2DK) routines are used to initialize drivers and the devices they control. init routines are executed during system initialization, and can be used in drivers that do not require system services to be initialized. start routines are executed after system services are enabled.

init routines can perform functions such as:

allocating memory for private buffering schemes

mapping a device into virtual address space

initializing hardware (for example, system generation or resetting the board)

Functions that may result in the caller sleeping, or that require user context, such as SV_WAIT(D3DK), may not be called. Any function that provides a flag to prevent it from sleeping must be called such that the function does not sleep. Also, init routines are executed before interrupts are enabled.

The following kernel functions can be called from the driver's init routine:

ASSERT	drv_usectohz	physmap
bcopy	drv_usecwait	physmap_free
btop/btopr	etoimajor	repinsb/repinsl/
bzero	getemajor	repinsw
cmn_err	geteminor	repoutsb/repoutsl/
dma_disable	getmajor	repoutsw
dma_enable	getminor	rmalloc
dma_free_buf	inb/inl/inw	rmallocmap
dma_free_cb	itoemajor	rmfreemap
dma_get_best_mode	kmem_alloc	rmfree
dma_get_buf	kmem_free	RWLOCK_ALLOC
dma_get_cb	kmem_zalloc	SLEEP_ALLOC
dma_prog	LOCK_ALLOC	SV_ALLOC
dma_stop	makedevice	vtop
dma_swsetup	max/min	
dma_swstart	outb/outl/outw	
drv_getparm	phalloc	
drv_hztousec	phfree	

NOTES

This entry point is optional.

RETURN VALUE

None.

SEE ALSO

start(D2DK)

NAME
　　intr – process a device interrupt

SYNOPSIS
　　void *prefix*intr(int *ivec*);

ARGUMENTS
　　ivec　　　Number used by the operating system to associate a driver's interrupt
　　　　　　handler with an interrupting device. The makeup and interpretation
　　　　　　of *ivec* is specific to each system implementation. In some systems,
　　　　　　this number may be the logical device number, or a combination of
　　　　　　logical device and logical controller numbers, used to map the correct
　　　　　　interrupt routine with a subdevice. In others, this number could be
　　　　　　the interrupt vector number.

DESCRIPTION
　　The intr routine is the interrupt handler for both block and character hardware
　　drivers. The interrupt handler is responsible for determining the reason for an
　　interrupt, servicing the interrupt, and waking up any base-level driver processes
　　sleeping on any events associated with the interrupt.

　　For example, when a disk drive has transferred information to the host to satisfy
　　a read request, the disk drive's controller generates an interrupt. The CPU ack-
　　nowledges the interrupt and calls the interrupt handler associated with that con-
　　troller and disk drive. The interrupt routine services the interrupt and then
　　wakes up the driver base-level process waiting for data. The base-level portion of
　　the driver then conveys the data to the user.

　　In general, most interrupt routines do the following tasks:

　　　　keep a record of interrupt occurrences

　　　　return immediately if no devices controlled by a driver caused the inter-
　　　　rupt (only for systems supporting shared interrupts)

　　　　interpret the interrupt routine argument *ivec*

　　　　reject requests for devices that are not served by the device's controller

　　　　process interrupts that happen without cause (called spurious interrupts)

　　　　handle all possible device errors

　　　　wake processes that are sleeping on any events associated with the inter-
　　　　rupt

　　There are also many tasks the intr routine must perform that are driver-type
　　and device specific. For example, the following types of drivers require different
　　functions from their intr routines:

　　　　A block driver dequeues requests and wakes up processes sleeping on an
　　　　I/O request.

　　　　A terminal driver receives and sends characters.

　　　　A printer driver ensures that characters are sent.

In addition, the functions of an **intr** routine are device dependent. You should know the exact chip set that produces the interrupt for your device. You need to know the exact bit patterns of the device's control and status register and how data is transmitted into and out of your computer. These specifics differ for every device you access.

The **intr** routine for an intelligent controller that does not use individual interrupt vectors for each subdevice must access the completion queue to determine which subdevice generated the interrupt. It must also update the status information, set/clear flags, set/clear error indicators, and so forth to complete the handling of a job. The code should also be able to handle a spurious completion interrupt identified by an empty completion queue. When the routine finishes, it should advance the unload pointer to the next entry in the completion queue.

If the driver called **biowait**(D3DK) or **SV_WAIT**(D3DK) to await the completion of an operation, the **intr** routine must call **biodone**(D3DK) or **SV_SIGNAL**(D3DK) to signal the process to resume.

The interrupt routine runs at the processor level associated with the interrupt level for the given device. Lower priority interrupts are deferred while the interrupt routine is active. Certain processor levels can block different interrupts. See **spl**(D3D) for more information.

NOTES

This entry point is only required for those drivers that interface to hardware that interrupts the host computer. It is not used with software drivers.

The **intr** routine must never:

> use functions that sleep

> drop the interrupt priority level below the level at which the interrupt routine was entered

> call any function or routine that requires user context (that is, if it accesses or alters information associated with the running process)

> **uiomove**(D3DK), **ureadc**(D3DK), and **uwritec**(D3DK) cannot be used in an interrupt routine when the **uio_segflg** member of the **uio**(D4DK) structure is set to **UIO_USERSPACE** (indicating a transfer between user and kernel space).

RETURN VALUE

None.

SEE ALSO

biodone(D3DK), spl(D3D), SV_SIGNAL(D3DK)

NAME

ioctl – control a character device

SYNOPSIS

```
#include <sys/types.h>
#include <sys/cred.h>
#include <sys/file.h>
#include <sys/errno.h>
```

int *prefix*ioctl(dev_t *dev*, int *cmd*, void **arg*, int *mode*, cred_t **crp*,
    int **rvalp*);

ARGUMENTS

dev   Device number.

cmd   Command argument the driver **ioctl** routine interprets as the operation to be performed.

arg   Passes parameters between the user and the driver. The interpretation of the argument is dependent on the command and the driver. For example, the argument can be an integer, or it can be the address of a user structure containing driver or hardware settings.

mode   Contains the file modes set when the device was opened. The driver can use this to determine if the device was opened for reading (**FREAD**), writing (**FWRITE**), etc. See **open**(D2DK) for a description of the values.

crp   Pointer to the user credential structure.

rvalp   Pointer to the return value for the calling process. The driver may elect to set the value if the **ioctl**(D2DK) succeeds.

DESCRIPTION

The **ioctl**(D2DK) routine provides non-STREAMS character drivers with an alternate entry point that can be used for almost any operation other than a simple transfer of data. Most often, **ioctl** is used to control device hardware parameters and establish the protocol used by the driver in processing data. I/O control commands are used to implement terminal settings, to format disk devices, to implement a trace driver for debugging, and to flush queues.

If the third argument, *arg*, is a pointer to user space, the driver can use **copyin**(D3DK) and **copyout**(D3DK) to transfer data between kernel and user space.

The **ioctl** routine is basically a **switch** statement, with each **case** definition corresponding to a different **ioctl** command identifying the action to be taken.

NOTES

This entry point is optional.

The **ioctl** routine has user context and can sleep.

STREAMS drivers do not have **ioctl** routines. The stream head converts I/O control commands to **M_IOCTL** messages, which are handled by the driver's **put**(D2DK) or **srv**(D2DK) routine.

An attempt should be made to keep the values for driver-specific I/O control commands distinct from others in the system. Each driver's I/O control commands are unique, but it is possible for user-level code to access a driver with an I/O control command that is intended for another driver, which can have serious results.

A common method to assign I/O control command values that are less apt to be duplicated is to compose the commands from some component unique to the driver (such as a module name or ID), and a counter, as in:

```
#define PREFIX        ('h'<<16|'d'<<8)
#define COMMAND1      (PREFIX|1)
#define COMMAND2      (PREFIX|2)
#define COMMAND3      (PREFIX|3)
```

RETURN VALUE

The **ioctl** routine should return 0 on success, or the appropriate error number on failure. The system call will usually return 0 on success or −1 on failure. However, the driver can choose to have the system call return a different value on success by passing the value through the *rvalp* pointer.

SEE ALSO

open(D2DK), copyin(D3DK), copyout(D3DK), drv_priv(D3DK), errnos(D5DK)

NAME

mmap – check virtual mapping for memory-mapped device

SYNOPSIS

```
#include <sys/types.h>
#include <sys/mman.h>
#include <sys/vm.h>

int prefixmmap(dev_t dev, off_t off, int prot);
```

ARGUMENTS

dev   Device whose memory is to be mapped.

off   Offset within device memory at which mapping begins.

prot   Protection flags from mman.h. Valid flags are:

PROT_READ	page can be read.
PROT_WRITE	page can be written.
PROT_EXEC	page can be executed.
PROT_USER	page is accessible from user-level.
PROT_ALL	all of the above.

DESCRIPTION

The mmap entry point provides a way to support character drivers for memory-mapped devices. A memory-mapped device has memory that can be mapped into a process's address space. The mmap(2) system call, when applied to a character special file, allows this device memory to be mapped into user space for direct access by the user application (no kernel buffering overhead is incurred.)

The mmap routine checks if the offset is within the range of pages supported by the device. For example, a device that has 512 bytes of memory that can be mapped into user space should not support offsets greater than, or equal to, 512. If the offset does not exist, then NOPAGE is returned. If the offset does exist, the mmap routine returns the physical page ID for the page at offset off in the device's memory.

A physical page ID is a machine-specific token that uniquely identifies a page of physical memory in the system (either system memory or device memory.) No assumptions should be made about the format of a physical page ID. The functions kvtoppid(D3DK) and phystoppid(D3D) can be used to get a physical page ID for a given address, depending on whether the address is virtual or physical.

NOTES

This entry point is optional.

The driver's mmap routine has user context and can sleep.

The driver mmap routine should only be supported for memory-mapped devices or pseudo-devices.

RETURN VALUE

If the protection and offset are valid for the device, the driver should return the physical page ID. Otherwise, NOPAGE should be returned.

SEE ALSO
    kvtoppid(D3DK), phystoppid(D3D)

    mmap(2)

NAME

open – gain access to a device

SYNOPSIS   [Block and Character]

```
#include <sys/types.h>
#include <sys/file.h>
#include <sys/errno.h>
#include <sys/open.h>
#include <sys/cred.h>
```

int *prefix*open(dev_t **devp,* int *oflag,* int *otyp,* cred_t **crp*);

ARGUMENTS

devp　　　　Pointer to a device number.

oflag　　　　Information passed from the user that instructs the driver on how to
open the file. The bit settings for the flag are found in **file.h**. Valid
settings are:

　　　　FEXCL　　　Interpreted in a driver-dependent manner. Some drivers
interpret this flag to mean open the device with exclusive
access (fail all other attempts to open the device.)

　　　　FNDELAY　　Open the device and return immediately without sleeping
(do not block the open even if there is a problem.)

　　　　FNONBLOCK　Open the device and return immediately without sleeping
(do not block the open even if there is a problem.)

　　　　FREAD　　　Open the device with read access permission.

　　　　FWRITE　　Open the device with write access permission.

otyp　　　　Parameter supplied so that the driver can determine how many times a
device was opened and for what reasons. All flags are defined in
open.h. The values are mutually exclusive.

　　　　OTYP_BLK　Open occurred through block interface for the device.

　　　　OTYP_CHR　Open occurred through the raw/character interface for
the device.

　　　　OTYP_LYR　Open a layered device. This flag is used when one driver
calls another driver's **open** routine.

crp　　　　Pointer to the user credential structure.

SYNOPSIS   [STREAMS]

```
#include <sys/types.h>
#include <sys/file.h>
#include <sys/stream.h>
#include <sys/errno.h>
#include <sys/cred.h>
```

int *prefix*open(queue_t **q,* dev_t **devp,* int *oflag,* int *sflag,* cred_t **crp*);

ARGUMENTS   [STREAMS]

q   Pointer to the queue used to reference the read side of the driver.

devp   Pointer to a device number. For modules, *devp* always points to the device number associated with the driver at the end (tail) of the stream.

oflag   Open flags. Valid values are the same as those listed above.

sflag   STREAMS flag. Values are mutually exclusive and are given as follows:

          CLONEOPEN   Indicates a clone open (see below). If the driver supports cloning, it must assign and return a device number of an unused device by changing the value of the device number to which *devp* points.

          MODOPEN   Indicates that an **open** routine is being called for a module, not a driver. This is useful in detecting configuration errors and in determining how the driver is being used, since STREAMS drivers can also be configured as STREAMS modules.

          0   Indicates a driver is being opened directly, without cloning.

crp   Pointer to the user credential structure.

DESCRIPTION

The driver's **open** routine is called to prepare a device for further access. It is called by the kernel during an **open**(2) or a **mount**(2) of the device special file. For non-STREAMS drivers, it can also be called from another (layered) driver. The STREAMS module **open** routine is called by the kernel during an **I_PUSH** **ioctl**(2) or an autopush-style open [see **autopush**(1M)].

The **open** routine could perform any of the following general functions, depending on the type of device and the service provided:

        enable interrupts

        allocate buffers or other resources needed to use the device

        lock an unsharable device

        notify the device of the open

        change the device number if this is a clone open

The **open** routine should verify that the minor number component of *devp* is valid, that the type of access requested by *otyp* and *oflag* is appropriate for the device, and, if required, check permissions using the user credentials pointed to by *crp* [see **drv_priv**(D3DK)].

Cloning is the process of the driver selecting an unused device for the user. It eliminates the need to poll many devices when looking for an unused one. Both STREAMS and Non-STREAMS drivers may implement cloning behavior by changing the device number pointed to by *devp*. A driver may designate certain minor devices as special clone entry points into the driver. When these are opened, the driver searches for an unused device and returns the new device number by changing the value of the device number to which *devp* points. Both the major device number and the minor device number can be changed, although usually just the minor number is changed. The major number is only changed when the clone controls more than one device.

Using this method of cloning, a STREAMS driver will never see *sflag* set to **CLONEOPEN**. A different method makes use of this flag. STREAMS drivers can take advantage of a special driver, known as the *clone driver*, to perform clone opens. This frees the driver from having to reserve special minors for the clone entry points. Here, the device node is actually that of the clone driver (the major number is the major number from the clone driver and the minor number is the major number from the real driver). When the clone driver is opened, it will call the real driver open routine with *sflag* set to **CLONEOPEN**.

NOTES

This entry point is required in all drivers.

The **open** routine has user context and can sleep.

Before returning, STREAMS drivers and modules must call **qprocson**(D3DK) to enable their **put**(D2DK) and service [**srv**(D2DK)] routines.

Support of cloning is optional.

For STREAMS drivers and modules, for a given device number (queue), only one instance of the **open** routine can be running at any given time. However, multiple opens on any two different device numbers (queues) can be running concurrently. It is the responsibility of the driver or module to synchronize access to its private data structures in this case. For clone opens, multiple clone opens can run concurrently, and it is the driver's responsibility to synchronize access to its private data structures, as well as allocation and deallocation of device numbers.

RETURN VALUE

The **open** routine should return 0 for success, or the appropriate error number.

SEE ALSO

close(D2DK), **drv_priv**(D3DK), **qprocson**(D3DK), **queue**(D4DK), **errnos**(D5DK)

NAME

print – display a driver message on the system console

SYNOPSIS

```
#include <sys/types.h>
#include <sys/errno.h>

int prefixprint(dev_t dev, char *str);
```

ARGUMENTS

dev   Device number.

str   Pointer to a NULL-terminated character string describing the problem.

DESCRIPTION

The **print** routine is called indirectly by the kernel for the block device when the kernel has detected an exceptional condition (such as out of space) in the device. The driver should print the message on the console along with any driver-specific information. To display the message on the console, the driver should use the **cmn_err**(D3DK) function.

NOTES

This entry point is optional.

The driver should not try to interpret the text string passed to it.

The driver's **print** routine should not call any functions that sleep.

RETURN VALUE

Ignored.

SEE ALSO

cmn_err(D3DK)

NAME

put – receive messages from the preceding queue

SYNOPSIS

```
#include <sys/types.h>
#include <sys/stream.h>
#include <sys/stropts.h>

int prefixrput(queue_t *q, mblk_t *mp);   /* read side */

int prefixwput(queue_t *q, mblk_t *mp);   /* write side */
```

ARGUMENTS

q   Pointer to the queue.
mp   Pointer to the message block.

DESCRIPTION

The primary task of the **put** routine is to coordinate the passing of messages from one queue to the next in a stream. The **put** routine is called by the preceding component (module, driver, or stream head) in the stream. **put** routines are designated "write" or "read" depending on the direction of message flow.

Modules and drivers must have write **put** routines. Modules must have read **put** routines, but drivers don't really need them because their interrupt handler can do the work intended for the read **put** routine. A message is passed to the **put** routine. If immediate processing is desired, the **put** routine can process the message, or it can enqueue it so that the service routine [see **srv**(D2DK)] can process it later.

The **put** routine must do at least one of the following when it receives a message:

Pass the message to the next component in the stream by calling the **putnext**(D3DK) function.

Process the message, if immediate processing is required (for example, high priority messages.)

Enqueue the message with the **putq**(D3DK) function for deferred processing by the service routine.

Typically, the **put** routine will switch on the message type, which is contained in **mp->b_datap->db_type**, taking different actions depending on the message type. For example, a **put** routine might process high priority messages and enqueue normal messages.

The **putq** function can be used as a module's **put** routine when no special processing is required and all messages are to be enqueued for the service routine.

Although it can be done in the service routine, drivers and modules usually handle queue flushing in their **put** routines. The canonical flushing algorithm for driver write put routines is as follows:

```
queue_t *q;      /* the write queue */

if (*mp->b_rptr & FLUSHBAND) { /* if driver recognizes bands */
      if (*mp->b_rptr & FLUSHW) {
            flushband(q, FLUSHDATA, *(mp->b_rptr + 1));
            *mp->b_rptr &= ~FLUSHW;
```

```
      }
      if (*mp->b_rptr & FLUSHR) {
            flushband(RD(q), FLUSHDATA, *(mp->b_rptr + 1));
            qreply(q, mp);
      } else {
            freemsg(mp);
      }
} else {
      if (*mp->b_rptr & FLUSHW) {
            flushq(q, FLUSHDATA);
            *mp->b_rptr &= ~FLUSHW;
      }
      if (*mp->b_rptr & FLUSHR) {
            flushq(RD(q), FLUSHDATA);
            qreply(q, mp);
      } else {
            freemsg(mp);
      }
}
```

The canonical flushing algorithm for module write put routines is as follows:

```
queue_t *q;      /* the write queue */

if (*mp->b_rptr & FLUSHBAND) { /* if module recognizes bands */
      if (*mp->b_rptr & FLUSHW)
            flushband(q, FLUSHDATA, *(mp->b_rptr + 1));
      if (*mp->b_rptr & FLUSHR)
            flushband(RD(q), FLUSHDATA, *(mp->b_rptr + 1));
} else {
      if (*mp->b_rptr & FLUSHW)
            flushq(q, FLUSHDATA);
      if (*mp->b_rptr & FLUSHR)
            flushq(RD(q), FLUSHDATA);
}
if (!SAMESTR(q)) {
      switch (*mp->b_rptr & FLUSHRW) {
      case FLUSHR:
            *mp->b_rptr = (*mp->b_rptr & ~FLUSHR) | FLUSHW;
            break;

      case FLUSHW:
            *mp->b_rptr = (*mp->b_rptr & ~FLUSHW) | FLUSHR;
            break;
      }
}
putnext(q, mp);
```

The algorithms for the read side are similar. In both examples, the **FLUSHBAND** flag need only be checked if the driver or module cares about priority bands.

NOTES

This entry point is required.

put routines do not have user context and so may not call any function that sleeps.

Multiple copies of the same **put** routine for a given queue, as well as the service routine for the queue, can be running concurrently. Drivers and modules are responsible for synchronizing access to their own private data structures accordingly.

No locks should be held when passing messages to other queues in the stream.

put procedures cannot be called directly. Drivers can use **put**(D3DK) for this purpose.

Drivers should free any messages they do not recognize.

Modules should pass on any messages they do not recognize.

Drivers should fail any unrecognized **M_IOCTL** messages by converting them into **M_IOCNAK** messages and sending them upstream.

Modules should pass on any unrecognized **M_IOCTL** messages.

RETURN VALUE

Ignored.

SEE ALSO

STREAMS Programmer's Guide

srv(D2DK), **flushband**(D3DK), **flushq**(D3DK), **putctl**(D3DK), **putctl1**(D3DK), **putnext**(D3DK), **putq**(D3DK), **qreply**(D3DK), **datab**(D4DK), **msgb**(D4DK), **queue**(D4DK)

NAME
           read – read data from a device

SYNOPSIS
           #include <sys/types.h>
           #include <sys/errno.h>
           #include <sys/uio.h>
           #include <sys/cred.h>

           int *prefix*read(dev_t *dev,* uio_t **uiop,* cred_t **crp*);

ARGUMENTS
           dev   Device number.

           uiop   Pointer to the **uio**(D4DK) structure that describes where the data is to
                        be stored in user space.

           crp   Pointer to the user credential structure for the I/O transaction.

DESCRIPTION
           The driver **read** routine is called during the **read**(2) system call. The **read** rou-
           tine is responsible for transferring data from the device to the user data area. The
           pointer to the user credentials, *crp*, is available so the driver can check to see if
           the user can read privileged information, if the driver provides access to any.
           The **uio** structure provides the information necessary to determine how much
           data should be transferred. The **uiomove**(D3DK) function provides a convenient
           way to copy data using the **uio** structure.

           Block drivers that provide a character interface can use **physiock**(D3DK) to per-
           form the data transfer with the driver's **strategy**(D2DK) routine.

NOTES
           This interface is optional.

           The **read** routine has user context and can sleep.

RETURN VALUE
           The **read** routine should return 0 for success, or the appropriate error number.

SEE ALSO
           strategy(D2DK), **write**(D2DK), **drv_priv**(D3DK), **physiock**(D3DK),
           uiomove(D3DK), **ureadc**(D3DK), **uio**(D4DK), **errnos**(D5DK)

NAME

size – return size of logical block device

SYNOPSIS

```
#include <sys/types.h>
#include <sys/param.h>

int prefixsize(dev_t dev);
```

ARGUMENTS

dev   The logical device number.

DESCRIPTION

The **size** entry point returns the number of **NBPSCTR**-byte units on a logical block device (partition). **NBPSCTR**, defined in **param.h**, is the number of bytes per logical disk sector. This routine is required for block drivers.

NOTES

The **size** routine has user context and can sleep.

RETURN VALUE

On success, the **size** routine should return the number of **NBPSCTR**-byte units on the logical block device specified by *dev*; on failure, **size** should return −1.

NAME

srv – service queued messages

SYNOPSIS

```
#include <sys/types.h>
#include <sys/stream.h>
#include <sys/stropts.h>

int prefixrsrv(queue_t *q);   /* read side */

int prefixwsrv(queue_t *q);   /* write side */
```

ARGUMENTS

q   Pointer to the queue.

DESCRIPTION

The service routine may be included in a STREAMS module or driver for a number of reasons. It provides greater control over the flow of messages in a stream by allowing the module or driver to reorder messages, defer the processing of some messages, or fragment and reassemble messages. Service routines also provide a way to recover from resource allocation failures.

A message is first passed to a module's or driver's **put**(D2DK) routine, which may or may not process it. The **put** routine can place the message on the queue for processing by the service routine.

Once a message has been enqueued, the STREAMS scheduler calls the service routine at some later time. Drivers and modules should not depend on the order in which service procedures are run. This is an implementation-dependent characteristic. In particular, applications should not rely on service procedures running before returning to user-level processing.

Every STREAMS queue [see **queue**(D4DK)] has limit values it uses to implement flow control. Tunable high and low water marks are checked to stop and restart the flow of message processing. Flow control limits apply only between two adjacent queues with service routines. Flow control occurs by service routines following certain rules before passing messages along. By convention, high priority messages are not affected by flow control.

STREAMS messages can be defined to have up to 256 different priorities to support some networking protocol requirements for multiple bands of data flow. At a minimum, a stream must distinguish between normal (priority band zero) messages and high priority messages (such as **M_IOCACK**). High priority messages are always placed at the head of the queue, after any other high priority messages already enqueued. Next are messages from all included priority bands, which are enqueued in decreasing order of priority. Each priority band has its own flow control limits. By convention, if a band is flow-controlled, all lower priority bands are also stopped.

Once a service routine is called by the STREAMS scheduler it must process all messages on its queue, until either the queue is empty, the stream is flow-controlled, or an allocation error occurs. Typically, the service routine will switch on the message type, which is contained in **mp->b_datap->db_type**, taking different actions depending on the message type. The framework for the canonical service procedure algorithm is as follows:

```
queue_t *q;
mblk_t *mp;

while ((mp = getq(q)) != NULL) {
      if (pcmsg(mp->b_datap->db_type) ||
        canputnext(q) {
            /* process the message */
            putnext(q, mp);
      } else {
            putbq(q, mp);
            return;
      }
}
```

If the module or driver cares about priority bands, the algorithm becomes:

```
queue_t *q;
mblk_t *mp;

while ((mp = getq(q)) != NULL) {
      if (pcmsg(mp->b_datap->db_type) ||
        bcanputnext(q, mp->b_band)) {
            /* process the message */
            putnext(q, mp);
      } else {
            putbq(q, mp);
            return;
      }
}
```

NOTES

This entry point is optional for modules and drivers, but multiplexing drivers are required to implement service routines for the upper and lower halves of the multiplexor. Furthermore, the only safe way to transfer messages between the upper and lower halves is to use **putq**(D3DK), **getq**(D3DK), **putbq**(D3DK), **insq**(D3DK), or **rmvq**(D3DK). In other words, multiplexing drivers must employ their service procedures to transfer messages between their upper and lower halves (that is, **putnext**(D3DK) cannot be called).

Each STREAMS module and driver can have a read and write service routine. If a service routine is not needed (because the **put** routine processes all messages), a **NULL** pointer should be placed in module's **qinit**(D4DK) structure.

If the service routine finishes running because of any reason other than flow control or an empty queue, then it must explicitly arrange for its rescheduling. For example, if an allocation error occurs during the processing of a message, the service routine can put the message back on the queue with **putbq**, and, before returning, arrange to have itself rescheduled [see **qenable**(D3DK)] at some later time [see **bufcall**(D3DK) and **timeout**(D3DK)].

Service routines do not have user context and so may not call any function that sleeps.

put routines can interrupt and run concurrently with service routines.

Only one copy of a queue's service routine will run at a time.

Drivers and modules should not call service routines directly. qenable(D3DK) should be used to schedule service routines to run.

Drivers should free any messages they do not recognize.

Modules should pass on any messages they do not recognize.

Drivers should fail any unrecognized M_IOCTL messages by converting them into M_IOCNAK messages and sending them upstream.

Modules should pass on any unrecognized M_IOCTL messages.

Service routines should never put high priority messages back on their queues.

RETURN VALUE

Ignored.

SEE ALSO

STREAMS Programmer's Guide
put(D2DK), bcanputnext(D3DK), bufcall(D3DK), canputnext(D3DK), getq(D3DK), pcmsg(D3DK), putbq(D3DK), putnext(D3DK), putq(D3DK), qenable(D3DK), timeout(D3DK), datab(D4DK), msgb(D4DK), qinit(D4DK), queue(D4DK)

NAME

start – initialize a device at system start-up

SYNOPSIS

void *prefix*start ( ) ;

DESCRIPTION

The **start** routine is called at system boot time after system services are available and interrupts have been enabled. It can be used to initialize the driver's data structures and/or hardware.

The **start** routine may perform the following types of activities:

initialize data structures for device access

allocate buffers for private buffering schemes

map the device into the system's virtual address space

initialize hardware (for example, perform a system generation and reset the board)

Functions that may result in the caller sleeping, or that require user context, such as **SV_WAIT**(D3DK), may not be called.

NOTES

This entry point is optional.

SEE ALSO

init(D2D)

NAME

strategy – perform block I/O

SYNOPSIS

```
#include <sys/types.h>
#include <sys/buf.h>

int prefixstrategy(struct buf *bp);
```

ARGUMENTS

bp　　　　　　Pointer to the buffer header.

DESCRIPTION

The **strategy** routine is called by the kernel to read and write blocks of data on the block device. **strategy** may also be called directly or indirectly (via a call to the kernel function **physiock**(D3DK)), to support the raw character interface of a block device from **read**(D2DK), **write**(D2DK) or **ioctl**(D2DK). The **strategy** routine's responsibility is to set up and initiate the data transfer.

Generally, the first validation test performed by the **strategy** routine is to see if the I/O is within the bounds of the device. If the starting block number, given by **bp->b_blkno**, is less than 0 or greater than the number of blocks on the device, **bioerror**(D3DK) should be used to set the buffer error number to **ENXIO**, the buffer should be marked done by calling **biodone**(D3DK), and the driver should return. If **bp->b_blkno** is equal to the number of blocks on the device and the operation is a write, indicated by the absence of the **B_READ** flag in **bp->b_flags** (!(bp->b_flags & B_READ)), then the same action should be taken. However, if the operation is a read and **bp->b_blkno** is equal to the number of blocks on the device, then the driver should set **bp->b_resid** equal to **bp->b_bcount**, mark the buffer done by calling **biodone**, and return. This will cause the read to return 0.

Once the I/O request has been validated, the **strategy** routine will queue the request. If there is not already a transfer under way, the I/O is started. Then the **strategy** routine returns. When the I/O is complete, the driver will call **biodone** to free the buffer and notify anyone who has called **biowait**(D3DK) to wait for the I/O to finish.

There are two kinds of I/O requests passed to **strategy** routines: normal block I/O requests and paged-I/O requests. Normal block I/O requests are identified by the absence of the **B_PAGEIO** flag in **bp->b_flags**. Here, the starting virtual address of the data transfer will be found in **bp->b_un.b_addr**. Paged-I/O requests are identified by the presence of the **B_PAGEIO** flag in **bp->b_flags**. These will not occur unless the driver has set the **D_NOBRKUP** flag [see **devflag**(D1D)]. The driver has several ways to perform a paged-I/O request.

If the driver wants to use virtual addresses, it can call **bp_mapin**(D3DK) to get a virtually contiguous mapping for the pages. If the driver wants to use physical addresses, it can also use **bp_mapin**, but only transfer one page at a time. The physical address can be obtained by calling **vtop**(D3D) for each page in the virtual range. The size of a page can be determined by calling **ptob**(D3DK). However, a more efficient way to use physical addresses is to use **getnextpg**(D3DK) and **pptophys**(D3D) for each page in the page list.

If the amount of data to be transferred is more than can be transferred, the driver can transfer as much as possible (if it supports partial reads and writes), use **bioerror** to set the buffer error number to EIO, and set **bp->b_resid** equal to the number of bytes not transferred. If all of the data were transferred, **bp->b_resid** should be set to 0.

NOTES

This entry point is required in all block drivers.

The **strategy** entry point has the necessary context to sleep, but it cannot assume it is called from the same context of the process that initiated the I/O request. Furthermore, the process that initiated the I/O might not even be in existence when the **strategy** routine is called.

RETURN VALUE

Ignored. Errors are returned by using **bioerror** to mark the buffer as being in error.

SEE ALSO

devflag(D1D), **read**(D2DK), **write**(D2DK), **biodone**(D3DK), **bioerror**(D3DK), **biowait**(D3DK), **bp_mapin**(D3DK), **getnextpg**(D3DK), **physiock**(D3DK), **pptophys**(D3D), **buf**(D4DK), **errnos**(D5DK)

NAME
write – write data to a device

SYNOPSIS
```
#include <sys/types.h>
#include <sys/errno.h>
#include <sys/uio.h>
#include <sys/cred.h>
```

int *prefix*write(dev_t *dev,* uio_t **uiop,* cred_t **crp*);

ARGUMENTS
dev   Device number.

uiop   Pointer to the **uio**(D4DK) structure that describes where the data is to be fetched from user space.

crp   Pointer to the user credential structure for the I/O transaction.

DESCRIPTION
The driver **write** routine is called during the **write**(2) system call. The **write** routine is responsible for transferring data from the user data area to the device. The pointer to the user credentials, *crp*, is available so the driver can check to see if the user can write privileged information, if the driver provides access to any. The **uio** structure provides the information necessary to determine how much data should be transferred. The **uiomove**(D3DK) function provides a convenient way to copy data using the **uio** structure.

Block drivers that provide a character interface can use **physiock**(D3DK) to perform the data transfer with the driver's **strategy**(D2DK) routine.

The write operation is intended to be synchronous from the caller's perspective. Minimally, the driver **write** routine should not return until the caller's buffer is no longer needed. For drivers that care about returning errors, the data should be committed to the device. For others, the data might only be copied to local staging buffers. Then the data will be committed to the device asynchronous to the user's request, losing the ability to return an error with the associated request.

NOTES
This interface is optional.

The **write** routine has user context and can sleep.

RETURN VALUE
The **write** routine should return 0 for success, or the appropriate error number.

SEE ALSO
read(D2DK), **strategy**(D2DK), **drv_priv**(D3DK), **physiock**(D3DK), **uiomove**(D3DK), **uwritec**(D3DK), **uio**(D4DK), **errnos**(D5DK)

NAME

    intro – introduction to kernel utility routines

SYNOPSIS

```
#include <sys/types.h>
#include <sys/ddi.h>
```

DESCRIPTION

    This section describes the kernel utility functions available for use by device drivers. Drivers must not call any kernel routines other than the ones described in this section.

    Unless otherwise stated, any kernel utility routine that sleeps will do so such that signals will not interrupt the sleep.

KERNEL UTILITY ROUTINES (D3)

KERNEL UTILITY ROUTINES (D3)

NAME

adjmsg – trim bytes from a message

SYNOPSIS

```
#include <sys/stream.h>
```

`int adjmsg(mblk_t *`*mp,* `int` *len*`);`

ARGUMENTS

mp   Pointer to the message to be trimmed.

len   The number of bytes to be removed.

DESCRIPTION

adjmsg removes bytes from a message. | *len*| (the absolute value of *len*) specifies how many bytes are to be removed. If *len* is greater than **0**, bytes are removed from the head of the message. If *len* is less than **0**, bytes are removed from the tail. **adjmsg** fails if | *len*| is greater than the number of bytes in *mp*. If *len* spans more than one message block in the message, the messages blocks must be the same type, or else **adjmsg** will fail.

RETURN VALUE

If the message can be trimmed successfully, 1 is returned. Otherwise, 0 is returned.

LEVEL

Base or Interrupt.

NOTES

Does not sleep.

Driver-defined basic locks, read/write locks, and sleep locks may be held across calls to this function.

If *len* is greater than the amount of data in a single message block, that message block is not freed. Rather, it is left linked in the message, and its read and write pointers are set equal to each other, indicating no data present in the block.

SEE ALSO

msgb(D4DK)

NAME

allocb – allocate a message block

SYNOPSIS

#include <sys/types.h>
#include <sys/stream.h>

mblk_t *allocb(int *size,* uint_t *pri*);

ARGUMENTS

size   The number of bytes in the message block.

pri   Priority of the request. This can take on one of three values: BPRI_LO,
            BPRI_MED, or BPRI_HI.

DESCRIPTION

allocb tries to allocate a STREAMS message block. Buffer allocation fails only
when the system is out of memory. If no buffer is available, the bufcall(D3DK)
function can help a module recover from an allocation failure.

The *pri* argument is a hint to the allocator indicating how badly the message is
needed. BPRI_LO should be used for normal data allocations. BPRI_MED should
be used for other non-critical allocations. BPRI_HI should be used for allocations
that absolutely must succeed, although success is not guaranteed. Some implementations may choose to ignore this parameter.

The following figure identifies the data structure members that are affected when
a message block is allocated.

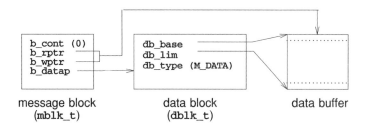

| message block   data block   data buffer |
| (mblk_t)   (dblk_t) |

RETURN VALUE

If successful, allocb returns a pointer to the allocated message block of type
M_DATA (defined in sys/stream.h). If a block cannot be allocated, a NULL pointer
is returned.

LEVEL

Base or Interrupt.

NOTES

Does not sleep.

Driver-defined basic locks, read/write locks, and sleep locks may be held across
calls to this function.

SEE ALSO

Programmer's Guide: STREAMS

bufcall(D3DK), **esballoc**(D3DK), **esbbcall**(D3DK), **freeb**(D3DK), **msgb**(D4DK)

EXAMPLE

Given a pointer to a queue (*q*) and an error number (*err*), the **send_error** routine sends an **M_ERROR** type message to the stream head.

If a message cannot be allocated, 0 is returned, indicating an allocation failure (line 7). Otherwise, the message type is set to **M_ERROR** (line 8). Line 9 increments the write pointer (**bp->b_wptr**) by the size (one byte) of the data in the message.

A message must be sent up the read side of the stream to arrive at the stream head. To determine whether *q* points to a read queue or a write queue, the **q->q_flag** member is tested to see if **QREADR** is set (line 10). If it is not set, *q* points to a write queue, and on line 11 the **RD**(D3DK) function is used to find the corresponding read queue. In line 12, the **putnext**(D3DK) function is used to send the message upstream. Then **send_error** returns 1 indicating success.

```
1    send_error(q, err)
2        queue_t *q;
3        uchar_t err;
4    {
5        mblk_t *bp;

6        if ((bp = allocb(1, BPRI_HI)) == NULL)
7                return(0);
8        bp->b_datap->db_type = M_ERROR;
9        *bp->b_wptr++ = err;
10       if (!(q->q_flag & QREADR))
11               q = RD(q);
12       putnext(q, bp);
13       return(1);
14   }
```

NAME

ASSERT – verify assertion

SYNOPSIS

```
#include <sys/debug.h>

void ASSERT(int expression);
```

ARGUMENTS

expression Expression to be evaluated.

DESCRIPTION

ASSERT is a debugging interface for verifying program invariants within code that is compiled with the DEBUG compilation option defined. *expression* is a boolean expression that the caller expects to evaluate to non-zero (that is, the caller is asserting that the expression has a non-zero value). If *expression* evaluates to non-zero, the ASSERT call has no effect. If *expression* evaluates to zero, ASSERT causes the system to panic with the following message:

PANIC: assertion failed: *expression*, file: *filename*, line: *lineno*

where *filename* is the name of the source file in which the failed assertion appears and *lineno* is the line number of the ASSERT call within the file.

When the DEBUG compilation option is not defined, ASSERT calls are not compiled into the code, and therefore have no effect.

RETURN VALUE

If *expression* evaluates to non-zero, ASSERT returns no value. If *expression* evaluates to zero, ASSERT panics the system.

LEVEL

Base or Interrupt.

NOTES

Does not sleep.

Driver-defined basic locks, read/write locks, and sleep locks may be held across calls to this function.

SEE ALSO

cmn_err(D3DK)

NAME

bcanput – test for flow control in specified priority band

SYNOPSIS

```
#include <sys/types.h>
#include <sys/stream.h>

int bcanput(queue_t *q, uchar_t pri);
```

ARGUMENTS

q   Pointer to the message queue.

pri   Message priority.

DESCRIPTION

bcanput tests if there is room for a message in priority band *pri* of the queue pointed to by *q*. The queue *must* have a service procedure.

If *pri* is 0, the **bcanput** call is equivalent to a call to **canput**.

It is possible because of race conditions to test for room using **bcanput** and get an indication that there is room for a message, and then have the queue fill up before subsequently enqueuing the message, causing a violation of flow control. This is not a problem, since the violation of flow control in this case is bounded.

RETURN VALUE

bcanput returns 1 if a message of priority *pri* can be placed on the queue. 0 is returned if a message of priority *pri* cannot be enqueued because of flow control within the priority band.

LEVEL

Base or Interrupt.

NOTES

Does not sleep.

The driver is responsible for both testing a queue with **bcanput** and refraining from placing a message on the queue if **bcanput** fails.

The caller cannot have the stream frozen [see **freezestr**(D3DK)] when calling this function.

Driver-defined basic locks, read/write locks, and sleep locks may be held across calls to this function.

The *q* argument may not reference **q_next** (for example, an argument of **q->q_next** is erroneous on a multiprocessor and is disallowed by the DDI/DKI). **bcanputnext(q)** is provided as a multiprocessor-safe equivalent to the common call **bcanput(q->q_next)**, which is no longer allowed [see **bcanputnext**(D3DK)].

SEE ALSO

bcanputnext(D3DK), canput(D3DK), canputnext(D3DK), putbq(D3DK), putnext(D3DK)

NAME

bcanputnext – test for flow control in a specified priority band

SYNOPSIS

```
#include <sys/types.h>
#include <sys/stream.h>

int bcanputnext(queue_t *q, uchar_t pri);
```

ARGUMENTS

q   Pointer to a message queue.

pri   Message priority.

DESCRIPTION

bcanputnext searches through the stream (starting at *q->q_next*) until it finds a queue containing a service routine, or until it reaches the end of the stream. If found, the queue containing the service routine is tested to see if a message in priority band *pri* can be enqueued. If the band is full, **bcanputnext** marks the queue to automatically back-enable the caller's service routine when the amount of data in messages on the queue has reached its low water mark.

If *pri* is 0, the **bcanputnext** call is equivalent to a call to **canputnext**.

It is possible because of race conditions to test for room using **bcanputnext** and get an indication that there is room for a message, and then have the queue fill up before subsequently enqueuing the message, causing a violation of flow control. This is not a problem since the violation of flow control in this case is bounded.

RETURN VALUE

bcanputnext returns 1 if a message of priority *pri* can be sent in the stream, or 0 if the priority band is flow-controlled. If **bcanputnext** reaches the end of the stream without finding a queue with a service routine, then it returns 1.

LEVEL

Base or Interrupt.

NOTES

Does not sleep.

The driver writer is responsible for both testing a queue with **bcanputnext** and refraining from placing a message on the queue if **bcanputnext** fails.

The caller cannot have the stream frozen [see **freezestr**(D3DK)] when calling this function.

Driver defined basic locks, read/write locks, and sleep locks may be held across calls to this function.

The *q* argument may not reference **q_next** (for example, an argument of **q->q_next** is erroneous on a multiprocessor and is disallowed by the DDI/DKI). **bcanputnext(q)** is provided as a multiprocessor-safe equivalent to the common call **bcanput(q->q_next)**, which is no longer allowed.

SEE ALSO

bcanput(D3DK), canput(D3DK), canputnext(D3DK), putbq(D3DK), putnext(D3DK)

NAME

bcopy – copy data between address locations in the kernel

SYNOPSIS

```
#include <sys/types.h>

void bcopy(caddr_t from, caddr_t to, size_t bcount);
```

ARGUMENTS

from   Source address from which the copy is made.

to   Destination address to which the copy is made.

bcount   Number of bytes to be copied.

DESCRIPTION

bcopy copies *bcount* bytes from one kernel address to another. It chooses the best algorithm based on address alignment and number of bytes to copy. If the input and output addresses overlap, the function executes, but the results are undefined.

RETURN VALUE

None.

LEVEL

Base or Interrupt.

NOTES

Does not sleep.

Driver-defined basic locks, read/write locks, and sleep locks may be held across calls to this function.

The source and destination address ranges must both be within the kernel address space and must be memory resident. No range checking is done. Since there is no mechanism by which drivers that conform to the rules of the DDI/DKI can obtain and use a kernel address which is not memory resident (an address which is paged out), DDI/DKI conforming drivers can assume that any address to which they have access is memory resident and therefore a valid argument to bcopy. Addresses within user address space are not valid arguments, and specifying such an address may cause the driver to corrupt the system in an unpredictable way. For copying between kernel and user space, drivers must use an appropriate function defined for that purpose (for example, copyin(D3DK), copyout(D3DK), uiomove(D3DK), ureadc(D3DK), or uwritec(D3DK)).

SEE ALSO

copyin(D3DK), copyout(D3DK), uiomove(D3DK), ureadc(D3DK), uwritec(D3DK)

EXAMPLE

An I/O request is made for data stored in a RAM disk. If the I/O operation is a read request, data are copied from the RAM disk to a buffer (line 9). If it is a write request, data are copied from a buffer to the RAM disk (line 15). The bcopy function is used since both the RAM disk and the buffer are part of the kernel address space.

```
1  #define RAMDNBLK    1000         /* number of blocks in the RAM disk */
2  #define RAMDBSIZ    NBPSCTR       /* bytes per block */
3  char ramdblks[RAMDNBLK][RAMDBSIZ]; /* blocks forming RAM disk */
       . . .
4
5  if (bp->b_flags & B_READ) {
6          /*
7           * read request - copy data from RAM disk to system buffer
8           */
9          bcopy(ramdblks[bp->b_blkno], bp->b_un.b_addr, bp->b_bcount);
10
11 } else {
12         /*
13          * write request - copy data from system buffer to RAM disk
14          */
15         bcopy(bp->b_un.b_addr, ramdblks[bp->b_blkno], bp->b_bcount);
16 }
```

NAME
 biodone – release buffer after block I/O and wakeup processes

SYNOPSIS
```
#include <sys/types.h>
#include <sys/buf.h>

void biodone(buf_t *bp);
```

ARGUMENTS
 bp   Pointer to the buffer header structure.

DESCRIPTION
 The **biodone** function is called by the driver when a block I/O request is complete. It is usually called from the driver's **strategy**(D2DK) routine or I/O completion handler [usually **intr**(D2D)].

 If the driver had specified an *iodone handler* by initializing the **b_iodone** field of the **buf**(D4DK) structure to the address of a function, that function is called with the single parameter, *bp*. Then **biodone** returns.

 If the driver had not specified an iodone handler, **biodone** will release the buffer back to the system. If there were any processes waiting for the I/O to complete, or for the buffer to be released, one is awakened.

RETURN VALUE
 None.

LEVEL
 Base or Interrupt.

NOTES
 Does not sleep.

 Driver-defined basic locks, read/write locks, and sleep locks may be held across calls to this function.

 If the buffer was allocated via **getrbuf**(D3DK), the driver must have specified an iodone handler.

SEE ALSO
 intr(D2D), **strategy**(D2DK), **biowait**(D3DK), **brelse**(D3DK), **freerbuf**(D3DK), **getrbuf**(D3DK), **buf**(D4DK)

EXAMPLE
 Generally, the first validation test performed by any block device **strategy** routine is a check to verify the bounds of the I/O request. If a **read** request is made for one block beyond the limits of the device (line 8), it will report an end-of-media condition (line 10). Otherwise, if the request is outside the limits of the device, the routine will report an error condition (line 12). In either case, the I/O operation is completed by calling **biodone** (line 14) and the driver returns.

```
1   #define RAMDNBLK    1000                /* Number of blocks in RAM disk */
2   #define RAMDBSIZ     512                /* Number of bytes per block */
3   char ramdblks[RAMDNBLK][RAMDBSIZ]; /* Array containing RAM disk */

4   ramdstrategy(bp)
5     register struct buf *bp;
6   {
7     register daddr_t blkno = bp->b_blkno;

8     if ((blkno < 0) || (blkno >= RAMDNBLK)) {
9         if ((blkno == RAMDNBLK) && (bp->b_flags & B_READ)) {
10            bp->b_resid = bp->b_bcount;      /* nothing read */
11        } else {
12            bioerror(bp, ENXIO);
13        }
14        biodone(bp);
15        return;
16    }
      . . .
```

NAME

bioerror – manipulate error field within a buffer header

SYNOPSIS

```
#include <sys/types.h>
#include <sys/buf.h>

void bioerror(buf_t *bp, int errno);
```

ARGUMENTS

bp　　　　Pointer to the buffer header.

errno　　　Error number to be set, or zero to indicate that the error field within the buffer header should be cleared.

DESCRIPTION

bioerror is used to manipulate the error field within a buffer header (buf(D4DK) structure). Driver code (for example, a strategy(D2DK) routine) that wishes to report an I/O error condition associated with the buffer pointed to by *bp* should call bioerror with *errno* set to the appropriate error number. This will set the appropriate field within the buffer header so that higher level code can detect the error and retrieve the error number using geterror(D3DK).

The error field within the buffer header can be cleared by calling bioerror with *errno* set to zero.

RETURN VALUE

None.

LEVEL

Base or Interrupt.

NOTES

Does not sleep.

Driver defined basic locks, read/write locks, and sleep locks may be held across calls to this function.

DDI/DKI conforming drivers are no longer permitted to manipulate the error field of the buf structure directly. bioerror must be used for this purpose.

SEE ALSO

strategy(D2DK), geteblk(D3DK), geterror(D3DK), getrbuf(D3DK), ngeteblk(D3DK), buf(D4DK), errnos(D5DK)

NAME

biowait – suspend processes pending completion of block I/O

SYNOPSIS

```
#include <sys/types.h>
#include <sys/buf.h>

int biowait(buf_t *bp);
```

ARGUMENTS

bp   Pointer to the buffer header structure.

DESCRIPTION

The **biowait** function suspends process execution during block I/O. Block drivers that have allocated their own buffers with **geteblk**(D3DK), **getrbuf**(D3DK), or **ngeteblk**(D3DK) can use **biowait** to suspend the current process execution while waiting for a read or write request to complete.

Drivers using **biowait** must use **biodone**(D3DK) in their I/O completion handlers to signal **biowait** when the I/O transfer is complete.

RETURN VALUE

If an error occurred during the I/O transfer, the error number is returned. Otherwise, on success, 0 is returned.

LEVEL

Base Only.

NOTES

Can sleep.

Driver-defined basic locks and read/write locks may not be held across calls to this function.

Driver defined sleep locks may be held across calls to this function.

SEE ALSO

intr(D2D), **strategy**(D2DK), **biodone**(D3DK), **geteblk**(D3DK), **getrbuf**(D3DK), **ngeteblk**(D3DK), **buf**(D4DK)

NAME

bp_mapin – allocate virtual address space for buffer page list

SYNOPSIS

```
#include <sys/types.h>
#include <sys/buf.h>

void bp_mapin(struct buf *bp);
```

ARGUMENTS

bp   Pointer to the buffer header structure.

DESCRIPTION

The **bp_mapin** function is used to map virtual address space to a page list maintained by the buffer header [see **buf**(D4DK)] during a paged-I/O request. A paged-I/O request is identified by the **B_PAGEIO** flag being set in the **b_flags** field of the buffer header passed to a driver's **strategy**(D2DK) routine. Before calling **bp_mapin**, the offset of the location in the first page where the I/O is to begin is stored in the **b_un.b_addr** field of the **buf** structure referenced by *bp* (for **strategy** routines, this is done for the driver by the system.)

bp_mapin allocates system virtual address space, maps that space to the page list, and returns the new virtual address in the **b_un.b_addr** field of the **buf** structure. This address is the virtual address of the start of the page mappings, plus the offset requested by the caller. After the I/O completes, the virtual address space can be deallocated using the **bp_mapout**(D3DK) function.

RETURN VALUE

None.

LEVEL

Base only.

NOTES

B_PAGEIO won't be set unless the driver has the **D_NOBRKUP** flag set [see **devflag**(D1D).]

This routine may sleep if virtual space is not immediately available.

Driver-defined basic locks and read/write locks may not be held across calls to this function.

Driver-defined sleep locks may be held across calls to this function.

SEE ALSO

devflag(D1D), **strategy**(D2DK), **bp_mapout**(D3DK), **buf**(D4DK)

NAME

bp_mapout – deallocate virtual address space for buffer page list

SYNOPSIS

```
#include <sys/types.h>
#include <sys/buf.h>

void bp_mapout(struct buf *bp);
```

ARGUMENTS

bp   Pointer to the buffer header structure.

DESCRIPTION

This function deallocates the system virtual address space associated with a buffer
header page list. The virtual address space must have been allocated by a previous call to **bp_mapin**(D3DK). Drivers should not reference any virtual addresses
in the mapped range after **bp_mapout** has been called.

RETURN VALUE

None.

LEVEL

Base or Interrupt.

NOTES

Driver-defined basic locks, read/write locks, and sleep locks may be held across
calls to this function.

SEE ALSO

bp_mapin(D3DK), **buf**(D4DK)

NAME

brelse – return a buffer to the system's free list

SYNOPSIS

```
#include <sys/types.h>
#include <sys/buf.h>

void brelse(struct buf *bp);
```

ARGUMENTS

bp   Pointer to the buffer header.

DESCRIPTION

The **brelse** function returns the buffer specified by *bp* to the system's buffer free list. If there were any processes waiting for this specific buffer to become free, or for any buffer to become available on the free list, one is awakened. The buffer specified by *bp* must have been previously allocated by a call to **geteblk**(D3DK) or **ngeteblk**(D3DK). **brelse** may not be called to release a buffer which has been allocated by any other means.

RETURN VALUE

None.

LEVEL

Base or Interrupt.

NOTES

Does not sleep.

Driver-defined basic locks, read/write locks, and sleep locks may be held across calls to this function.

SEE ALSO

clrbuf(D3DK), **biodone**(D3DK), **biowait**(D3DK), **geteblk**(D3DK), **ngeteblk**(D3DK), **buf**(D4DK)

NAME

btop – convert size in bytes to size in pages (round down)

SYNOPSIS

```
#include <sys/types.h>
#include <sys/ddi.h>

ulong_t btop(ulong_t numbytes);
```

ARGUMENTS

numbytes Size in bytes to convert to equivalent size in pages.

DESCRIPTION

btop returns the number of pages that are contained in the specified number of bytes, with downward rounding if the byte count is not a page multiple.

For example, if the page size is 2048, then btop(4096) and btop(4097) both return 2, and btop(4095) returns 1.

btop(0) returns 0.

RETURN VALUE

The return value is the number of pages. There are no invalid input values, and therefore no error return values.

LEVEL

Base or Interrupt.

NOTES

Does not sleep.

Driver-defined basic locks, read/write locks, and sleep locks may be held across calls to this function.

SEE ALSO

btopr(D3DK), ptob(D3DK)

NAME

btopr – convert size in bytes to size in pages (round up)

SYNOPSIS

```
#include <sys/types.h>
#include <sys/ddi.h>

ulong_t btopr(ulong_t numbytes);
```

ARGUMENTS

numbytes   Size in bytes to convert to equivalent size in pages.

DESCRIPTION

btopr returns the number of pages that are contained in the specified number of bytes, with upward rounding if the byte count is not a page multiple.

For example, if the page size is 2048, then btopr(4096) and btopr(4095) both return 2, and btopr(4097) returns 3.

btopr(0) returns 0.

RETURN VALUE

The return value is the number of pages. There are no invalid input values, and therefore no error return values.

LEVEL

Base or Interrupt.

NOTES

Does not sleep.

Driver-defined basic locks, read/write locks, and sleep locks may be held across calls to this function.

SEE ALSO

btop(D3DK), ptob(D3DK)

NAME

bufcall – call a function when a buffer becomes available

SYNOPSIS

```
#include <sys/types.h>
#include <sys/stream.h>

toid_t bufcall(uint_t size, int pri, void (*func)(), long arg);
```

ARGUMENTS

size Number of bytes in the buffer to be allocated (from the failed **allocb**(D3DK) request).

pri   Priority of the **allocb** allocation request (**BPRI_LO**, **BPRI_MED**, or **BPRI_HI**).

func Function or driver routine to be called when a buffer becomes available.

arg   Argument to the function to be called when a buffer becomes available.

DESCRIPTION

bufcall serves as a **timeout** call of indeterminate length. When a buffer alloca-tion request fails, **bufcall** can be used to schedule the routine, *func*, to be called with the argument, *arg*, when a buffer of at least *size* bytes becomes available.

When *func* runs, all interrupts from STREAMS devices will be blocked on the pro-cessor on which it is running. *func* will have no user context and may not call any function that sleeps.

RETURN VALUE

If successful, **bufcall** returns a non-zero value that identifies the scheduling request. This non-zero identifier may be passed to **unbufcall**(D3DK) to cancel the request. If any failure occurs, **bufcall** returns 0.

LEVEL

Base or Interrupt.

NOTES

Does not sleep.

Driver-defined basic locks, read/write locks, and sleep locks may be held across calls to this function.

Even when *func* is called, **allocb** can still fail if another module or driver had allocated the memory before *func* was able to call **allocb**.

SEE ALSO

allocb(D3DK), **esballoc**(D3DK), **esbbcall**(D3DK), **itimeout**(D3DK), **unbufcall**(D3DK)

EXAMPLE

The purpose of this service routine [see **srv**(D2DK)] is to add a header to all **M_DATA** messages. We assume only **M_DATA** messages are added to its queue. Service routines must process all messages on their queues before returning, or arrange to be rescheduled.

While there are messages to be processed (line 21), we check to see if we can send the message on in the stream. If not, we put the message back on the queue (line 23) and return. The STREAMS flow control mechanism will re-enable us later when messages can be sent. If **canputnext**(D3DK) succeeded, we try to allocate a buffer large enough to hold the header (line 26). If no buffer is available, the service routine must be rescheduled later, when a buffer is available. We put the original message back on the queue (line 28), lock the private data structure, and use **bufcall** to attempt the rescheduling (lines 30 and 31). If **bufcall** succeeds, we set the **m_type** field in the module's private data structure to **BUFCALL**. If **bufcall** failed, we use **itimeout**(D3DK) to reschedule us instead (line 33). **modcall** will be called in about a half second [**drv_usectohz(500000)**]. When the rescheduling has been done, we unlock the private data structure and return.

When **modcall** runs, it will lock the private data structure and set the **m_type** field to zero, indicating that there is no outstanding request. Then the data structure is unlocked and the queue's service routine is scheduled to run by calling **qenable**(D3DK) (line 59).

If the buffer allocation is successful, we initialize the header (lines 41–43), make the message type **M_PROTO** (line 45), link the **M_DATA** message to it (line 46), and pass it on (line 47).

See **unbufcall**(D3DK) for the other half of this example.

```
 1   struct hdr {
 2       uint_t h_size;
 3       int     h_version;
 4   };
 5   struct mod {
 6       toid_t m_id;
 7       char    m_type;
 8       lock_t *m_lock;
         . . .
 9   };
10   #define TIMEOUT  1
11   #define BUFCALL  2
     . . .
12   modsrv(q) /* assume only M_DATA messages enqueued here */
13         queue_t *q;
14   {
15       mblk_t *bp;
16       mblk_t *mp;
17       struct hdr *hp;
18       struct mod *modp;
19       pl_t pl;

20       modp = (struct mod *)q->q_ptr;
21       while ((mp = getq(q)) != NULL) {
22             if (!canputnext(q)) {
23                   putbq(q, mp);
24                   return;
25             }
26             bp = allocb(sizeof(struct hdr), BPRI_MED);
27             if (bp == NULL) {
28                   putbq(q, mp);
29                   pl = LOCK(modp->m_lock, plstr);
30                   modp->m_id = bufcall(sizeof(struct hdr), BPRI_MED, modcall,
31                         (long)q);
32                   if (modp->m_id == 0) {
33                         modp->m_id = itimeout(modcall, q, drv_usectohz(500000), plstr);
```

```
34                      modp->m_type = TIMEOUT;
35                  } else {
36                      modp->m_type = BUFCALL;
37                  }
38                  UNLOCK(modp->m_lock, pl);
39                  return;
40              }
41          hp = (struct hdr *)bp->b_wptr;
42          hp->h_size = msgdsize(mp);
43          hp->h_version = 1;
44          bp->b_wptr += sizeof(struct hdr);
45          bp->b_datap->db_type = M_PROTO;
46          bp->b_cont = mp;
47          putnext(q, bp);
48      }
49  }
50  modcall(q)
51      queue_t *q;
52  {
53      struct mod *modp;
54      pl_t pl;

55      modp = (struct mod *)q->q_ptr;
56      pl = LOCK(modp->m_lock, plstr);
57      modp->m_type = 0;
58      UNLOCK(modp->m_lock, pl);
59      qenable(q);
60  }
```

NAME

bzero – clear memory for a given number of bytes

SYNOPSIS

```
#include <sys/types.h>

void bzero(caddr_t addr, size_t bytes);
```

ARGUMENTS

addr   Starting virtual address of memory to be cleared.

bytes   The number of bytes to clear.

DESCRIPTION

The **bzero** function clears a contiguous portion of memory by filling the memory with zeros. It chooses the best algorithm based on address alignment and number of bytes to clear.

RETURN VALUE

None.

LEVEL

Base or Interrupt.

NOTES

Does not sleep.

Driver-defined basic locks, read/write locks, and sleep locks may be held across calls to this function.

There are no alignment restrictions on *addr*, and no length restrictions on *bytes*, other than the address range specified must be within the kernel address space and must be memory resident. No range checking is done. Since there is no mechanism by which drivers that conform to the rules of the DDI/DKI can obtain and use a kernel address that is not memory resident (an address that is paged out), DDI/DKI conforming drivers can assume that any address to which they have access is memory resident and therefore a valid argument to **bzero**. An address within user address space is not a valid argument, and specifying such an address may cause the driver to corrupt the system in an unpredictable way.

SEE ALSO

bcopy(D3DK), clrbuf(D3DK), kmem_zalloc(D3DK)

EXAMPLE

In a driver **close**(D2DK) routine, rather than clear each individual member of its private data structure, the driver could use **bzero** as shown here:

```
bzero((caddr_t)&drv_dat[getminor(dev)], sizeof(struct drvr_data));
```

NAME

canput – test for room in a message queue

SYNOPSIS

```
#include <sys/stream.h>

int canput(queue_t *q);
```

ARGUMENTS

q　　　　　　　Pointer to the message queue.

DESCRIPTION

canput tests if there is room for a message in the queue pointed to by *q*. The queue *must* have a service procedure.

It is possible because of race conditions to test for room using canput and get an indication that there is room for a message, and then have the queue fill up before subsequently enqueuing the message, causing a violation of flow control. This is not a problem, since the violation of flow control in this case is bounded.

RETURN VALUE

canput returns 1 if a message can be placed on the queue. 0 is returned if a message cannot be enqueued because of flow control.

LEVEL

Base or Interrupt.

NOTES

Does not sleep.

The driver is responsible for both testing a queue with canput and refraining from placing a message on the queue if canput fails.

The caller cannot have the stream frozen [see freezestr(D3DK)] when calling this function.

Driver-defined basic locks, read/write locks, and sleep locks may be held across calls to this function.

The *q* argument may not reference q_next (for example, an argument of q->q_next is erroneous on a multiprocessor and is disallowed by the DDI/DKI). canputnext(q) is provided as a multiprocessor-safe equivalent to the common call canput(q->q_next), which is no longer allowed [see canputnext(D3DK)].

SEE ALSO

bcanput(D3DK), bcanputnext(D3DK), canputnext(D3DK), putbq(D3DK), putnext(D3DK)

NAME

canputnext – test for flow control in a stream

SYNOPSIS

```
#include <sys/stream.h>

int canputnext(queue_t *q);
```

ARGUMENTS

q　　　　　Pointer to a message queue.

DESCRIPTION

canputnext searches through the stream (starting at q->q_next) until it finds a queue containing a service routine, or until it reaches the end of the stream. If found, the queue containing the service routine is tested to see if there is room for a message in the queue. If the queue is full, canputnext marks the queue to automatically back-enable the caller's service routine when the amount of data in messages on the queue has reached its low water mark.

It is possible because of race conditions to test for room using canputnext and get an indication that there is room for a message, and then have the queue fill up before subsequently enqueuing the message, causing a violation of flow control. This is not a problem since the violation of flow control in this case is bounded.

RETURN VALUE

canputnext returns 1 if a message can be sent in the stream, or 0 if the stream is flow-controlled. If canputnext reaches the end of the stream without finding a queue with a service routine, then it returns 1.

LEVEL

Base or Interrupt.

NOTES

Does not sleep.

The driver writer is responsible for both testing a queue with canputnext and refraining from placing a message on the queue if canputnext fails.

The caller cannot have the stream frozen [see freezestr(D3DK)] when calling this function.

Driver defined basic locks, read/write locks, and sleep locks may be held across calls to this function.

The q argument may not reference q_next (e.g. an argument of q->q_next is erroneous on a multiprocessor and is disallowed by the DDI/DKI). canputnext(q) is provided as a multiprocessor-safe equivalent to the common call canput(q->q_next), which is no longer allowed.

SEE ALSO

bcanput(D3DK), bcanputnext(D3DK), canput(D3DK), putbq(D3DK), putnext(D3DK)

NAME

clrbuf – erase the contents of a buffer

SYNOPSIS

```
#include <sys/types.h>
#include <sys/buf.h>

void clrbuf(buf_t *bp);
```

ARGUMENTS

bp   Pointer to the buffer header structure.

DESCRIPTION

The **clrbuf** function zeros a buffer and sets the **b_resid** member of the **buf**(D4DK) structure to 0. Zeros are placed in the buffer starting at the address specified by **b_un.b_addr** for a length of **b_bcount** bytes.

If the buffer has the **B_PAGEIO** flag set in the **b_flags** field, then **clrbuf** should not be called until the proper virtual space has been allocated by a call to **bp_mapin**(D3DK).

RETURN VALUE

None.

LEVEL

Base or Interrupt.

NOTES

Does not sleep.

Driver-defined basic locks, read/write locks, and sleep locks may be held across calls to this function.

SEE ALSO

bp_mapin(D3DK), **buf**(D4DK)

NAME

cmn_err – display an error message or panic the system

SYNOPSIS

```
#include <sys/cmn_err.h>

void cmn_err( int level, char *format, . . . /* args */) ;
```

ARGUMENTS

level   *level* indicates the severity of the error condition. Valid levels are:

    CE_CONT   used to continue a previous message or to display an informative message not connected with an error.

    CE_NOTE   used to display a message preceded with **NOTICE:** . This message is used to report system events that do not necessarily require action, but may interest the system administrator. For example, a message saying that a sector on a disk needs to be accessed repeatedly before it can be accessed correctly might be noteworthy.

    CE_WARN   used to display a message preceded with **WARNING:** . This message is used to report system events that require immediate attention, such as those where if an action is not taken, the system may panic. For example, when a peripheral device does not initialize correctly, this level should be used.

    CE_PANIC   used to display a message preceded with **PANIC:** , and panic the system. Drivers should use this level only for debugging or in the case of severe errors that indicate that the system cannot continue to function. This level halts processing.

format The message to be displayed. By default, the message is sent both to the system console and to the circular kernel buffer, **putbuf**. If the first character in *format* is an exclamation point ("!"), the message goes only to **putbuf**. If the first character in *format* is a circumflex ("^"), the message goes only to the console. The size of the kernel buffer **putbuf** is defined by the kernel variable **putbufsz**. Driver developers or administrators can read the **putbuf** buffer using appropriate debugging or administrative tools (for example, **crash**(1M)).

        cmn_err appends **\n** to each *format* string, even when a message is sent to **putbuf**, except when *level* is **CE_CONT**.

        Valid conversion specifications are %**s**, %**u**, %**d**, %**o**, and %**x**. The **cmn_err** function is otherwise similar to the **printf**(3S) library subroutine in its interpretation of the *format* string, except that **cmn_err** does not accept length specifications in conversion specifications. For example, %**3d** is invalid and will be treated as a literal string, resulting in a mismatch of arguments.

args   the set of arguments passed with the message being displayed. Any argument within the range of supported conversion specifications can be passed.

DESCRIPTION

cmn_err displays a specified message on the console and/or stores it in the kernel buffer **putbuf**. **cmn_err** can also panic the system.

At times, a driver may encounter error conditions requiring the attention of a system console monitor. These conditions may mean halting the system; however, this must be done with caution. Except during the debugging stage, or in the case of a serious, unrecoverable error, a driver should never stop the system.

The **cmn_err** function with the **CE_CONT** argument can be used by driver developers as a driver code debugging tool. However, using **cmn_err** in this capacity can change system timing characteristics.

RETURN VALUE

None.

LEVEL

Base or Interrupt.

NOTES

Does not sleep.

If *level* is **CE_PANIC**, then driver defined basic locks, read/write locks, and sleep locks may not be held across calls to this function. For other levels, locks may be held.

SEE ALSO

print(D2DK)

crash(1M) in the *System Administrator's Reference Manual*

printf(3S) in the *Programmer's Reference Manual*

EXAMPLE

The **cmn_err** function can record tracing and debugging information only in the **putbuf** buffer (lines 12 and 13) or display problems with a device only on the system console (lines 17 and 18).

```
 1  struct  device { /* device registers layout */
        . . .
 2      int status;    /* device status word */
 3  };

 4  extern struct device xx_dev[]; /* physical device registers */
 5  extern int xx_cnt;             /* number of physical devices */
        . . .
 6  int
 7  xxopen(dev_t *devp, int flag, int otyp, cred_t *crp)
 8  {
 9      register struct device *dp;

10      dp = xx_dev[getminor(*devp)];      /* get dev registers */
11  #ifdef DEBUG                           /* in debugging mode, log function call */
12      cmn_err(CE_NOTE, "!xxopen function call, dev = 0x%x", *devp);
13      cmn_err(CE_CONT, "! flag = 0x%x", flag);
14  #endif

15      /* display device power failure on system console */
```

```
16      if ((dp->status & POWER) == OFF)
17          cmn_err(CE_WARN, "^xxopen: Power is OFF on device %d port %d",
18              getemajor(*devp), geteminor(*devp));
```

NAME

copyb – copy a message block

SYNOPSIS

```
#include <sys/stream.h>

mblk_t *copyb(mblk_t *bp);
```

ARGUMENTS

bp   Pointer to the message block from which data are copied.

DESCRIPTION

copyb allocates a new message block, and copies into it the data from the block pointed to by *bp*. The new block will be at least as large as the block being copied. The **b_rptr** and **b_wptr** members of the message block pointed to by *bp* are used to determine how many bytes to copy.

RETURN VALUE

If successful, copyb returns a pointer to the newly allocated message block containing the copied data. Otherwise, it returns a **NULL** pointer.

LEVEL

Base or Interrupt.

NOTES

Does not sleep.

Driver-defined basic locks, read/write locks, and sleep locks may be held across calls to this function.

SEE ALSO

allocb(D3DK), copymsg(D3DK), msgb(D4DK)

EXAMPLE

This example illustrates how copyb can be used during message retransmission. If there are no messages to retransmit, we return (line 21). Otherwise, we lock the retransmission list (line 23). For each retransmission record in the list, we test to see if either the message has already been retransmitted, or if the downstream queue is full (by calling canputnext(D3DK) on line 26). If either is true, we skip the current retransmission record and continue searching the list. Otherwise, we use copyb(D3DK) to copy a header message block (line 30), and dupmsg(D3DK) to duplicate the data to be retransmitted (line 32).

If either operation fails, we clean up and break out of the loop. Otherwise, we update the new header block with the correct destination address (line 37), link the message to be retransmitted to it (line 38), mark the retransmission record as having sent the message (line 39), unlock the retransmission list (line 40), and send the message downstream (line 41). Then we go back and lock the list again and start searching for more messages to retransmit.

This continues until we are either at the end of the retransmission list, or unable to send a message because of allocation failure. With the list still locked, we clear all the flags for sent messages (lines 44 and 45). Finally, we unlock the list lock and reschedule a **timeout** at the next valid interval (line 47) and return. Since we are using itimeout(D3DK), **retransmit** will run at the specified processor level, plstr.

```
1   struct retrns {
2       mblk_t          *r_mp;          /* message to retransmit */
3       long            r_address;      /* destination address */
4       queue_t         *r_outq;        /* output queue */
5       struct retrns   *r_next;        /* next retransmission */
6       uchar_t         r_sent;         /* message sent */
7   };
8   struct protoheader {
9       long            h_address;      /* destination address */
        ...
10  };
11  mblk_t *header;
12  lock_t *retranslck;
13  struct retrns *rlist;
    ...
14  retransmit()
15  {
16      register mblk_t *bp, *mp;
17      register struct retrns *rp;
18      struct protoheader *php;
19      pl_t pl;

20      if (!rlist)
21              return;
22  loop:
23      pl = LOCK(retranslck, plstr);
24      rp = rlist;
25      while (rp) {
26              if (rp->r_sent || !canputnext(rp->r_outq)) {
27                      rp = rp->r_next;
28                      continue;
29              }
30              if ((bp = copyb(header)) == NULL)
31                      break;
32              if ((mp = dupmsg(rp->r_mp)) == NULL) {
33                      freeb(bp);
34                      break;
35              }
36              php = (struct protoheader *)bp->b_rptr;
37              php->h_address = rp->r_address;
38              bp->bp_cont = mp;
39              rp->r_sent = 1;
40              UNLOCK(retranslck, pl);
41              putnext(rp->r_outq, bp);
42              goto loop;
43      }
44      for (rp = rlist; rp; rp = rp->r_next)
45              rp->r_sent = 0;
46      UNLOCK(retranslck, pl);
47      (void) itimeout(retransmit, 0, RETRNS_TIME, plstr);
48  }
```

NAME

copyin – copy data from a user buffer to a driver buffer

SYNOPSIS

```
#include <sys/types.h>

int copyin(caddr_t userbuf, caddr_t driverbuf, size_t count);
```

ARGUMENTS

userbuf   User source address from which copy is made.

driverbuf   Driver destination address to which copy is made.

count   Number of bytes to copy.

DESCRIPTION

copyin copies *count* bytes of data from the user virtual address specified by *userbuf* to the kernel virtual address specified by *driverbuf*. The driver must ensure that adequate space is allocated for the destination address.

copyin chooses the best algorithm based on address alignment and number of bytes to copy. Although the source and destination addresses are not required to be word aligned, word aligned addresses may result in a more efficient copy.

RETURN VALUE

If the copy is successful, 0 is returned. Otherwise, –1 is returned to indicate that the specified user address range is not valid.

LEVEL

Base Only.

NOTES

May sleep.

Drivers usually convert a return value of –1 into an **EFAULT** error.

Driver-defined basic locks and read/write locks may not be held across calls to this function.

Driver-defined sleep locks may be held across calls to this function.

When holding sleep locks across calls to this function, drivers must be careful to avoid creating a deadlock. During the data transfer, page fault resolution might result in another I/O to the same device. For example, this could occur if the driver controls the disk drive used as the swap device.

The driver destination buffer must be completely within the kernel address space, or the system can panic.

SEE ALSO

bcopy(D3DK), copyout(D3DK), uiomove(D3DK), ureadc(D3DK), uwritec(D3DK)

EXAMPLE

A driver ioctl(D2DK) routine (line 5) can be used to get or set device attributes or registers. If the specified command is **XX_SETREGS** (line 9), the driver copies user data to the device registers (line 11). If the user address is invalid, an error code is returned.

```
1  struct  device {  /* device registers layout */
       ...
2      int command;   /* device command word */
3  };

4  extern struct device xx_dev[];  /* physical device registers */
       ...
5  xxioctl(dev_t dev, int cmd, void *arg, int mode, cred_t *crp, int *rvp)
6  {
7      register struct device *dp;

8      switch (cmd) {
9      case XX_SETREGS:       /* copy user program data to device registers */
10         dp = &xx_dev[getminor(dev)];
11         if (copyin(arg, (caddr_t)dp, sizeof(struct device)))
12             return (EFAULT);
13         break;
```

NAME

copymsg – copy a message

SYNOPSIS

```
#include <sys/stream.h>

mblk_t *copymsg(mblk_t *mp);
```

ARGUMENTS

mp　　　　Pointer to the message to be copied.

DESCRIPTION

copymsg forms a new message by allocating new message blocks, copies the contents of the message referred to by *mp* (using the copyb(D3DK) function), and returns a pointer to the new message.

RETURN VALUE

If successful, copymsg returns a pointer to the new message. Otherwise, it returns a NULL pointer.

LEVEL

Base or Interrupt.

NOTES

Does not sleep.

Driver-defined basic locks, read/write locks, and sleep locks may be held across calls to this function.

SEE ALSO

allocb(D3DK), copyb(D3DK), msgb(D4DK)

EXAMPLE

The routine lctouc converts all the lower case ASCII characters in the message to upper case. If the reference count is greater than one (line 8), then the message is shared, and must be copied before changing the contents of the data buffer. If the call to copymsg fails (line 9), we return NULL (line 10). Otherwise, we free the original message (line 11). If the reference count was equal to one, the message can be modified. For each character (line 16) in each message block (line 15), if it is a lower case letter, we convert it to an upper case letter (line 18). When done, we return a pointer to the converted message (line 21).

```
 1  mblk_t *lctouc(mp)
 2      mblk_t *mp;
 3  {
 4      mblk_t *cmp;
 5      mblk_t *tmp;
 6      uchar_t *cp;
 7
 8      if (mp->b_datap->db_ref > 1) {
 9              if ((cmp = copymsg(mp)) == NULL)
10                      return(NULL);
11              freemsg(mp);
12      } else {
13              cmp = mp;
14      }
```

```
15    for (tmp = cmp; tmp; tmp = tmp->b_next) {
16          for (cp = tmp->b_rptr; cp < tmp->b_wptr; cp++) {
17                if ((*cp <= 'z') && (*cp >= 'a'))
18                      *cp -= 0x20;
19          }
20    }
21    return(cmp);
22 }
```

NAME

copyout – copy data from a driver buffer to a user buffer

SYNOPSIS

```
#include <sys/types.h>

int copyout(caddr_t driverbuf, caddr_t userbuf, size_t count);
```

ARGUMENTS

driverbuf　Driver source address from which copy is made.

userbuf　User destination address to which copy is made.

count　Number of bytes to copy.

DESCRIPTION

copyout copies *count* bytes of data from the kernel virtual address specified by *driverbuf* to the user virtual address specified by *userbuf*.

copyout chooses the best algorithm based on address alignment and number of bytes to copy. Although the source and destination addresses are not required to be word aligned, word aligned addresses may result in a more efficient copy.

RETURN VALUE

If the copy is successful, 0 is returned. Otherwise, −1 is returned to indicate that the specified user address range is not valid.

LEVEL

Base Only.

NOTES

May sleep.

Drivers usually convert a return value of −1 into an **EFAULT** error.

Driver-defined basic locks and read/write locks may not be held across calls to this function.

Driver-defined sleep locks may be held across calls to this function.

When holding sleep locks across calls to this function, drivers must be careful to avoid creating a deadlock. During the data transfer, page fault resolution might result in another I/O to the same device. For example, this could occur if the driver controls the disk drive used as the swap device.

The driver source buffer must be completely within the kernel address space, or the system can panic.

SEE ALSO

bcopy(D3DK), copyin(D3DK), uiomove(D3DK), ureadc(D3DK), uwritec(D3DK)

EXAMPLE

A driver ioctl(D2DK) routine (line 5) can be used to get or set device attributes or registers. If the specified command is **XX_GETREGS** (line 9), the driver copies the current device register values to a user data area (line 11). If the user address is invalid, an error code is returned.

```
1   struct  device { /* device registers layout */
       ...
2      int status;   /* device status word */
3   };

4   extern struct device xx_dev[]; /* physical device registers */
       ...
5   xxioctl(dev_t dev, int cmd, void *arg, int mode, cred_t *crp, int *rvp)
6   {
7      register struct device *dp;

8      switch (cmd) {
9      case XX_GETREGS:      /* copy device registers to user program */
10             dp = &xx_dev[getminor(dev)];
11             if (copyout((caddr_t)dp, arg, sizeof(struct device)))
12                     return (EFAULT);
13             break;
```

NAME

datamsg – test whether a message is a data message

SYNOPSIS

```
#include <sys/types.h>
#include <sys/stream.h>
#include <sys/ddi.h>

int datamsg(uchar_t type);
```

ARGUMENTS

type   The type of message to be tested. The **db_type** field of the **datab** structure contains the message type. This field may be accessed through the message block using **mp->b_datap->db_type**.

DESCRIPTION

The **datamsg** function tests the type of message to determine if it is a data message type (**M_DATA**, **M_DELAY**, **M_PROTO**, or **M_PCPROTO**).

RETURN VALUE

datamsg returns 1 if the message is a data message and 0 if the message is any other type.

LEVEL

Base or Interrupt.

NOTES

Does not sleep.

Driver-defined basic locks, read/write locks, and sleep locks may be held across calls to this function.

SEE ALSO

allocb(D3DK), **datab**(D4DK), **msgb**(D4DK), **messages**(D5DK)

EXAMPLE

The **put**(D2DK) routine enqueues all data messages for handling by the **srv**(D2DK) (service) routine. All non-data messages are handled in the **put** routine.

```
 1  xxxput(q, mp)
 2      queue_t *q;
 3      mblk_t *mp;
 4  {
 5      if (datamsg(mp->b_datap->db_type)) {
 6              putq(q, mp);
 7              return;
 8      }
 9      switch (mp->b_datap->db_type) {
10      case M_FLUSH:
        ...
11      }
12  }
```

NAME

delay – delay process execution for a specified number of clock ticks

SYNOPSIS

`void delay(long ticks);`

ARGUMENTS

ticks   The number of clock ticks to delay.

DESCRIPTION

`delay` causes the caller to sleep for the amount of time specified by *ticks*, which is in units of clock ticks. The exact length of the delay is not guaranteed but it will not be less than *ticks* clock ticks. The length of a clock tick can vary across different implementations and therefore drivers should not include any hard-coded assumptions about the length of a tick. The **drv_usectohz**(D3DK) and **drv_hztousec**(D3DK) functions can be used, as necessary, to convert between clock ticks and microseconds (implementation independent units).

The **delay** function calls **itimeout**(D3DK) to schedule a wakeup after the specified amount of time has elapsed. **delay** then goes to sleep until **itimeout** wakes up the sleeping process.

RETURN VALUE

None.

LEVEL

Base Only.

NOTES

Function sleeps.

Driver-defined basic locks and read/write locks may not be held across calls to this function.

Driver-defined sleep locks may be held across calls to this function, but this is discouraged because it can adversely affect performance by forcing any other processes contending for the lock to sleep for the duration of the delay.

SEE ALSO

drv_hztousec(D3DK), **drv_usectohz**(D3DK), **drv_usecwait**(D3DK), **itimeout**(D3DK), **untimeout**(D3DK)

NAME

dma_pageio – break up an I/O request into manageable units

SYNOPSIS

```
#include <sys/buf.h>

void dma_pageio(void (*strat)(), buf_t *bp);
```

ARGUMENTS

strat   Address of the **strategy**(D2DK) routine to call to complete the I/O transfer.

bp   Pointer to the buffer header structure.

DESCRIPTION

dma_pageio breaks up a data transfer request from **physiock**(D3DK) into units of contiguous memory. This function enhances the capabilities of the direct memory access controller (DMAC).

RETURN VALUE

None.

LEVEL

Base Only.

NOTES

Can sleep.

Driver-defined basic locks and read/write locks may not be held across calls to this function.

Driver defined sleep locks may be held across calls to this function.

When the transfer completes, any allocated buffers are freed.

The interrupt priority level is not maintained across calls to **dma_pageio**.

SEE ALSO

read(D2DK), **strategy**(D2DK), **write**(D2DK), **physiock**(D3DK), **buf**(D4DK)

EXAMPLE

The following example shows how **dma_pageio** is used when reading or writing disk data. The driver's **read**(D2DK) and **write**(D2DK) entry points use **physiock** to check the validity of the I/O and perform the data transfer. The **strategy**(D2DK) routine passed to **physiock** just calls **dma_pageio** to perform the data transfer one page at a time.

```
 1   struct dsize {
 2      daddr_t nblocks;        /* number of blocks in disk partition */
 3      int cyloff;             /* starting cylinder # of partition */
 4   } my_sizes[2] = {
 5      20448, 21,              /* partition 0 = cyl 21-305 */
 6      21888, 1               /* partition 1 = cyl  1-305 */
 7   };

 8   int
 9   my_read(dev, uiop, crp)
10      dev_t dev;
11      uio_t *uiop;
12      cred_t *crp;
13   {
14      register int nblks;

15      nblks = my_sizes[getminor(dev)].nblocks;
16      return(physiock(my_breakup, 0, dev, B_READ, nblks, uiop));
17   }

18   int
19   my_write(dev, uiop, crp)
20      dev_t dev;
21      uio_t *uiop;
22      cred_t *crp;
23   {
24      register int nblks;

25      nblks = my_sizes[getminor(dev)].nblocks;
26      return(physiock(my_breakup, 0, dev, B_WRITE, nblks, uiop));
27   }

28   static void
29   my_breakup(bp)
30      register buf_t *bp;
31   {
32      dma_pageio(my_strategy, bp);
33   }
```

NAME

    drv_getparm – retrieve kernel state information

SYNOPSIS

    `#include <sys/types.h>`
    `#include <sys/ddi.h>`

    `int drv_getparm(ulong_t` *parm,* `ulong_t *`*value_p*`);`

ARGUMENTS

    parm   The kernel parameter to be obtained. Possible values are:

            LBOLT   Read the number of clock ticks since the last system reboot. The difference between the values returned from successive calls to retrieve this parameter provides an indication of the elapsed time between the calls in units of clock ticks. The length of a clock tick can vary across different implementations, and therefore drivers should not include any hard-coded assumptions about the length of a tick. The **drv_hztousec**(D3DK) and **drv_usectohz**(D3DK) functions can be used, as necessary, to convert between clock ticks and microseconds (implementation independent units).

            UPROCP   Retrieve a pointer to the process structure for the current process. The value returned in *value_p* is of type (`proc_t *`) and the only valid use of the value is as an argument to **vtop**(D3D). Since this value is associated with the current process, the caller must have process context (that is, must be at base level) when attempting to retrieve this value. Also, this value should only be used in the context of the process in which it was retrieved.

            UCRED   Retrieve a pointer to the credential structure describing the current user credentials for the current process. The value returned in *value_p* is of type (`cred_t *`) and the only valid use of the value is as an argument to **drv_priv**(D3DK). Since this value is associated with the current process, the caller must have process context (i.e. must be at base level) when attempting to retrieve this value. Also, this value should only be used in the context of the process in which it was retrieved.

            TIME   Read the time in seconds. This is the same time value that is returned by the **time**(2) system call. The value is defined as the time in seconds since `00:00:00` **GMT, January 1, 1970**. This definition presupposes that the administrator has set the correct system date and time.

    value_p   A pointer to the data space into which the value of the parameter is to be copied.

DESCRIPTION

drv_getparm returns the value of the parameter specified by *parm* in the location pointed to by *value_p*.

drv_getparm does not explicitly check to see whether the driver has the appropriate context when the function is called. It is the responsibility of the driver to use this function only when it is appropriate to do so and to correctly declare the data space needed.

RETURN VALUE

If the function is successful, 0 is returned. Otherwise −1 is returned to indicate that *parm* specified an invalid parameter.

LEVEL

Base only when using the **UPROCP** or **UCRED** argument values.

Base or interrupt when using the **LBOLT** or **TIME** argument values.

NOTES

Does not sleep.

Driver-defined basic locks, read/write locks, and sleep locks may be held across calls to this function.

SEE ALSO

drv_hztousec(D3DK), drv_priv(D3DK), drv_usectohz(D3DK), vtop(D3D)

time(2) in the *Programmer's Reference Manual*

NAME

   drv_hztousec – convert clock ticks to microseconds

SYNOPSIS

   #include <sys/types.h>
   #include <sys/ddi.h>

   clock_t drv_hztousec(clock_t *ticks*);

ARGUMENTS

   ticks   The number of clock ticks to convert to equivalent microseconds.

DESCRIPTION

   drv_hztousec converts the length of time expressed by *ticks*, which is in units of
   clock ticks, into units of microseconds.

   Several functions either take time values expressed in clock ticks as arguments
   [**itimeout**(D3DK), **delay**(D3DK)] or return time values expressed in clock ticks
   [**drv_getparm**(D3DK)]. The length of a clock tick can vary across different implementations, and therefore drivers should not include any hard-coded assumptions
   about the length of a tick. **drv_hztousec** and the complementary function
   drv_usectohz(D3DK) can be used, as necessary, to convert between clock ticks
   and microseconds.

RETURN VALUE

   The number of microseconds equivalent to the *ticks* argument. No error value is
   returned. If the microsecond equivalent to *ticks* is too large to be represented as a
   clock_t, then the maximum **clock_t** value will be returned.

LEVEL

   Base or Interrupt.

NOTES

   Does not sleep.

   Driver-defined basic locks, read/write locks, and sleep locks may be held across
   calls to this function.

   The time value returned by **drv_getparm** with an **LBOLT** argument will fre-
   quently be too large to represent in microseconds as a **clock_t**. When using
   drv_getparm together with **drv_hztousec** to time operations, drivers can help
   avoid overflow by converting the difference between return values from successive calls to **drv_getparm** instead of trying to convert the return values them-
   selves.

SEE ALSO

   delay(D3DK), **drv_getparm**(D3DK), **drv_usectohz**(D3DK), **dtimeout**(D3D),
   itimeout(D3DK)

NAME

    drv_priv – determine whether credentials are privileged

SYNOPSIS

    `int drv_priv(cred_t *`*crp*`);`

ARGUMENTS

    crp   Pointer to the user credential structure.

DESCRIPTION

    The **drv_priv** function determines whether the credentials specified by the credential structure pointed to by *crp* identify a privileged process. This function should only be used when file access modes and special minor device numbers are insufficient to provide the necessary protection for the driver operation being performed. Calls to **drv_priv** should replace all calls to **suser** and any explicit checks for effective user ID equal to zero in driver code.

    A credential structure pointer is passed into various driver entry point functions (**open**(D2DK), **close**(D2DK), **read**(D2DK), **write**(D2DK), and **ioctl**(D2DK)) and can also be obtained by calling **drv_getparm**(D3DK) from base level driver code.

RETURN VALUE

    This routine returns 0 if the specified credentials identify a privileged process and **EPERM** otherwise.

LEVEL

    Base or Interrupt.

NOTES

    Does not sleep.

    Driver-defined basic locks, read/write locks, and sleep locks may be held across calls to this function.

    The only valid use for a credential structure pointer is as an argument to **drv_priv**. The contents of a credential structure are not defined by the DDI/DKI and a driver may not examine the contents of the structure directly.

NAME
>   drv_setparm – set kernel state information

SYNOPSIS
>   #include <sys/types.h>
>   #include <sys/ddi.h>
>
>   int drv_setparm(ulong_t *parm*, ulong_t *value*);

ARGUMENTS
>   *parm*   The kernel parameter to be updated. Possible values are:
>
>   SYSCANC   Add *value* to the count of the number of characters received from a terminal device after the characters have been processed to remove special characters such as *break* or *backspace*.
>
>   SYSMINT   Add *value* to the count of the number of modem interrupts received.
>
>   SYSOUTC   Add *value* to the count of the number of characters output to a terminal device.
>
>   SYSRAWC   Add *value* to the count of the number of characters received from a terminal device, before canonical processing has occurred.
>
>   SYSRINT   Add *value* to the count of the number of interrupts generated by data ready to be received from a terminal device.
>
>   SYSXINT   Add *value* to the count of the number of interrupts generated by data ready to be transmitted to a terminal device.
>
>   *value*   The value to be added to the parameter.

DESCRIPTION
>   drv_setparm verifies that *parm* corresponds to a kernel parameter that may be modified. If the value of *parm* corresponds to a parameter that may not be modified, –1 is returned. Otherwise, the parameter is incremented by *value*.
>
>   No checking is performed to determine the validity of *value*. It is the driver's responsibility to guarantee the correctness of *value*.

RETURN VALUE
>   If the function is successful, 0 is returned. Otherwise, –1 is returned to indicate that *parm* specified an invalid parameter.

LEVEL
>   Base or Interrupt.

NOTES
>   Does not sleep.
>
>   Driver-defined basic locks, read/write locks, and sleep locks may be held across calls to this function.

SEE ALSO
>   drv_getparm(D3DK)

NAME

    drv_usectohz – convert microseconds to clock ticks

SYNOPSIS

    `#include <sys/types.h>`
    `#include <sys/ddi.h>`

    `clock_t drv_usectohz(clock_t` *microsecs*`);`

ARGUMENTS

    microsecs   The number of microseconds to convert to equivalent clock ticks.

DESCRIPTION

    drv_usectohz converts the length of time expressed by *microsecs*, which is in units of microseconds, into units of clock ticks.

    Several functions either take time values expressed in clock ticks as arguments [**itimeout**(D3DK), **delay**(D3DK)] or return time values expressed in clock ticks [**drv_getparm**(D3DK)]. The length of a clock tick can vary across different implementations, and therefore drivers should not include any hard-coded assumptions about the length of a tick. **drv_usectohz** and the complementary function **drv_hztousec**(D3DK) can be used, as necessary, to convert between microseconds and clock ticks.

RETURN VALUE

    The value returned is the smallest number of clock ticks that represent a time interval equal to or greater than the *microsecs* argument. No error value is returned. If the number of ticks equivalent to the *microsecs* argument is too large to be represented as a **clock_t**, then the maximum **clock_t** value will be returned.

LEVEL

    Base or Interrupt.

NOTES

    Does not sleep.

    Driver-defined basic locks, read/write locks, and sleep locks may be held across calls to this function.

SEE ALSO

    delay(D3DK), **drv_getparm**(D3DK), **drv_hztousec**(D3DK), **dtimeout**(D3D), **itimeout**(D3DK)

NAME
   drv_usecwait – busy-wait for specified interval
SYNOPSIS
   #include <sys/types.h>
   #include <sys/ddi.h>

   void drv_usecwait(clock_t *microsecs*);
ARGUMENTS
   microsecs   The number of microseconds to busy-wait.

DESCRIPTION
   drv_usecwait causes the caller to busy-wait for at least the number of
   microseconds specified by *microsecs*. The amount of time spent busy-waiting may
   be greater than the time specified by *microsecs* but will not be less.
   drv_usecwait should only be used to wait for short periods of time (less than a
   clock tick) or when it is necessary to wait without sleeping (for example, at interrupt level). When the desired delay is at least as long as clock tick and it is possible to sleep, the delay(D3DK) function should be used instead since it will not
   waste processor time busy-waiting as drv_usecwait does.

   Because excessive busy-waiting is wasteful the driver should only make calls to
   drv_usecwait as needed, and only for as much time as needed. drv_usecwait
   does not raise the interrupt priority level; if the driver wishes to block interrupts
   for the duration of the wait, it is the driver's responsibility to set the priority level
   before the call and restore it to its original value afterward.

RETURN VALUE
   None.

LEVEL
   Base or Interrupt.

NOTES
   Does not sleep.

   Driver-defined basic locks, read/write locks, and sleep locks may be held across
   calls to this function.

   Busy-waiting can increase the preemption latency experienced by high priority
   processes. Since short and bounded preemption latency can be critical in a real
   time environment, drivers intended for use in such an environment should not
   use this interface or should limit the length of the wait to an appropriately short
   length of time.

SEE ALSO
   delay(D3DK), drv_hztousec(D3DK), drv_usectohz(D3DK), itimeout(D3DK),
   untimeout(D3DK)

NAME

dtimeout – execute a function on a specified processor, after a specified length of time

SYNOPSIS

```
#include <sys/types.h>

toid_t dtimeout(void (*fn)(), void *arg, long ticks, pl_t pl,
                processorid_t processor);
```

ARGUMENTS

fn   Function to execute on the specified processor when the time increment expires.

arg   Argument to the function.

ticks   Number of clock ticks to wait before the function is called.

pl   The interrupt priority level at which the function will be called. *pl* must specify a priority level greater than or equal to *pltimeout*; thus, *plbase* cannot be used. See **LOCK_ALLOC**(D3DK) for a list of values for *pl*.

processor Processor on which the function must execute.

DESCRIPTION

dtimeout causes the function specified by *fn* to be called after the time interval specified by *ticks*, on the processor specified by *processor*, at the interrupt priority level specified by *pl*. *arg* will be passed as the only argument to function *fn*. The **dtimeout** call returns immediately without waiting for the specified function to execute.

This directed timeout capability provides a form of dynamic processor binding for driver code.

The length of time before the function is called is not guaranteed to be exactly equal to the requested time, but will be at least *ticks–1* clock ticks in length. The function specified by *fn* must neither sleep nor reference process context.

RETURN VALUE

If the function specified by *fn* is successfully scheduled, **dtimeout** returns a non-zero identifier that can be passed to **untimeout** to cancel the request. If the function could not be scheduled on the specified processor, **dtimeout** returns a value of 0.

LEVEL

Base or Interrupt.

NOTES

Does not sleep.

Driver defined basic locks, read/write locks, and sleep locks may be held across calls to this function.

Drivers should be careful to cancel any pending **timeout** functions that access data structures before these structures are de-initialized or deallocated.

After the time interval has expired, *fn* only runs if the processor is at base level.

Otherwise, *fn* is deferred until some time in the near future.

If **dtimeout** is called holding a lock that is contended for by *fn*, the caller must hold the lock at a processor level greater than the base processor level.

A *ticks* argument of 0 has the same effect as a *ticks* argument of 1. Both will result in an approximate wait of between 0 and 1 tick (possibly longer).

SEE ALSO

    `itimeout`(D3DK), `LOCK_ALLOC`(D3DK), `untimeout`(D3DK)

NAME
dupb – duplicate a message block

SYNOPSIS
#include <sys/stream.h>

mblk_t *dupb(mblk_t *bp);

ARGUMENTS
bp   Pointer to the message block to be duplicated.

DESCRIPTION
dupb creates a new message block structure to reference the message block pointed to by *bp*. Unlike **copyb**(D3DK), **dupb** does not copy the information in the data block, but creates a new structure to point to it.

The following figure shows how the **db_ref** field of the data block structure has been changed from 1 to 2, reflecting the increase in the number of references to the data block. The new message block contains the same information as the first. Note that **b_rptr** and **b_wptr** are copied from *bp*, and that **db_ref** is incremented.

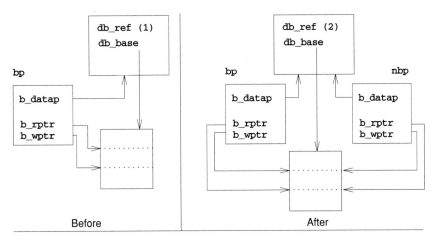

nbp=dupb(bp);

RETURN VALUE
If successful, **dupb** returns a pointer to the new message block. Otherwise, it returns a **NULL** pointer.

LEVEL
Base or Interrupt

NOTES
Does not sleep.

Driver-defined basic locks, read/write locks, and sleep locks may be held across calls to this function.

SEE ALSO

copyb(D3DK), dupmsg(D3DK), datab(D4DK), msgb(D4DK)

NAME

dupmsg – duplicate a message

SYNOPSIS

```
#include <sys/stream.h>

mblk_t *dupmsg(mblk_t *mp);
```

ARGUMENTS

mp   Pointer to the message.

DESCRIPTION

dupmsg forms a new message by duplicating the message blocks in the message pointed to by *mp* and linking them via their **b_cont** pointers.

RETURN VALUE

If successful, dupmsg returns a pointer to the new message. Otherwise, it returns a **NULL** pointer.

LEVEL

Base or Interrupt.

Driver-defined basic locks, read/write locks, and sleep locks may be held across calls to this function.

NOTES

Does not sleep.

SEE ALSO

copyb(D3DK), copymsg(D3DK), dupb(D3DK), datab(D4DK), msgb(D4DK)

EXAMPLE

See the copyb(D3DK) manual page for an example of dupmsg.

NAME

enableok – allow a queue to be serviced

SYNOPSIS

```
#include <sys/stream.h>
#include <sys/ddi.h>

void enableok(queue_t *q);
```

ARGUMENTS

q   Pointer to the queue.

DESCRIPTION

The **enableok** function allows the service routine of the queue pointed to by *q* to be rescheduled for service. It cancels the effect of a previous use of the **noenable**(D3DK) function on *q*.

RETURN VALUE

None.

LEVEL

Base or Interrupt.

NOTES

Does not sleep.

Driver-defined basic locks, read/write locks, and sleep locks may be held across calls to this function.

The caller cannot have the stream frozen [see **freezestr**(D3DK)] when calling this function.

SEE ALSO

srv(D2DK), **noenable**(D3DK), **qenable**(D3DK), **queue**(D4DK)

EXAMPLE

The **qrestart** routine uses two STREAMS functions to re-enable a queue that has been disabled. The **enableok** function removes the restriction that prevented the queue from being scheduled when a message was enqueued. Then, if there are messages on the queue, it is scheduled by calling **qenable**(D3DK).

```
1  void
2  qrestart(q)
3       register queue_t *q;
4  {
5       enableok(q);
6       if (q->q_first)
7               qenable(q);
8  }
```

NAME

esballoc – allocate a message block using an externally-supplied buffer

SYNOPSIS

```
#include <sys/types.h>
#include <sys/stream.h>

mblk_t *esballoc(uchar_t *base, int size, int pri, frtn_t *fr_rtnp);
```

ARGUMENTS

base   Address of driver-supplied data buffer.

size   Number of bytes in data buffer.

pri   Priority of allocation request (used to allocate the message and data blocks.) Valid values are **BPRI_LO**, **BPRI_MED**, and **BPRI_HI**.

fr_rtnp   Pointer to the free-routine data structure.

DESCRIPTION

esballoc creates a STREAMS message and attaches a driver-supplied data buffer in place of a STREAMS data buffer. It allocates a message and data block header only. The driver-supplied data buffer, pointed to by *base*, is used as the data buffer for the message.

When **freeb**(D3DK) is called to free the message, on the last reference to the message, the driver's free-routine, specified by the **free_func** field in the **free_rtn**(D4DK) structure, is called with one argument, specified by the **free_arg** field, to free the data buffer.

Instead of requiring a specific number of arguments, the **free_arg** field is defined of type **char ***. This way, the driver can pass a pointer to a structure if more than one argument is needed.

When the **free_func** function runs, interrupts from all STREAMS devices will be blocked. It has no user context and may not call any routine that sleeps. The function may not access any dynamically allocated data structures that might no longer exist when it runs.

RETURN VALUE

On success, a pointer to the newly allocated message block is returned. On failure, **NULL** is returned.

LEVEL

Base or Interrupt.

NOTES

Does not sleep.

Driver-defined basic locks, read/write locks, and sleep locks may be held across calls to this function.

SEE ALSO

allocb(D3DK), **freeb**(D3DK), **free_rtn**(D4DK)

NAME

esbbcall – call a function when an externally-supplied buffer can be allocated

SYNOPSIS

```
#include <sys/types.h>
#include <sys/stream.h>

toid_t esbbcall(int pri, void (*func)(), long arg);
```

ARGUMENTS

pri   Priority of the **esballoc**(D3DK) allocation request (**BPRI_LO**, **BPRI_MED**, or **BPRI_HI**.)

func Function to be called when a buffer becomes available.

arg   Argument to the function to be called when a buffer becomes available.

DESCRIPTION

esbbcall, like **bufcall**(D3DK), serves as a **timeout** call of indeterminate length. If **esballoc**(D3DK) is unable to allocate a message block header and a data block header to go with its externally supplied data buffer, **esbbcall** can be used to schedule the routine *func*, to be called with the argument *arg* when memory becomes available.

When *func* runs, all interrupts from STREAMS devices will be blocked on the processor on which it is running. *func* will have no user context and may not call any function that sleeps.

RETURN VALUE

If successful, **esbbcall** returns a non-zero value that identifies the scheduling request. This non-zero identifier may be passed to **unbufcall**(D3DK) to cancel the request. If any failure occurs, **esbbcall** returns 0.

LEVEL

Base or Interrupt.

NOTES

Does not sleep.

Driver-defined basic locks, read/write locks, and sleep locks may be held across calls to this function.

Even when *func* is called, **esballoc** can still fail if another module or driver had allocated the memory before *func* was able to call **allocb**.

SEE ALSO

allocb(D3DK), **bufcall**(D3DK), **esballoc**(D3DK), **itimeout**(D3DK), **unbufcall**(D3DK)

NAME

etoimajor – convert external to internal major device number

SYNOPSIS

```
#include <sys/types.h>
#include <sys/ddi.h>

major_t etoimajor(major_t emaj);
```

ARGUMENTS

emaj　　　　External major number.

DESCRIPTION

etoimajor converts the external major number (*emaj*) to an internal major number. See **getemajor**(D3DK) for a description of external and internal major numbers.

RETURN VALUE

etoimajor returns the internal major number or **NODEV** if the external major number is invalid.

LEVEL

Base or Interrupt.

NOTES

Does not sleep.

Driver-defined basic locks, read/write locks, and sleep locks may be held across calls to this function.

SEE ALSO

getemajor(D3DK), **geteminor**(D3DK), **getmajor**(D3DK), **getminor**(D3DK), **itoemajor**(D3DK), **makedevice**(D3DK)

NAME

flushband – flush messages in a specified priority band

SYNOPSIS

```
#include <sys/types.h>
#include <sys/stream.h>

void flushband(queue_t *q, uchar_t pri, int flag);
```

ARGUMENTS

q   Pointer to the queue.

pri   Priority band of messages to be flushed.

flag   Determines messages to flush. Valid *flag* values are:

         FLUSHDATA   Flush only data messages (types **M_DATA**, **M_DELAY**, **M_PROTO**, and **M_PCPROTO**).

         FLUSHALL   Flush all messages.

DESCRIPTION

The **flushband** function flushes messages associated with the priority band specified by *pri*. If *pri* is **0**, only normal and high priority messages are flushed. Otherwise, messages are flushed from the band *pri* according to the value of *flag*.

RETURN VALUE

None.

LEVEL

Base or Interrupt.

NOTES

Does not sleep.

Driver-defined basic locks, read/write locks, and sleep locks may be held across calls to this function.

The caller cannot have the stream frozen [see **freezestr**(D3DK)] when calling this function.

SEE ALSO

put(D2DK), **flushq**(D3DK), queue(D4DK)

EXAMPLE

See put(D2DK) for an example of **flushband**.

NAME

flushq – flush messages on a queue

SYNOPSIS

```
#include <sys/stream.h>

void flushq(queue_t *q, int flag);
```

ARGUMENTS

q   Pointer to the queue to be flushed.

flag   Determines messages to flush. Valid *flag* values are:

FLUSHDATA Flush only data messages (types M_DATA, M_DELAY, M_PROTO, and M_PCPROTO).

FLUSHALL   Flush all messages.

DESCRIPTION

flushq frees messages on a queue by calling freemsg(D3DK) for each message. If the queue's count falls below the low water mark and someone wants to write to the queue, the nearest upstream or downstream service procedure is enabled.

RETURN VALUE

None.

LEVEL

Base or Interrupt.

NOTES

Does not sleep.

Driver-defined basic locks, read/write locks, and sleep locks may be held across calls to this function.

The caller cannot have the stream frozen [see freezestr(D3DK)] when calling this function.

SEE ALSO

put(D2DK), flushband(D3DK), freemsg(D3DK), putq(D3DK), queue(D4DK)

EXAMPLE

See put(D2DK) for an example of flushq.

NAME

freeb – free a message block

SYNOPSIS

```
#include <sys/stream.h>

void freeb(mblk_t *bp);
```

ARGUMENTS

bp   Pointer to the message block to be deallocated.

DESCRIPTION

freeb deallocates a message block. If the reference count of the **db_ref** member of the **datab**(D4DK) structure is greater than 1, **freeb** decrements the count and returns. Otherwise, if **db_ref** equals 1, it deallocates the message block and the corresponding data block and buffer.

If the data buffer to be freed was allocated with **esballoc**(D3DK), the driver is notified that the attached data buffer needs to be freed by calling the free-routine [see **free_rtn**(D4DK)] associated with the data buffer. Once this is accomplished, **freeb** releases the STREAMS resources associated with the buffer.

RETURN VALUE

None.

LEVEL

Base or Interrupt.

NOTES

Does not sleep.

Driver-defined basic locks, read/write locks, and sleep locks may be held across calls to this function.

SEE ALSO

allocb(D3DK), dupb(D3DK), esballoc(D3DK), datab(D4DK), free_rtn(D4DK), msgb(D4DK)

EXAMPLE

See copyb(D3DK) for an example of **freeb**.

NAME

freemsg – free a message

SYNOPSIS

#include <sys/stream.h>

void freemsg(mblk_t *mp);

ARGUMENTS

mp   Pointer to the message to be deallocated.

DESCRIPTION

freemsg frees all message blocks, data blocks, and data buffers associated with the message pointed to by mp. freemsg walks down the b_cont list [see msgb(D4DK)], calling freeb(D3DK) for every message block in the message.

RETURN VALUE

None.

LEVEL

Base or Interrupt.

NOTES

Does not sleep.

Driver-defined basic locks, read/write locks, and sleep locks may be held across calls to this function.

SEE ALSO

freeb(D3DK), msgb(D4DK)

EXAMPLE

See copymsg(D3DK) for an example of freemsg.

NAME

freerbuf – free a raw buffer header

SYNOPSIS

```
#include <sys/buf.h>
#include <sys/ddi.h>

void freerbuf(buf_t *bp);
```

ARGUMENTS

bp   Pointer to a previously allocated buffer header structure.

DESCRIPTION

freerbuf frees a raw buffer header previously allocated by **getrbuf**(D3DK). It may not be used on a buffer header obtained through any other interface. It is typically called from a driver's *iodone handler*, specified in the **b_iodone** field of the **buf**(D4DK) structure.

RETURN VALUE

None.

LEVEL

Base or Interrupt.

NOTES

Does not sleep.

Driver-defined basic locks, read/write locks, and sleep locks may be held across calls to this function.

SEE ALSO

biodone(D3DK), **biowait**(D3DK), **getrbuf**(D3DK), **buf**(D4DK)

NAME

`freezestr` – freeze the state of a stream

SYNOPSIS

```
#include <sys/types.h>
#include <sys/stream.h>

pl_t freezestr(queue_t *q);
```

ARGUMENTS

q Pointer to a message queue.

DESCRIPTION

`freezestr` sets the interrupt priority level to `plstr` (if the current level is lower than `plstr` and the implementation requires that interrupts be blocked while the stream is frozen) and freezes the state of the stream containing the queue specified by q. Freezing the stream prevents any further entries into open, close, put, and service procedures on the stream and prevents any messages from being placed on or taken off any queues in the stream (except by the caller of `freezestr`). Freezing the stream does not automatically stop all functions that are running within the stream; functions will continue to run until they attempt to perform some operation which changes the state of the stream, at which point they will be forced to wait for the stream to be unfrozen by a call to unfreezestr(D3DK).

Drivers and modules must freeze the stream while they manipulate its queues directly. This includes searching the queues and for the duration of any calls to insq(D3DK), rmvq(D3DK), strqset(D3DK), and strqget(D3DK).

RETURN VALUE

`freezestr` returns the previous interrupt priority level which is typically used in a subsequent call to **unfreezestr**.

LEVEL

Base or Interrupt.

NOTES

Does not sleep.

Calling `freezestr` to freeze a stream that is already frozen by the caller will result in deadlock.

Driver defined basic locks, read/write locks, and sleep locks may be held across calls to this function.

`freezestr` should be used sparingly as it is rarely necessary to freeze a stream (most modules do not need to manipulate their queues directly) and freezing a stream can have a significant negative effect on performance.

SEE ALSO

unfreezestr(D3DK)

EXAMPLE

See insq(D3DK) for an example of **freezestr**.

NAME

geteblk – get an empty buffer

SYNOPSIS

```
#include <sys/types.h>
#include <sys/buf.h>

buf_t *geteblk();
```

DESCRIPTION

geteblk retrieves a buffer [see buf(D4DK)] from the buffer cache and returns a pointer to the buffer header. If a buffer is not available, geteblk sleeps until one is available.

When the driver strategy(D2DK) routine receives a buffer header from the kernel, all the necessary members are already initialized. However, when a driver allocates buffers for its own use, it must set up some of the members before calling its strategy routine.

The following list describes the state of these members when the buffer header is received from geteblk:

b_flags	is set to indicate the transfer is from the user's buffer to the kernel. The driver must set the B_READ flag if the transfer is from the kernel to the user's buffer.
b_edev	is set to NODEV and must be initialized by the driver.
b_bcount	is set to 1024.
b_un.b_addr	is set to the buffer's virtual address.
b_blkno	is not initialized by geteblk, and must be initialized by the driver

Typically, block drivers do not allocate buffers. The buffer is allocated by the kernel, and the associated buffer header is used as an argument to the driver strategy routine. However, to implement some special features, such as ioctl(D2DK) commands that perform I/O, the driver may need its own buffer space. The driver can get the buffer space from the system by using geteblk or ngeteblk(D3DK). Or the driver can choose to use its own memory for the buffer and only allocate a buffer header with getrbuf(D3DK).

RETURN VALUE

A pointer to the buffer header structure is returned.

LEVEL

Base Only.

NOTES

Can sleep.

Driver-defined basic locks and read/write locks may not be held across calls to this function.

Driver-defined sleep locks may be held across calls to this function.

Buffers allocated via **geteblk** must be freed using either **brelse**(D3DK) or **biodone**(D3DK).

SEE ALSO
   biodone(D3DK), **biowait**(D3DK), **brelse**(D3DK), **ngeteblk**(D3DK), **buf**(D4DK)

NAME

getemajor – get external major device number

SYNOPSIS

```
#include <sys/types.h>
#include <sys/ddi.h>

major_t getemajor(dev_t dev);
```

ARGUMENTS

dev   External device number.

DESCRIPTION

getemajor returns the external major number given a device number, *dev*. External major numbers are visible to the user. Internal major numbers are only visible in the kernel. Since the range of major numbers may be large and sparsely populated, the kernel keeps a mapping between external and internal major numbers to save space.

All driver entry points are passed device numbers using external major numbers.

Usually, a driver with more than one external major number will have only one internal major number. However, some system implementations map one-to-one between external and internal major numbers. Here, the internal major number is the same as the external major number and the driver may have more than one internal major number.

RETURN VALUE

The external major number.

LEVEL

Base or Interrupt.

NOTES

Does not sleep.

Driver-defined basic locks, read/write locks, and sleep locks may be held across calls to this function.

SEE ALSO

etoimajor(D3DK), geteminor(D3DK), getmajor(D3DK), getminor(D3DK), makedevice(D3DK)

NAME

geteminor – get external minor device number

SYNOPSIS

```
#include <sys/types.h>
#include <sys/ddi.h>

minor_t geteminor(dev_t dev);
```

ARGUMENTS

dev   External device number.

DESCRIPTION

geteminor returns the external minor number given a device number, *dev*. External minor numbers are visible to the user. Internal minor numbers are only visible in the kernel. Since a driver can support more than one external major device that map to the same internal major device, the kernel keeps a mapping between external minor numbers and internal minor numbers to allow drivers to index arrays more easily. For example, a driver may support two devices, each with five minor numbers. The user may see each set of minor numbers numbered from zero to four, but the driver sees them as one set of minor numbers numbered from zero to nine.

All driver entry points are passed device numbers using external minor numbers.

Systems that map external major device numbers one-to-one with internal major numbers also map external minor numbers one-to-one with internal minor numbers.

RETURN VALUE

The external minor number.

LEVEL

Base or Interrupt.

NOTES

Does not sleep.

Driver-defined basic locks, read/write locks, and sleep locks may be held across calls to this function.

SEE ALSO

etoimajor(D3DK), getemajor(D3DK), getmajor(D3DK), getminor(D3DK), makedevice(D3DK)

NAME

> `geterror` – retrieve error number from a buffer header

SYNOPSIS

> `#include <sys/buf.h>`
>
> `int geterror(struct buf *`*bp*`);`

ARGUMENTS

> *bp*   Pointer to the buffer header.

DESCRIPTION

> `geterror` is called to retrieve the error number from the error field of a buffer header (`buf`(D4DK) structure).

RETURN VALUE

> An error number indicating the error condition of the I/O request is returned. If the I/O request completed successfully, 0 is returned.

LEVEL

> Base or Interrupt.

NOTES

> Does not sleep.
>
> Driver-defined basic locks, read/write locks, and sleep locks may be held across calls to this function.

SEE ALSO

> `buf`(D4DK), `errnos`(D5DK)

NAME

getmajor – get internal major device number

SYNOPSIS

```
#include <sys/types.h>
#include <sys/ddi.h>

major_t getmajor(dev_t dev);
```

ARGUMENTS

dev   Device number.

DESCRIPTION

The **getmajor** function extracts the internal major number from a device number. See **getemajor**(D3DK) for an explanation of external and internal major numbers.

RETURN VALUE

The internal major number.

LEVEL

Base or Interrupt.

NOTES

No validity checking is performed. If *dev* is invalid, an invalid number is returned.

Does not sleep.

Driver-defined basic locks, read/write locks, and sleep locks may be held across calls to this function.

SEE ALSO

etoimajor(D3DK), **getemajor**(D3DK), **geteminor**(D3DK), **getminor**(D3DK), **makedevice**(D3DK)

NAME

　　getminor – get internal minor device number

SYNOPSIS

　　#include <sys/types.h>
　　#include <sys/ddi.h>

　　minor_t getminor(dev_t *dev*);

ARGUMENTS

　　dev　　　　　Device number.

DESCRIPTION

　　The **getminor** function extracts the internal minor number from a device number.
　　See **getemajor**(D3DK) for an explanation of external and internal major numbers.

RETURN VALUE

　　The internal minor number.

LEVEL

　　Base or Interrupt.

NOTES

　　No validity checking is performed. If *dev* is invalid, an invalid number is
　　returned.

　　Does not sleep.

　　Driver-defined basic locks, read/write locks, and sleep locks may be held across
　　calls to this function.

SEE ALSO

　　etoimajor(D3DK), **getemajor**(D3DK), **geteminor**(D3DK), **getmajor**(D3DK),
　　makedevice(D3DK)

NAME
    getnextpg – get next page pointer

SYNOPSIS
    #include <sys/types.h>
    #include <vm/page.h>
    #include <sys/buf.h>

    page_t *getnextpg(buf_t *bp, page_t *pp);

ARGUMENTS
    bp   Pointer to the buffer header structure.

    pp   Pointer to the previous page structure returned.

DESCRIPTION
    getnextpg will return a pointer to the next page in a buffer header's page list
    [see buf(D4DK)] during a paged-I/O request. A paged-I/O request is identified
    by the B_PAGEIO flag being set in the b_flags field of the buffer header passed
    to a driver's strategy(D2DK) routine.

    Given a buffer header, bp, and a pointer to the page, pp, returned from the previ-
    ous call to getnextpg, the next page is returned. If pp is NULL, the first page in
    the page list is returned.

RETURN VALUE
    On success, a pointer to the next page structure in the page list is returned. If the
    end of the list is reached, NULL is returned.

LEVEL
    Base or Interrupt.

NOTES
    B_PAGEIO won't be set unless the driver has the D_NOBRKUP flag set [see
    devflag(D1D).]

    Does not sleep.

    Driver defined basic locks, read/write locks, and sleep locks may be held across
    calls to this function.

SEE ALSO
    devflag(D1D), strategy(D2DK), bp_mapin(D3DK), bp_mapout(D3DK),
    pptophys(D3D), buf(D4DK)

NAME

getq – get the next message from a queue

SYNOPSIS

```
#include <sys/stream.h>

mblk_t *getq(queue_t *q);
```

ARGUMENTS

q　　　　　　　Pointer to the queue from which the message is to be retrieved.

DESCRIPTION

getq is used by service [see srv(D2DK)] routines to retrieve queued messages. It gets the next available message from the top of the queue pointed to by q. getq handles flow control, restarting I/O that was blocked as needed.

RETURN VALUE

If there is a message to retrieve, getq returns a pointer to it. If no message is queued, getq returns a NULL pointer.

LEVEL

Base or Interrupt.

NOTES

Does not sleep.

Driver-defined basic locks, read/write locks, and sleep locks may be held across calls to this function.

The caller cannot have the stream frozen [see freezestr(D3DK)] when calling this function.

SEE ALSO

srv(D2DK), bcanput(D3DK), canput(D3DK), putbq(D3DK), putq(D3DK), qenable(D3DK), rmvq(D3DK)

EXAMPLE

See srv(D2DK) for an example of getq.

NAME

getrbuf – get a raw buffer header

SYNOPSIS

```
#include <sys/buf.h>
#include <sys/kmem.h>
#include <sys/ddi.h>

buf_t *getrbuf(long flag);
```

ARGUMENTS

flag   Indicates whether caller should sleep for free space. If *flag* is set to **KM_SLEEP**, the caller will sleep if necessary until memory is available. If *flag* is set to **KM_NOSLEEP**, the caller will not sleep, but **getrbuf** will return **NULL** if memory is not immediately available.

DESCRIPTION

getrbuf allocates the space for a buffer header [see **buf**(D4DK)]. It is used when a block driver is performing raw I/O (character interface) and needs to set up a buffer header that is not associated with a system-provided data buffer. The driver provides its own memory for the data buffer.

After allocating the buffer header, the caller must set the **b_iodone** field to the address of an *iodone handler* to be invoked when the I/O is complete [see **biodone**(D3DK)]. The caller must also initialize the following fields:

b_flags   must be set to indicate the direction of data transfer. Initially, it is set to indicate the transfer is from the user's buffer to the kernel. The driver must set the **B_READ** flag if the transfer is from the kernel to the user's buffer.

b_edev   must be initialized to the proper device number.

b_bcount   must be set to the number of bytes to transfer.

b_un.b_addr   must be set to the virtual address of the caller-supplied buffer.

b_blkno   must be set to the block number to be accessed.

b_resid   must be set to the same value as **b_bcount**.

b_bufsize   can be used to remember the size of the data buffer associated with the buffer header.

Typically, block drivers do not allocate buffers. The buffer is allocated by the kernel, and the associated buffer header is used as an argument to the driver **strategy** routine. However, to implement some special features, such as **ioctl**(D2DK) commands that perform I/O, the driver may need its own buffer space. The driver can get the buffer space from the system by using **geteblk**(D3DK) or **ngeteblk**(D3DK). Or the driver can choose to use its own memory for the buffer and only allocate a buffer header with **getrbuf**.

RETURN VALUE

Upon successful completion, **getrbuf** returns a pointer to the allocated buffer header. If **KM_NOSLEEP** is specified and sufficient memory is not immediately available, **getrbuf** returns a **NULL** pointer.

LEVEL

Base only if *flag* is set to **KM_SLEEP**. Base or interrupt if *flag* is set to **KM_NOSLEEP**.

NOTES

May sleep if *flag* is set to **KM_SLEEP**.

Driver-defined basic locks and read/write locks may be held across calls to this function if *flag* is **KM_NOSLEEP**, but may not be held if *flag* is **KM_SLEEP**.

Driver-defined sleep locks may be held across calls to this function regardless of the value of *flag*.

SEE ALSO

biodone(D3DK), **biowait**(D3DK), **freerbuf**(D3DK), **buf**(D4DK)

NAME

inb – read a byte from a 8 bit I/O port

SYNOPSIS

```
#include <sys/types.h>

uchar_t inb(int port);
```

ARGUMENTS

port   A valid 8 bit I/O port.

DESCRIPTION

This function provides a C language interface to the machine instruction that reads a byte from an 8 bit I/O port using the I/O address space, instead of the memory address space.

RETURN VALUE

Returns the value of the byte read from the I/O port.

LEVEL

Base or Interrupt.

NOTES

Does not sleep.

Driver-defined basic locks, read/write locks, and sleep locks may be held across calls to this function.

This function may not be meaningful on all implementations because some implementations may not support I/O-mapped I/O.

SEE ALSO

Programmer's Reference Manual

Integrated Software Development Guide

inl(D3D), inw(D3D), outb(D3D), outl(D3D), outw(D3D), repinsb(D3D), repinsd(D3D), repinsw(D3D), repoutsb(D3D), repoutsd(D3D), repoutsw(D3D)

NAME

inl – read a 32 bit word from a 32 bit I/O port

SYNOPSIS

```
#include <sys/types.h>

ulong_t inl(int port);
```

ARGUMENTS

port   A valid 32 bit I/O port.

DESCRIPTION

This function provides a C language interface to the machine instruction that
reads a 32 bit word from a 32 bit I/O port using the I/O address space, instead
of the memory address space.

RETURN VALUE

Returns the value of the 32 bit word read from the I/O port.

LEVEL

Base or Interrupt.

NOTES

Does not sleep.

Driver-defined basic locks, read/write locks, and sleep locks may be held across
calls to this function.

This function may not be meaningful on all implementations because some implementations may not support I/O-mapped I/O.

SEE ALSO

Programmer's Reference Manual

Integrated Software Development Guide

inb(D3D), inw(D3D), outb(D3D), outl(D3D), outw(D3D), repinsb(D3D),
repinsd(D3D), repinsw(D3D), repoutsb(D3D), repoutsd(D3D), repoutsw(D3D)

NAME

insq – insert a message into a queue

SYNOPSIS

```
#include <sys/stream.h>
```

int insq(queue_t *q, mblk_t *emp, mblk_t *nmp);

ARGUMENTS

q   Pointer to the queue containing message emp.

emp   Pointer to the existing message before which the new message is to be inserted.

nmp   Pointer to the new message to be inserted.

DESCRIPTION

insq inserts a message into a queue. The message to be inserted, nmp, is placed in the queue pointed to by q, immediately before the message, emp. If emp is NULL, the new message is placed at the end of the queue. All flow control parameters are updated. The service procedure is scheduled to run unless disabled by a previous call to noenable(D3DK).

Messages are ordered in the queue based on their priority, as described in srv(D2DK). If an attempt is made to insert a message out of order in the queue, then nmp is not enqueued.

RETURN VALUE

If nmp was successfully enqueued, insq returns 1. Otherwise, insq returns 0.

LEVEL

Base or Interrupt.

NOTES

Does not sleep.

Driver-defined basic locks, read/write locks, and sleep locks may be held across calls to this function.

The caller must have the stream frozen [see freezestr(D3DK)] when calling this function.

The insertion can fail if there is not enough memory to allocate the accounting data structures used with messages whose priority bands are greater than zero.

If emp is non-NULL, it must point to a message in the queue pointed to by q, or a system panic could result.

SEE ALSO

srv(D2DK), freezestr(D3DK), getq(D3DK), putbq(D3DK), putq(D3DK), rmvq(D3DK), unfreezestr(D3DK)

EXAMPLE

This routine illustrates the use of insq to insert a message into the middle of a queue. This routine can be used to strip all the M_PROTO headers off all messages on a queue. First, we freeze the stream (line 7) so the state of the queue does not change while we are searching it. Then we traverse the list of messages on the queue, looking for M_PROTO messages (line 11). When one is found, we remove it from the queue using rmvq(D3DK) (line 12). If there is no data portion of the message (line 13), we free the entire message using **freemsg**(D3DK). Otherwise, for every **M_PROTO** message block in the message, we strip the **M_PROTO** block off using **unlinkb**(D3DK) (line 17) and free the message block using **freeb**(D3DK). When the header has been stripped, the data portion of the message is inserted back into the queue where it was originally found (line 21). Finally, when we are done searching the queue, we unfreeze the stream (line 26).

```
1  void
2  striproto(q)
3     queue_t *q;
4  {
5     register mblk_t *emp, *nmp, *mp;
6     pl_t pl;

7     pl = freezestr(q);
8     mp = q->q_first;
9     while (mp) {
10          emp = mp->b_next;
11          if (mp->b_datap->db_type == M_PROTO) {
12                  rmvq(q, mp);
13                  if (msgdsize(mp) == 0) {
14                          freemsg(mp);
15                  } else {
16                          while (mp->b_datap->db_type == M_PROTO) {
17                                  nmp = unlinkb(mp);
18                                  freeb(mp);
19                                  mp = nmp;
20                          }
21                          insq(q, emp, mp);
22                  }
23          }
24          mp = emp;
25     }
26     unfreezestr(q, pl);
27  }
```

NAME

inw – read a 16 bit short word from a 16 bit I/O port

SYNOPSIS

```
#include <sys/types.h>

ushort_t inw(int port);
```

ARGUMENTS

port   A valid 16 bit I/O port.

DESCRIPTION

This function provides a C language interface to the machine instruction that reads a 16 bit short word from a 16 bit I/O port using the I/O address space, instead of the memory address space.

RETURN VALUE

Returns the value of the 16 bit short word read from the I/O port.

LEVEL

Base or Interrupt.

NOTES

Does not sleep.

Driver-defined basic locks, read/write locks, and sleep locks may be held across calls to this function.

This function may not be meaningful on all implementations because some implementations may not support I/O-mapped I/O.

SEE ALSO

Programmer's Reference Manual

Integrated Software Development Guide

inb(D3D), inl(D3D), outb(D3D), outl(D3D), outw(D3D), repinsb(D3D), repinsd(D3D), repinsw(D3D), repoutsb(D3D), repoutsd(D3D), repoutsw(D3D)

NAME

itimeout – execute a function after a specified length of time

SYNOPSIS

```
#include <sys/types.h>
```

toid_t itimeout(void (*fn)(), void *arg, long ticks, pl_t pl);

ARGUMENTS

fn   Function to execute when the time increment expires.

arg   Argument to the function.

ticks   Number of clock ticks to wait before the function is called.

pl   The interrupt priority level at which the function will be called. pl
            must specify a priority level greater than or equal to pltimeout; thus,
            plbase cannot be used. See **LOCK_ALLOC**(D3DK) for a list of values for
            pl.

DESCRIPTION

itimeout causes the function specified by fn to be called after the time interval
specified by ticks, at the interrupt priority level specified by pl. arg will be passed
as the only argument to function fn. The itimeout call returns immediately
without waiting for the specified function to execute.

The length of time before the function is called is not guaranteed to be exactly
equal to the requested time, but will be at least ticks–1 clock ticks in length. The
function specified by fn must neither sleep nor reference process context.

RETURN VALUE

If the function specified by fn is successfully scheduled, itimeout returns a non-
zero identifier that can be passed to untimeout to cancel the request. If the function could not be scheduled, itimeout returns a value of 0.

LEVEL

Base or Interrupt.

NOTES

Does not sleep.

Driver defined basic locks, read/write locks, and sleep locks may be held across
calls to this function.

Drivers should be careful to cancel any pending timeout functions that access
data structures before these structures are de-initialized or deallocated.

After the time interval has expired, fn only runs if the processor is at base level.
Otherwise, fn is deferred until some time in the near future.

If itimeout is called holding a lock that is contended for by fn, the caller must
hold the lock at a processor level greater than the base processor level.

A ticks argument of 0 has the same effect as a ticks argument of 1. Both will
result in an approximate wait of between 0 and 1 tick (possibly longer).

SEE ALSO

      dtimeout(D3D), LOCK_ALLOC(D3DK), untimeout(D3DK)

EXAMPLE

      See copyb(D3DK) for an example of itimeout.

NAME

itoemajor – convert internal to external major device number

SYNOPSIS

```
#include <sys/types.h>
#include <sys/ddi.h>
```

`major_t itoemajor(major_t` *imaj,* `major_t` *prevemaj)*`;`

ARGUMENTS

imaj   Internal major number.

prevemaj   Most recently obtained external major number (or **NODEV**, if this is the
             first time the function has been called).

DESCRIPTION

itoemajor converts the internal major number to the external major number.
The external-to-internal major number mapping can be many-to-one, and so any
internal major number may correspond to more than one external major number.
By repeatedly invoking this function and passing the most recent external major
number obtained, the driver can obtain all possible external major number values.
See **getemajor**(D3DK) for an explanation of external and internal major numbers.

RETURN VALUE

External major number, or **NODEV**, if all have been searched.

LEVEL

Base or Interrupt.

NOTES

Does not sleep.

Driver-defined basic locks, read/write locks, and sleep locks may be held across
calls to this function.

SEE ALSO

etoimajor(D3DK), getemajor(D3DK), geteminor(D3DK), getmajor(D3DK),
getminor(D3DK), makedevice(D3DK)

NAME
kmem_alloc – allocate space from kernel free memory

SYNOPSIS
```
#include <sys/types.h>
#include <sys/kmem.h>

void *kmem_alloc(size_t size, int flag);
```

ARGUMENTS
size   Number of bytes to allocate.

flag   Specifies whether the caller is willing to sleep waiting for memory. If *flag* is set to **KM_SLEEP**, the caller will sleep if necessary until the specified amount of memory is available. If *flag* is set to **KM_NOSLEEP**, the caller will not sleep, but **kmem_alloc** will return **NULL** if the specified amount of memory is not immediately available.

DESCRIPTION
kmem_alloc allocates *size* bytes of kernel memory and returns a pointer to the allocated memory.

RETURN VALUE
Upon successful completion, **kmem_alloc** returns a pointer to the allocated memory. If **KM_NOSLEEP** is specified and sufficient memory is not immediately available, **kmem_alloc** returns a **NULL** pointer. If *size* is set to 0, **kmem_alloc** returns **NULL** regardless of the value of *flag*.

LEVEL
Base only if *flag* is set to **KM_SLEEP**. Base or interrupt if *flag* is set to **KM_NOSLEEP**.

NOTES
May sleep if *flag* is set to **KM_SLEEP**.

Driver-defined basic locks and read/write locks may be held across calls to this function if *flag* is **KM_NOSLEEP** but may not be held if *flag* is **KM_SLEEP**.

Driver-defined sleep locks may be held across calls to this function regardless of the value of *flag*.

Kernel memory is a limited resource and should be used judiciously. Memory allocated using **kmem_alloc** should be freed as soon as possible. Drivers should not use local freelists for memory or similar schemes that cause the memory to be held for longer than necessary.

Since holding memory allocated using **kmem_alloc** for extended periods of time (e.g allocating memory at system startup and never freeing it) can have an adverse effect on overall memory usage and system performance, memory needed for such extended periods should be statically allocated whenever possible.

The address returned by a successful call to **kmem_alloc** is word-aligned.

SEE ALSO
kmem_free(D3DK), **kmem_zalloc**(D3DK)

NAME

kmem_free – free previously allocated kernel memory

SYNOPSIS

```
#include <sys/types.h>
#include <sys/kmem.h>

void kmem_free(void *addr, size_t size);
```

ARGUMENTS

addr   Address of the allocated memory to be returned. *addr* must specify the same address that was returned by the corresponding call to **kmem_alloc**(D3DK) or **kmem_zalloc**(D3DK) which allocated the memory.

size   Number of bytes to free. The *size* parameter must specify the same number of bytes as was allocated by the corresponding call to **kmem_alloc** or **kmem_zalloc**.

DESCRIPTION

kmem_free returns *size* bytes of previously allocated kernel memory. The *addr* and *size* arguments must specify exactly one complete area of memory that was allocated by a call to **kmem_alloc** or **kmem_zalloc** (that is, the memory cannot be freed piecemeal).

RETURN VALUE

None.

LEVEL

Base or Interrupt.

NOTES

Does not sleep.

Driver-defined basic locks, read/write locks, and sleep locks may be held across calls to this function.

SEE ALSO

kmem_alloc(D3DK), **kmem_zalloc**(D3DK)

NAME

kmem_zalloc – allocate and clear space from kernel free memory

SYNOPSIS

```
#include <sys/types.h>
#include <sys/kmem.h>

void *kmem_zalloc(size_t size, int flag);
```

ARGUMENTS

size   Number of bytes to allocate.

flag   Specifies whether the caller is willing to sleep waiting for memory. If *flag* is set to **KM_SLEEP**, the caller will sleep if necessary until the specified amount of memory is available. If *flag* is set to **KM_NOSLEEP**, the caller will not sleep, but **kmem_zalloc** will return **NULL** if the specified amount of memory is not immediately available.

DESCRIPTION

kmem_zalloc allocates *size* bytes of kernel memory, clears the memory by filling it with zeros, and returns a pointer to the allocated memory.

RETURN VALUE

Upon successful completion, **kmem_zalloc** returns a pointer to the allocated memory. If **KM_NOSLEEP** is specified and sufficient memory is not immediately available, **kmem_zalloc** returns a **NULL** pointer. If *size* is set to 0, **kmem_zalloc** returns **NULL** regardless of the value of *flag*.

LEVEL

Base only if *flag* is set to **KM_SLEEP**. Base or interrupt if *flag* is set to **KM_NOSLEEP**.

NOTES

May sleep if *flag* is set to **KM_SLEEP**.

Driver-defined basic locks and read/write locks may be held across calls to this function if *flag* is **KM_NOSLEEP** but may not be held if *flag* is **KM_SLEEP**.

Driver-defined sleep locks may be held across calls to this function regardless of the value of *flag*.

Kernel memory is a limited resource and should be used judiciously. Memory allocated using **kmem_zalloc** should be freed as soon as possible. Drivers should not use local freelists for memory or similar schemes that cause the memory to be held for longer than necessary.

Since holding memory allocated using **kmem_zalloc** for extended periods of time (e.g allocating memory at system startup and never freeing it) can have an adverse effect on overall memory usage and system performance, memory needed for such extended periods should be statically allocated whenever possible.

The address returned by a successful call to **kmem_zalloc** is word-aligned.

SEE ALSO

kmem_alloc(D3DK), kmem_free(D3DK)

NAME

    kvtoppid – get physical page ID for kernel virtual address

SYNOPSIS

    `#include <sys/types.h>`
    `#include <sys/vmparam.h>`

    `ppid_t kvtoppid(caddr_t` *addr*`);`

ARGUMENTS

    addr   The kernel virtual address for which the physical page ID is to be returned.

DESCRIPTION

    This routine can be used to obtain a physical page ID suitable to be used as the return value of the driver's **mmap**(D2DK) entry point. **kvtoppid** returns the physical page ID corresponding to the virtual address *addr*.

    A physical page ID is a machine-specific token that uniquely identifies a page of physical memory in the system (either system memory or device memory.) No assumptions should be made about the format of a physical page ID.

RETURN VALUE

    If *addr* is valid, the corresponding physical page ID is returned. Otherwise, **NOPAGE** is returned.

LEVEL

    Base or interrupt.

NOTES

    Does not sleep.

    Driver defined basic locks, read/write locks, and sleep locks may be held across calls to this function.

SEE ALSO

    mmap(D2DK), **intro**(D3DK), **phystoppid**(D3D)

NAME
linkb – concatenate two message blocks

SYNOPSIS
```
#include <sys/stream.h>

void linkb(mblk_t *mp1, mblk_t *mp2);
```

ARGUMENTS
mp1   Pointer to the message to which *mp2* is to be added.

mp2   Pointer to the message to be added.

DESCRIPTION
linkb appends the message *mp2* to the tail of message *mp1*. The continuation pointer (b_cont) of the last message block in the first message is set to point to the second message:

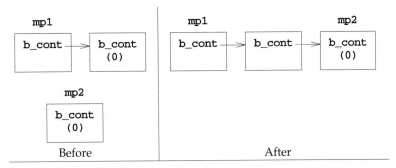

linkb(mp1, mp2);

RETURN VALUE
None.

LEVEL
Base or Interrupt.

NOTES
Does not sleep.

Driver-defined basic locks, read/write locks, and sleep locks may be held across calls to this function.

SEE ALSO
unlinkb(D3DK), msgb(D4DK)

NAME

LOCK – acquire a basic lock

SYNOPSIS

```
#include <sys/types.h>
#include <sys/ksynch.h>

pl_t LOCK(lock_t *lockp, pl_t pl);
```

ARGUMENTS

lockp   Pointer to the basic lock to be acquired.

pl   The interrupt priority level to be set while the lock is held by the caller. Because some implementations require that interrupts that might attempt to acquire the lock be blocked on the processor on which the lock is held, portable drivers must specify a *pl* value that is sufficient to block out any interrupt handler that might attempt to acquire this lock. See the description of the *min_pl* argument to **LOCK_ALLOC**(D3DK) for additional discussion and a list of the valid values for *pl*. Implementations which do not require that the interrupt priority level be raised during lock acquisition may choose to ignore this argument.

DESCRIPTION

LOCK sets the interrupt priority level in accordance with the value specified by *pl* (if required by the implementation) and acquires the lock specified by *lockp*. If the lock is not immediately available, the caller will wait until the lock is available. It is implementation defined whether the caller will block during the wait. Some implementations may cause the caller to spin for the duration of the wait, while on others the caller may block at some point.

RETURN VALUE

Upon acquiring the lock, **LOCK** returns the previous interrupt priority level (**plbase - plhi**).

LEVEL

Base or Interrupt.

NOTES

Basic locks are not recursive. A call to **LOCK** attempting to acquire a lock that is currently held by the calling context will result in deadlock.

Calls to **LOCK** should honor the ordering defined by the lock hierarchy [see **LOCK_ALLOC**(D3DK)] in order to avoid deadlock.

Driver defined sleep locks may be held across calls to this function.

Driver defined basic locks and read/write locks may be held across calls to this function subject to the hierarchy and recursion restrictions described above.

When called from interrupt level, the *pl* argument must not specify a priority level below the level at which the interrupt handler is running.

SEE ALSO

LOCK_ALLOC(D3DK), **LOCK_DEALLOC**(D3DK), **TRYLOCK**(D3DK), **UNLOCK**(D3DK)

NAME

LOCK_ALLOC – allocate and initialize a basic lock

SYNOPSIS

```
#include <sys/types.h>
#include <sys/kmem.h>
#include <sys/ksynch.h>

lock_t *LOCK_ALLOC(uchar_t hierarchy, pl_t min_pl, lkinfo_t *lkinfop, int flag);
```

ARGUMENTS

hierarchy Hierarchy value which asserts the order in which this lock will be acquired relative to other basic and read/write locks. This assertion is enforced by the system when the driver is compiled with the **DEBUG** and **_LOCKTEST** compilation options defined. *hierarchy* must be within the range 1 through 32 inclusive and must be chosen such that locks are normally acquired in order of increasing *hierarchy* number. In other words, when acquiring a basic lock using any function other than **TRYLOCK**(D3DK), the lock being acquired must have a *hierarchy* value that is strictly greater than the *hierarchy* values associated with all locks currently held by the calling context.

Implementations of lock testing may differ in whether they assume a separate range of *hierarchy* values for each interrupt priority level or a single range that spans all interrupt priority levels. In order to be portable across different implementations, drivers which may acquire locks at more than one interrupt priority level should define the *hierarchy* among those locks such that the *hierarchy* is strictly increasing with increasing priority level (e.g. if M is the maximum *hierarchy* value defined for any lock that may be acquired at priority level N, then M + 1 should be the minimum hierarchy value defined for any lock that may be acquired at any priority level greater than N).

min_pl Minimum priority level argument which asserts the minimum priority level that will be passed in with any attempt to acquire this lock [see **LOCK**(D3DK)]. This assertion may be enforced by the system when the driver is compiled with the **DEBUG** and **_LOCKTEST** compilation options defined. Implementations which do not require that the interrupt priority level be raised during lock acquisition may choose not to enforce the *min_pl* assertion, even when the appropriate compilation options have been defined. The valid values for this argument are as follows:

plbase	Block no interrupts
pltimeout	Block functions scheduled by itimeout and dtimeout
pldisk	Block disk device interrupts
plstr	Block STREAMS interrupts
plhi	Block all interrupts

The notion of a *min_pl* assumes a defined order of priority levels. The following partial order is defined:

```
plbase < pltimeout <= pldisk,plstr <= plhi
```

The ordering of **pldisk** and **plstr** relative to each other is not defined.

Setting a given priority level will block interrupts associated with that level as well as any levels that are defined to be less than or equal to the specified level. In order to be portable a driver should not acquire locks at different priority levels where the relative order of those priority levels is not defined above.

The *min_pl* argument should specify a priority level that would be sufficient to block out any interrupt handler that might attempt to acquire this lock. In addition, potential deadlock problems involving multiple locks should be considered when defining the *min_pl* value. For example, if the normal order of acquisition of locks A and B (as defined by the lock hierarchy) is to acquire A first and then B, lock B should never be acquired at a priority level less than the *min_pl* for lock A. Therefore, the *min_pl* for lock B should be greater than or equal to the *min_pl* for lock A.

Note that the specification of *min_pl* with a **LOCK_ALLOC** call does not actually cause any interrupts to be blocked upon lock acquisition, it simply asserts that subsequent **LOCK** calls to acquire this lock will pass in a priority level at least as great as *min_pl*.

lkinfop   Pointer to a **lkinfo**(D4DK) structure. The **lk_name** member of the **lkinfo** structure points to a character string defining a name that will be associated with the lock for the purpose of statistics gathering. The name should begin with the driver prefix and should be unique to the lock or group of locks for which the driver wishes to collect a uniquely identifiable set of statistics (i.e. if a given name is shared by a group of locks, the statistics of individual locks within the group will not be uniquely identifiable). There are no flags defined within the **lk_flags** member of the **lkinfo** structure for use with **LOCK_ALLOC**.

The *lkinfop* pointer is recorded in a statistics buffer along with the lock statistics when the driver is compiled with the **DEBUG** and **_MPSTATS** compilation options defined. A given **lkinfo** structure may be shared among multiple basic locks and read/write locks but a **lkinfo** structure may not be shared between a basic lock and a sleep lock. The caller must ensure that the **lk_flags** and **lk_pad** members of the **lkinfo** structure are zeroed out before passing it to **LOCK_ALLOC**.

flag   Specifies whether the caller is willing to sleep waiting for memory. If *flag* is set to **KM_SLEEP**, the caller will sleep if necessary until sufficient memory is available. If *flag* is set to **KM_NOSLEEP**, the caller will not sleep, but **LOCK_ALLOC** will return **NULL** if sufficient memory is not immediately available. Under the **_MPSTATS** compilation option, if **KM_NOSLEEP** is specified and sufficient memory can be immediately allocated for the lock itself but not for an accompanying statistics buffer, **LOCK_ALLOC** will return a pointer to the allocated lock but individual statistics will not be collected for the lock.

DESCRIPTION

LOCK_ALLOC dynamically allocates and initializes an instance of a basic lock. The lock is initialized to the unlocked state.

RETURN VALUE

Upon successful completion, LOCK_ALLOC returns a pointer to the newly allocated lock. If KM_NOSLEEP is specified and sufficient memory is not immediately available, LOCK_ALLOC returns a NULL pointer.

LEVEL

Base only if *flag* is set to KM_SLEEP. Base or interrupt if *flag* is set to KM_NOSLEEP.

NOTES

May sleep if flag is set to KM_SLEEP.

Driver defined basic locks and read/write locks may be held across calls to this function if *flag* is KM_NOSLEEP but may not be held if *flag* is KM_SLEEP.

Driver defined sleep locks may be held across calls to this function regardless of the value of *flag*.

SEE ALSO

LOCK(D3DK), LOCK_DEALLOC(D3DK), TRYLOCK(D3DK), UNLOCK(D3DK), lkinfo(D4DK)

NAME

LOCK_DEALLOC – deallocate an instance of a basic lock

SYNOPSIS

```
#include <sys/types.h>
#include <sys/ksynch.h>

void LOCK_DEALLOC(lock_t *lockp);
```

ARGUMENTS

lockp   Pointer to the basic lock to be deallocated.

DESCRIPTION

LOCK_DEALLOC deallocates the basic lock specified by *lockp*.

RETURN VALUE

None.

LEVEL

Base or Interrupt.

NOTES

Does not sleep.

Attempting to deallocate a lock that is currently locked or is being waited for is an error and will result in undefined behavior.

Driver defined basic locks (other than the one being deallocated), read/write locks, and sleep locks may be held across calls to this function.

SEE ALSO

LOCK(D3DK), LOCK_ALLOC(D3DK), TRYLOCK(D3DK), UNLOCK(D3DK)

NAME

makedevice – make device number from major and minor numbers

SYNOPSIS

```
#include <sys/types.h>
#include <sys/ddi.h>

dev_t makedevice(major_t majnum, minor_t minnum);
```

ARGUMENTS

majnum   Major number.

minnum   Minor number.

DESCRIPTION

The **makedevice** function creates a device number from a major and minor device number. **makedevice** should be used to create device numbers so that the driver will port easily to releases that treat device numbers differently.

RETURN VALUE

The device number, containing both the major number and the minor number, is returned. No validation of the major or minor numbers is performed.

LEVEL

Base or Interrupt.

NOTES

Does not sleep.

Driver-defined basic locks, read/write locks, and sleep locks may be held across calls to this function.

SEE ALSO

getemajor(D3DK), geteminor(D3DK), getmajor(D3DK), getminor(D3DK)

EXAMPLE

In the following example, **makedevice** is used to create the device number selected during a clone open. If the **CLONEOPEN** flag is set (line 11), we lock the list of minor devices (line 12) and search through the list, looking for a minor device that is available (lines 13-14). If we find an unused minor, we break off the search, mark the minor as being in use (line 20), unlock the list, create a new device number, and store it in the memory location pointed to by **devp** (line 22). If no unused minor was found, we unlock the list and return the error **ENXIO**.

```
1   xxxopen(q, devp, oflag, sflag, crp)
2       queue_t *q;
3       dev_t *dev;
4       int oflag;
5       int sflag;
6       cred_t *crp;
7   {
8       minor_t minnum;
9       pl_t pl;
10      extern lock_t *xxxminlock;

11      if (sflag == CLONEOPEN) {
12              pl = LOCK(xxxminlock, plstr);
13              for (minnum = 0; minnum < XXXMAXMIN; minnum++)
```

```
14                      if (!INUSE(minnum))
15                              break;
16              if (minnum >= XXXMAXMIN) {
17                      UNLOCK(xxxminlock, pl);
18                      return(ENXIO);
19              } else {
20                      SETINUSE(minnum);
21                      UNLOCK(xxxminlock, pl);
22                      *devp = makedevice(getemajor(*devp), minnum);
23              }
24      }
        ...
```

NAME

> max – return the larger of two integers

SYNOPSIS

> ```
> #include <sys/ddi.h>
> ```
>
> int max(int *int1,* int *int2*);

ARGUMENTS

> *int1, int2*   The integers to be compared.

DESCRIPTION

> max compares two integers and returns the larger of two. If the *int1* and *int2* arguments are not of the specified type the results are undefined.
>
> Also, this interface may be implemented in a way that causes the arguments to be evaluated multiple times, so callers should beware of side effects.

RETURN VALUE

> The larger of the two integers.

LEVEL

> Base or Interrupt.

NOTES

> Does not sleep.
>
> Driver-defined basic locks, read/write locks, and sleep locks may be held across calls to this function.

SEE ALSO

> min(D3DK)

NAME

min – return the lesser of two integers

SYNOPSIS

`#include <sys/ddi.h>`

`int min(int` *int1,* `int` *int2*`);`

ARGUMENTS

int1, int2   The integers to be compared.

DESCRIPTION

min compares two integers and returns the lesser of the two. If the *int1* and *int2* arguments are not of the specified type the results are undefined.

Also, this interface may be implemented in a way that causes the arguments to be evaluated multiple times, so callers should beware of side effects.

RETURN VALUE

The lesser of the two integers.

LEVEL

Base or Interrupt.

NOTES

Does not sleep.

Driver-defined basic locks, read/write locks, and sleep locks may be held across calls to this function.

SEE ALSO

max(D3DK)

NAME

    `msgdsize` – return number of bytes of data in a message

SYNOPSIS

    `#include <sys/stream.h>`

    `int msgdsize(mblk_t *`*mp*`);`

ARGUMENTS

    mp   Pointer to the message to be evaluated.

DESCRIPTION

    `msgdsize` counts the number of bytes of data in the message pointed to by *mp*. Only bytes included in message blocks of type **M_DATA** are included in the count.

RETURN VALUE

    The number of bytes of data in the message.

LEVEL

    Base or Interrupt.

NOTES

    Does not sleep.

    Driver-defined basic locks, read/write locks, and sleep locks may be held across calls to this function.

SEE ALSO

    msgb(D4DK)

EXAMPLE

    See insq(D3DK) for an example of **msgdsize**.

NAME

msgpullup – concatenate bytes in a message

SYNOPSIS

```
#include <sys/stream.h>

mblk_t *msgpullup(mblk_t *mp, int len);
```

ARGUMENTS

mp   Pointer to the message whose blocks are to be concatenated.

len   Number of bytes to concatenate.

DESCRIPTION

msgpullup concatenates and aligns the first *len* data bytes of the message pointed to by *mp*, copying the data into a new message. The original message is unaltered. If *len* equals −1, all data are concatenated. If *len* bytes of the same message type cannot be found, msgpullup fails and returns NULL.

RETURN VALUE

On success, a pointer to the new message is returned; on failure, NULL is returned.

LEVEL

Base or Interrupt

NOTES

Does not sleep.

Driver-defined basic locks, read/write locks, and sleep locks may be held across calls to this function.

SEE ALSO

allocb(D3DK), msgb(D4DK)

NAME

　　`ngeteblk` – get an empty buffer of the specified size

SYNOPSIS

　　`#include <sys/types.h>`
　　`#include <sys/buf.h>`

　　`buf_t *ngeteblk(size_t` *bsize*`);`

DESCRIPTION

　　`ngeteblk` retrieves a buffer [see **buf**(D4DK)] of size *bsize* from the buffer cache and returns a pointer to the buffer header. If a buffer is not available, `ngeteblk` dynamically allocates one. If memory is not immediately available, `ngeteblk` will sleep until enough memory has been freed to allocate the buffer.

　　When the driver **strategy**(D2DK) routine receives a buffer header from the kernel, all the necessary members are already initialized. However, when a driver allocates buffers for its own use, it must set up some of the members before calling its **strategy** routine.

　　The following list describes the state of these members when the buffer header is received from `ngeteblk`:

　　b_flags　　　is set to indicate the transfer is from the user's buffer to the kernel. The driver must set the **B_READ** flag if the transfer is from the kernel to the user's buffer.

　　b_edev　　　is set to **NODEV** and must be initialized by the driver.

　　b_bcount　　is set to *bsize*.

　　b_un.b_addr　is set to the buffer's virtual address.

　　b_blkno　　　is not initialized by `ngeteblk`, and must be initialized by the driver

　　Typically, block drivers do not allocate buffers. The buffer is allocated by the kernel, and the associated buffer header is used as an argument to the driver **strategy** routine. However, to implement some special features, such as **ioctl**(D2DK) commands that perform I/O, the driver may need its own buffer space. The driver can get the buffer space from the system by using **geteblk**(D3DK) or `ngeteblk`. Or the driver can choose to use its own memory for the buffer and only allocate a buffer header with **getrbuf**(D3DK).

RETURN VALUE

　　A pointer to the buffer header structure is returned.

LEVEL

　　Base Only.

NOTES

　　Can sleep.

　　Driver-defined basic locks and read/write locks may not be held across calls to this function.

Driver-defined sleep locks may be held across calls to this function.

Buffers allocated via **ngeteblk** must be freed using either **brelse**(D3DK) or **biodone**(D3DK).

SEE ALSO

biodone(D3DK), **biowait**(D3DK), **brelse**(D3DK), **geteblk**(D3DK), **buf**(D4DK)

NAME

noenable – prevent a queue from being scheduled

SYNOPSIS

```
#include <sys/stream.h>
#include <sys/ddi.h>

void noenable(queue_t *q);
```

ARGUMENTS

q   Pointer to the queue.

DESCRIPTION

The **noenable** function prevents the service routine of the queue pointed to by *q* from being scheduled for service by **insq**(D3DK), **putbq**(D3DK), or **putq**(D3DK), when enqueuing a message that is not a high priority message. This restriction can be lifted with the **enableok**(D3DK) function.

noenable does not prevent the queue's service routine from being scheduled when a high priority message is enqueued, or by an explicit call to **qenable**(D3DK).

RETURN VALUE

None.

LEVEL

Base or Interrupt.

NOTES

Does not sleep.

Driver-defined basic locks, read/write locks, and sleep locks may be held across calls to this function.

The caller cannot have the stream frozen [see **freezestr**(D3DK)] when calling this function.

SEE ALSO

srv(D2DK), **enableok**(D3DK), **insq**(D3DK), **putbq**(D3DK), **putq**(D3DK), **qenable**(D3DK), **queue**(D4DK)

NAME

OTHERQ – get pointer to queue's partner queue

SYNOPSIS

```
#include <sys/stream.h>
#include <sys/ddi.h>

queue_t *OTHERQ(queue_t *q);
```

ARGUMENTS

q Pointer to the queue.

DESCRIPTION

The OTHERQ function returns a pointer to the other of the two **queue** structures
that make up an instance of a STREAMS module or driver. If q points to the
read queue the write queue will be returned, and vice versa.

RETURN VALUE

OTHERQ returns a pointer to a queue's partner.

LEVEL

Base or Interrupt.

NOTES

Does not sleep.

Driver-defined basic locks, read/write locks, and sleep locks may be held across
calls to this function.

SEE ALSO

RD(D3DK), WR(D3DK)

EXAMPLE

This routine sets the minimum packet size, the maximum packet size, the high
water mark, and the low water mark for the read and write queues of a given
module or driver. It is passed either one of the queues. This could be used if a
module or driver wished to update its queue parameters dynamically.

```
1  void
2  set_q_params(queue_t *q, long min, long max, ulong_t hi, ulong_t lo)
3  {
4      register pl_t pl;

5      pl = freezestr(q);
6      (void) strqset(q, QMINPSZ, 0, min);
7      (void) strqset(q, QMAXPSZ, 0, max);
8      (void) strqset(q, QHIWAT, 0, hi);
9      (void) strqset(q, QLOWAT, 0, lo);
10     (void) strqset(OTHERQ(q), QMINPSZ, 0, min);
11     (void) strqset(OTHERQ(q), QMAXPSZ, 0, max);
12     (void) strqset(OTHERQ(q), QHIWAT, 0, hi);
13     (void) strqset(OTHERQ(q), QLOWAT, 0, lo);
14     unfreezestr(q, pl);
15 }
```

NAME
> outb – write a byte to an 8 bit I/O port

SYNOPSIS
> `#include <sys/types.h>`
>
> `void outb(int` *port,* `uchar_t` *data*`);`

ARGUMENTS
> *port*   A valid 8 bit I/O port.
>
> *data*   The 8 bit value to be written to the port.

DESCRIPTION
> This function provides a C language interface to the machine instruction that writes a byte to an 8 bit I/O port using the I/O address space, instead of the memory address space.

RETURN VALUE
> None.

LEVEL
> Base or Interrupt.

NOTES
> Does not sleep.
>
> Driver-defined basic locks, read/write locks, and sleep locks may be held across calls to this function.
>
> This function may not be meaningful on all implementations because some implementations may not support I/O-mapped I/O.

SEE ALSO
> *Programmer's Reference Manual*
>
> *Integrated Software Development Guide*
>
> **inb**(D3D), **inl**(D3D), **inw**(D3D), **outl**(D3D), **outw**(D3D), **repinsb**(D3D), **repinsd**(D3D), **repinsw**(D3D), **repoutsb**(D3D), **repoutsd**(D3D), **repoutsw**(D3D)

NAME

outl – write a 32 bit long word to a 32 bit I/O port

SYNOPSIS

```
#include <sys/types.h>

void outl(int port, ulong_t  data);
```

ARGUMENTS

port   A valid 32 bit I/O port.

data   The 32 bit value to be written to the port.

DESCRIPTION

This function provides a C language interface to the machine instruction that writes a 32 bit long word to a 32 bit I/O port using the I/O address space, instead of the memory address space.

RETURN VALUE

None.

LEVEL

Base or Interrupt.

NOTES

Does not sleep.

Driver-defined basic locks, read/write locks, and sleep locks may be held across calls to this function.

This function may not be meaningful on all implementations because some implementations may not support I/O-mapped I/O.

SEE ALSO

Programmer's Reference Manual

Integrated Software Development Guide

inb(D3D), inl(D3D), inw(D3D), outb(D3D), outw(D3D), repinsb(D3D), repinsd(D3D), repinsw(D3D), repoutsb(D3D), repoutsd(D3D), repoutsw(D3D)

NAME

outw – write a 16 bit short word to a 16 bit I/O port

SYNOPSIS

`#include <sys/types.h>`

`void outw(int` *port,* `ushort_t` *data*`);`

ARGUMENTS

port   A valid 16 bit I/O port.

data   The 16 bit value to be written to the port.

DESCRIPTION

This function provides a C language interface to the machine instruction that writes a 16 bit short word to a 16 bit I/O port using the I/O address space, instead of the memory address space.

RETURN VALUE

None.

LEVEL

Base or Interrupt.

NOTES

Does not sleep.

Driver-defined basic locks, read/write locks, and sleep locks may be held across calls to this function.

This function may not be meaningful on all implementations because some implementations may not support I/O-mapped I/O.

SEE ALSO

Programmer's Reference Manual

Integrated Software Development Guide

inb(D3D), inl(D3D), inw(D3D), outb(D3D), outl(D3D), repinsb(D3D),
repinsd(D3D), repinsw(D3D), repoutsb(D3D), repoutsd(D3D), repoutsw(D3D)

NAME

pcmsg – test whether a message is a priority control message

SYNOPSIS

```
#include <sys/types.h>
#include <sys/stream.h>
#include <sys/ddi.h>

int pcmsg(uchar_t type);
```

ARGUMENTS

type   The type of message to be tested.

DESCRIPTION

The **pcmsg** function tests the type of message to determine if it is a priority control message (also known as a high priority message.) The **db_type** field of the **datab**(D4DK) structure contains the message type. This field may be accessed through the message block using **mp->b_datap->db_type**.

RETURN VALUE

pcmsg returns 1 if the message is a priority control message and 0 if the message is any other type.

LEVEL

Base or Interrupt.

NOTES

Does not sleep.

Driver defined basic locks, read/write locks, and sleep locks may be held across calls to this function.

SEE ALSO

allocb(D3DK), **datab**(D4DK), **msgb**(D4DK), **messages**(D5DK)

EXAMPLE

The service routine processes messages on the queue. If the message is a high priority message, or if it is a normal message and the stream is not flow-controlled, the message is processed and passed along in the stream. Otherwise, the message is placed back on the head of the queue and the service routine returns.

```
1    xxxsrv(q)
2          queue_t *q;
3    {
4          mblk_t *mp;

5          while ((mp = getq(q)) != NULL) {
6                if (pcmsg(mp->b_datap->db_type) || canputnext(q)) {
7                      /* process message */
8                      putnext(q, mp);
9                } else {
10                     putbq(q, mp);
11                     return;
12                }
13         }
14   }
```

NAME

phalloc – allocate and initialize a pollhead structure

SYNOPSIS

```
#include <sys/poll.h>
#include <sys/kmem.h>

struct pollhead *phalloc(int flag);
```

ARGUMENTS

flag   Specifies whether the caller is willing to sleep waiting for memory. If *flag* is set to **KM_SLEEP**, the caller will sleep if necessary until sufficient memory is available. If *flag* is set to **KM_NOSLEEP**, the caller will not sleep, but **phalloc** will return **NULL** if sufficient memory is not immediately available.

DESCRIPTION

phalloc allocates and initializes a **pollhead** structure for use by non-STREAMS character drivers that wish to support polling. The *flag* argument indicates whether the caller is willing to sleep waiting for memory as described above.

RETURN VALUE

Upon successful completion, **phalloc** returns a pointer to the newly allocated **pollhead** structure. If **KM_NOSLEEP** is specified and sufficient memory is not immediately available, **phalloc** returns a **NULL** pointer.

LEVEL

Base only if *flag* is set to **KM_SLEEP**. Base or interrupt if *flag* is set to **KM_NOSLEEP**.

NOTES

May sleep if flag is set to **KM_SLEEP**.

Driver defined basic locks and read/write locks may be held across calls to this function if *flag* is **KM_NOSLEEP** but may not be held if *flag* is **KM_SLEEP**.

Driver defined sleep locks may be held across calls to this function regardless of the value of *flag*.

DDI/DKI conforming drivers may only use **pollhead** structures which have been allocated and initialized using **phalloc**. Use of **pollhead** structures which have been obtained by any other means is prohibited.

SEE ALSO

chpoll(D2DK), phfree(D3DK)

NAME

phfree – free a pollhead structure

SYNOPSIS

```
#include <sys/poll.h>
#include <sys/kmem.h>

void phfree(struct pollhead *php);
```

ARGUMENTS

php   Pointer to the **pollhead** structure to be freed. The structure pointed to by *php* must have been previously allocated by a call to **phalloc**(D3DK).

DESCRIPTION

phfree frees the **pollhead** structure specified by *php*.

RETURN VALUE

None.

LEVEL

Base or Interrupt.

NOTES

Does not sleep.

Driver defined basic locks, read/write locks, and sleep locks may be held across calls to this function.

DDI/DKI conforming drivers may only use **pollhead** structures which have been allocated and initialized using **phalloc**. Use of **pollhead** structures which have been obtained by any other means is prohibited.

SEE ALSO

chpoll(D2DK), **phalloc**(D3DK)

NAME

physiock – validate and issue raw I/O request

SYNOPSIS

```
#include <sys/types.h>
#include <sys/buf.h>
#include <sys/uio.h>

int physiock(int (*strat)(), buf_t *bp, dev_t dev, int rwflag,
    daddr_t nblocks, uio_t *uiop);
```

ARGUMENTS

strat   Address of the driver **strategy**(D2DK) routine.

bp   Pointer to the **buf**(D4DK) structure describing the I/O request. If set to **NULL**, then a buffer is allocated from the buffer pool and returned to the free list after the transfer completes.

dev   External device number.

rwflag Flag indicating whether the access is a read or a write. If set to **B_READ**, the direction of the data transfer will be from the kernel to the user's buffer. If set to **B_WRITE**, the direction of the data transfer will be from the user's buffer to the kernel.

nblocks Number of blocks that a logical device can support. One block is equal to **NBPSCTR** bytes. **NBPSCTR** is defined in **sys/param.h**.

uiop   Pointer to the **uio**(D4DK) structure that defines the user space of the I/O request.

DESCRIPTION

physiock is called by the character interface (**ioctl**(D2DK), **read**(D2DK), and **write**(D2DK)) routines of block drivers to help perform unbuffered I/O while maintaining the buffer header as the interface structure.

physiock performs the following functions:

Verifies the requested transfer is valid by checking if the offset is at or past the end of the device.

Sets up a buffer header describing the transfer.

Faults pages in and locks the pages impacted by the I/O transfer so they can't be swapped out.

Calls the driver **strategy** routine passed to it (*strat*).

Sleeps until the transfer is complete and is awakened by a call to **biodone**(D3DK) from the driver's I/O completion handler.

Performs the necessary cleanup and updates, then returns to the driver routine.

A transfer using **physiock** is considered valid if the specified data location exists on the device, and the user has specified a storage area large enough that exists in user memory space.

RETURN VALUE

physiock returns 0 if the result is successful, or the appropriate error number on failure. If a partial transfer occurs, the **uio** structure is updated to indicate the amount not transferred and an error is returned. **physiock** returns the **ENXIO** error if an attempt is made to read beyond the end of the device. If a read is performed at the end of the device, 0 is returned. **ENXIO** is also returned if an attempt is made to write at or beyond the end of a the device. **EFAULT** is returned if user memory is not valid. **EAGAIN** is returned if **physiock** could not lock pages for DMA.

LEVEL

Base Only.

NOTES

Can sleep.

Driver-defined basic locks and read/write locks may not be held across calls to this function.

Driver-defined sleep locks may be held across calls to this function.

Some device drivers need *nblocks* to be arbitrarily large (for example, for tapes whose sizes are unknown). In this case, *nblocks* should be no larger than (2^{22})-1.

SEE ALSO

ioctl(D2DK), read(D2DK), strategy(D2DK), write(D2DK), dma_pageio(D3D), buf(D4DK), uio(D4DK)

EXAMPLE

See dma_pageio(D3D) for an example of **physiock**.

NAME

   physmap – obtain virtual address mapping for physical addresses

SYNOPSIS

   #include <sys/types.h>
   #include <sys/kmem.h>

   caddr_t physmap(paddr_t *physaddr*, ulong_t *nbytes*, uint_t *flags*);

ARGUMENTS

   physaddr   Starting physical address to map.

   nbytes   Number of bytes to map.

   flags   Flags indicating whether the caller is willing to sleep. Values are
                 found in **sys/kmem.h** and may be either of the following: **KM_SLEEP** if
                 physmap is allowed to sleep waiting for resources, or **KM_NOSLEEP** if it
                 is not allowed to sleep.

DESCRIPTION

   physmap allocates a virtual address mapping for a given range of physical
   addresses. It is generally used from a driver's **init**(D2D) or **start**(D2DK) routine to get a pointer to device memory (for memory-mapped I/O). The range of
   virtual addresses will be cache-inhibited.

RETURN VALUE

   On success, **physmap** returns a virtual address that can be used to access *nbytes*
   bytes corresponding to physical address *physaddr*. If **KM_NOSLEEP** is specified and
   sufficient virtual space is not immediately available, **physmap** returns **NULL**.

LEVEL

   Base only if *flags* is set to **KM_SLEEP**. Base or interrupt if *flags* is set to
   KM_NOSLEEP.

NOTES

   May sleep if *flags* is set to **KM_SLEEP**.

   Driver-defined basic locks and read/write locks may be held across calls to this
   function if *flags* is **KM_NOSLEEP**, but may not be held if *flags* is **KM_SLEEP**.

   Driver-defined sleep locks may be held across calls to this function regardless of
   the value of *flags*.

SEE ALSO

   init(D2D), **start**(D2DK), **physmap_free**(D3D)

NAME
physmap_free – free virtual address mapping for physical addresses

SYNOPSIS
```
#include <sys/types.h>
#include <sys/kmem.h>

void physmap_free(caddr_t vaddr, ulong_t nbytes, uint_t flags);
```

ARGUMENTS
vaddr   Virtual address for which the mapping will be released.

nbytes   Number of bytes in the mapping.

flags   For future use (must be set to 0.)

DESCRIPTION
physmap_free releases a mapping allocated by a previous call to **physmap**. The *nbytes* argument must be identical to that given to **physmap**. Currently, no flags are supported and the *flags* argument must be set to zero. Generally, **physmap_free** will never be called, since drivers usually keep the mapping forever, but it is provided if a driver wants to dynamically allocate and free mappings.

RETURN VALUE
None.

LEVEL
Base or Interrupt.

NOTES
Does not sleep.

Driver-defined basic locks, read/write locks, and sleep locks may be held across calls to this function.

SEE ALSO
physmap(D3D)

NAME

`phystoppid` – get physical page ID for physical address

SYNOPSIS

```
#include <sys/types.h>
#include <sys/vmparam.h>

ppid_t phystoppid(paddr_t addr);
```

ARGUMENTS

addr   The physical address for which the physical page ID is to be returned.

DESCRIPTION

This routine can be used to obtain a physical page ID suitable to be used as the return value of the driver's `mmap`(D2DK) entry point. `phystoppid` returns the physical page ID corresponding to the physical address *addr*.

A physical page ID is a machine-specific token that uniquely identifies a page of physical memory in the system (either system memory or device memory.) No assumptions should be made about the format of a physical page ID.

RETURN VALUE

If *addr* is valid, the corresponding physical page ID is returned. Otherwise, `NOPAGE` is returned.

LEVEL

Base or interrupt.

NOTES

Does not sleep.

Driver defined basic locks, read/write locks, and sleep locks may be held across calls to this function.

SEE ALSO

`mmap`(D2DK), `intro`(D3DK), `kvtoppid`(D3DK)

NAME

pollwakeup – inform polling processes that an event has occurred

SYNOPSIS

```
#include <sys/poll.h>

void pollwakeup(struct pollhead *php, short event);
```

ARGUMENTS

php   Pointer to a **pollhead** structure.

event   Event to notify the process about.

DESCRIPTION

The **pollwakeup** function provides non-STREAMS character drivers with a way to notify processes polling for the occurrence of an event. **pollwakeup** should be called from the driver for each occurrence of an event. Events are described in chpoll(D2DK).

The **pollhead** structure will usually be associated with the driver's private data structure for the particular minor device where the event has occurred.

RETURN

None.

LEVEL

Base or Interrupt.

NOTES

Does not sleep.

Driver-defined basic locks, read/write locks, and sleep locks may be held across calls to this function.

pollwakeup should only be called with one event at a time.

SEE ALSO

chpoll(D2DK)

poll(2) in the *Programmer's Reference Manual*

NAME

pptophys – convert page pointer to physical address

SYNOPSIS

```
#include <sys/types.h>
#include <vm/page.h>

paddr_t pptophys(page_t *pp);
```

ARGUMENTS

pp   Pointer to the page structure.

DESCRIPTION

pptophys will convert a pointer to a page structure to a physical address. Block drivers can use this address for physical DMA operations during paged-I/O requests. A paged-I/O request is identified by the **B_PAGEIO** flag being set in the **b_flags** field of the buffer header [see **buf**(D4DK)] passed to a driver's **strategy**(D2DK) routine. The pointer to the page structure can be obtained by calling **getnextpg**(D3DK).

RETURN VALUE

The physical address represented by the page structure pointed to by *pp*.

LEVEL

Base or Interrupt.

NOTES

B_PAGEIO won't be set unless the driver has the **D_NOBRKUP** flag set [see **devflag**(D1D).]

Does not sleep.

Driver defined basic locks, read/write locks, and sleep locks may be held across calls to this function.

SEE ALSO

devflag(D1D), **strategy**(D2DK), **getnextpg**(D3DK), **buf**(D4DK)

NAME

proc_ref – obtain a reference to a process for signaling

SYNOPSIS

```
void *proc_ref();
```

DESCRIPTION

A non-STREAMS character driver can call **proc_ref** to obtain a reference to the process in whose context it is running. The value returned can be used in subsequent calls to **proc_signal**(D3DK) to post a signal to the process. The return value should not be used in any other way (i.e. the driver should not attempt to interpret its meaning.)

RETURN VALUE

An identifier that can be used in calls to **proc_signal** and **proc_unref**(D3DK).

LEVEL

Base only.

NOTES

Processes can exit even though they are referenced by drivers. In this event, reuse of the identifier will be deferred until all driver references are given up.

There must be a matching call to **proc_unref** for every call to **proc_ref**, when the driver no longer needs to reference the process. This is typically done as part of **close**(D2DK) processing.

Requires user context.

Does not sleep.

Driver defined basic locks, read/write locks, and sleep locks may be held across calls to this function.

SEE ALSO

proc_signal(D3DK), **proc_unref**(D3DK)

NAME

proc_signal – send a signal to a process

SYNOPSIS

```
#include <sys/signal.h>

int proc_signal(void *pref, int sig);
```

ARGUMENTS

pref   Identifier obtained by a previous call to **proc_ref**(D3DK).

sig   Signal number to be sent. Valid signal numbers are listed in **signals**(D5DK).

DESCRIPTION

The **proc_signal** function can be used to post a signal to the process represented by *pref*. This will interrupt any process blocked in **SV_WAIT_SIG**(D3DK) or **SLEEP_LOCK_SIG**(D3DK) at the time the signal is posted, causing those functions to return prematurely in most cases. If the process has exited then this function has no effect.

RETURN VALUE

If the process still exists, 0 is returned. Otherwise, −1 is returned to indicate that the process no longer exists.

LEVEL

Base or Interrupt

NOTES

STREAMS drivers and modules should not use this mechanism for signaling processes. Instead, they can send **M_SIG** or **M_PCSIG** STREAMS messages to the stream head.

proc_signal must not be used to send **SIGTSTP** to a process.

Does not sleep.

Driver defined basic locks, read/write locks, and sleep locks may be held across calls to this function.

SEE ALSO

proc_ref(D3DK), **proc_unref**(D3DK), **signals**(D5DK)

NAME

proc_unref – release a reference to a process

SYNOPSIS

void proc_unref(void *pref);

ARGUMENTS

pref   Identifier obtained by a previous call to proc_ref(D3DK).

DESCRIPTION

The proc_unref function can be used to release a reference to a process identified by the parameter *pref*. There must be a matching call to proc_unref for every previous call to proc_ref(D3DK).

RETURN VALUE

None.

LEVEL

Base or Interrupt.

NOTES

Processes can exit even though they are referenced by drivers. In this event, reuse of *pref* will be deferred until all driver references are given up.

Does not sleep.

Driver defined basic locks, read/write locks, and sleep locks may be held across calls to this function.

SEE ALSO

proc_ref(D3DK), proc_signal(D3DK)

NAME
ptob – convert size in pages to size in bytes

SYNOPSIS
#include <sys/types.h>
#include <sys/ddi.h>

ulong_t ptob(ulong_t *numpages*);

ARGUMENTS
numpages   Size in pages to convert to equivalent size in bytes.

DESCRIPTION
ptob returns the number of bytes that are contained in the specified number of pages. For example, if the page size is 2048, then ptob(2) returns 4096. ptob(0) returns 0.

RETURN VALUE
The return value is the number of bytes in the specified number of pages. There is no checking done on the input value and overflow is not detected. In the case of a page count whose corresponding byte count cannot be represented by a ulong_t the higher order bits are truncated.

LEVEL
Base or Interrupt.

NOTES
Does not sleep.

Driver-defined basic locks, read/write locks, and sleep locks may be held across calls to this function.

SEE ALSO
btop(D3DK), btopr(D3DK)

NAME

put – call a put procedure

SYNOPSIS

```
#include <sys/stream.h>

void put(queue_t *q, mblk_t *mp);
```

ARGUMENTS

q   Pointer to a message queue.

mp   Pointer to the message block being passed.

DESCRIPTION

put calls the put procedure (**put**(D2DK) entry point) for the queue specified by *q*, passing it the arguments *q* and *mp*. It is typically used by a driver or module to call its own put procedure so that the proper accounting is done in the stream.

RETURN VALUE

None.

LEVEL

Base or Interrupt.

NOTES

Does not sleep.

The caller cannot have the stream frozen [see **freezestr**(D3DK)] when calling this function.

Driver defined basic locks, read/write locks, and sleep locks may not be held across calls to this function.

DDI/DKI conforming drivers and modules are no longer permitted to call put procedures directly, but must call through the appropriate STREAMS utility function—for example, **put**(D3DK), **putnext**(D3DK), **putctl**(D3DK), **putnextctl**(D3DK), **qreply**(D3DK). **put(q, mp)** is provided as a DDI/DKI-conforming equivalent to a direct call to a **put** procedure, which is no longer allowed.

SEE ALSO

put(D2DK), **putctl**(D3DK), **putctl1**(D3DK), **putnext**(D3DK), **putnextctl**(D3DK), **putnextctl1**(D3DK), **qreply**(D3DK)

NAME

　　putbq – place a message at the head of a queue

SYNOPSIS

　　`#include <sys/stream.h>`

　　`int putbq(queue_t *q, mblk_t *bp);`

ARGUMENTS

　　q　　　　Pointer to the queue.

　　bp　　　Pointer to the message.

DESCRIPTION

　　putbq puts a message back at the head of a queue. If messages of a higher priority are on the queue, then *bp* is placed at the head of its corresponding priority band. See **srv**(D2DK) for more information about message priorities.

　　All flow control parameters are updated. The queue's service routine is scheduled if it has not been disabled by a previous call to **noenable**(D3DK).

　　putbq is usually called when **bcanputnext**(D3DK) or **canputnext**(D3DK) determines that the message cannot be passed on to the next stream component.

RETURN VALUE

　　putbq returns 1 on success and 0 on failure.

LEVEL

　　Base or Interrupt.

NOTES

　　Does not sleep.

　　Driver-defined basic locks, read/write locks, and sleep locks may be held across calls to this function.

　　The caller cannot have the stream frozen [see **freezestr**(D3DK)] when calling this function.

　　putbq can fail if there is not enough memory to allocate the accounting data structures used with messages whose priority bands are greater than zero.

　　High priority messages should never be put back on a queue from within a service routine.

SEE ALSO

　　srv(D2DK), **bcanputnext**(D3DK), **canputnext**(D3DK), **getq**(D3DK), **insq**(D3DK), **putq**(D3DK), **rmvq**(D3DK), **msgb**(D4DK), **queue**(D4DK)

EXAMPLE

　　See **bufcall**(D3DK) for an example of **putbq**.

NAME

> `putctl` – send a control message to a queue

SYNOPSIS

> `#include <sys/stream.h>`
>
> `int putctl(queue_t *q, int type);`

ARGUMENTS

> *q*   Pointer to the queue to which the message is to be sent.
>
> *type*   Message type (must be control).

DESCRIPTION

> `putctl` tests the *type* argument to make sure a data type has not been specified, and then attempts to allocate a message block. `putctl` fails if *type* is **M_DATA**, **M_PROTO**, or **M_PCPROTO**, or if a message block cannot be allocated. If successful, `putctl` calls the **put**(D2DK) routine of the queue pointed to by *q*, passing it the allocated message.

RETURN VALUE

> On success, 1 is returned. Otherwise, if *type* is a data type, or if a message block cannot be allocated, 0 is returned.

LEVEL

> Base or Interrupt.

NOTES

> Does not sleep.
>
> The caller cannot have the stream frozen [see **freezestr**(D3DK)] when calling this function.
>
> Driver-defined basic locks, read/write locks, and sleep locks may not be held across calls to this function.
>
> The *q* argument to **putctl** and **putnextctl**(D3DK) may not reference **q_next** (e.g. an argument of **q->q_next** is erroneous on a multiprocessor and is disallowed by the DDI/DKI). **putnextctl(q, type)** is provided as a multiprocessor-safe equivalent to the common call **putctl(q->q_next, type)**, which is no longer allowed.

SEE ALSO

> put(D2DK), put(D3DK), putctl1(D3DK), putnextctl(D3DK), putnextctl1(D3DK)

EXAMPLE

> The **pass_ctl** routine is used to pass control messages to one's own queue. **M_BREAK** messages are handled with **putctl** (line 9). **putctl1** (line 11) is used for **M_DELAY** messages, so that *param* can be used to specify the length of the delay. If an invalid message type is detected, **pass_ctl** returns 0, indicating failure (line 13).

```
1  int
2  pass_ctl(wrq, type, param)
3     queue_t *wrq;
4     uchar_t type;
5     uchar_t param;
```

```
 6  {

 7      switch (type) {
 8      case M_BREAK:
 9              return(putctl(wrq, M_BREAK));

10      case M_DELAY:
11              return(putctl1(wrq, M_DELAY, param));

12      default:
13              return(0);
14      }
15  }
```

NAME

putctl1 – send a control message with a one-byte parameter to a queue

SYNOPSIS

```
#include <sys/stream.h>

int putctl1(queue_t *q, int type, int param);
```

ARGUMENTS

q   Pointer to the queue to which the message is to be sent.

type   Message type (must be control).

param   One-byte parameter.

DESCRIPTION

putctl1, like putctl(D3DK), tests the *type* argument to make sure a data type has not been specified, and attempts to allocate a message block. The *param* parameter can be used, for example, to specify the signal number when an **M_PCSIG** message is being sent. putctl1 fails if **type** is **M_DATA**, **M_PROTO**, or **M_PCPROTO**, or if a message block cannot be allocated. If successful, putctl1 calls the **put**(D2DK) routine of the queue pointed to by *q*, passing it the allocated message.

RETURN VALUE

On success, 1 is returned. Otherwise, if *type* is a data type, or if a message block cannot be allocated, 0 is returned.

LEVEL

Base or Interrupt.

NOTES

Does not sleep.

The caller cannot have the stream frozen [see **freezestr**(D3DK)] when calling this function.

Driver-defined basic locks, read/write locks, and sleep locks may not be held across calls to this function.

The *q* argument to **putctl1** and **putnextctl1**(D3DK) may not reference **q_next** (e.g. an argument of **q->q_next** is erroneous on a multiprocessor and is disallowed by the DDI/DKI). **putnextctl1(q, type, param)** is provided as a multiprocessor-safe equivalent to the common call **putctl1(q->q_next, type, param)**, which is no longer allowed.

SEE ALSO

put(D2DK), put(D3DK), putctl(D3DK), putnextctl(D3DK), putnextctl1(D3DK)

EXAMPLE

See putctl(D3DK) for an example of putctl1.

NAME

putnext – send a message to the next queue

SYNOPSIS

```
#include <sys/stream.h>
#include <sys/ddi.h>

int putnext(queue_t *q, mblk_t *mp);
```

ARGUMENTS

q 　　　　Pointer to the queue from which the message mp will be sent.

mp 　　　Pointer to the message to be passed.

DESCRIPTION

The **putnext** function is used to pass a message to the **put**(D2DK) routine of the next queue ($q–>q\_next$) in the stream.

RETURN VALUE

Ignored.

LEVEL

Base or Interrupt.

NOTES

Does not sleep.

Driver-defined basic locks, read/write locks, and sleep locks may not be held across calls to this function.

The caller cannot have the stream frozen [see **freezestr**(D3DK)] when calling this function.

SEE ALSO

put(D2DK), **putnextctl**(D3DK), **putnextctl1**(D3DK)

EXAMPLE

See **allocb**(D3DK) for an example of **putnext**.

NAME

putnextctl – send a control message to a queue

SYNOPSIS

```
#include <sys/stream.h>

int putnextctl(queue_t *q, int type);
```

ARGUMENTS

q   Pointer to the queue from which the message is to be sent.

type   Message type (must be control type).

DESCRIPTION

putnextctl tests the *type* argument to make sure a data type has not been specified, and then attempts to allocate a message block. putnextctl fails if *type* is M_DATA, M_PROTO, or M_PCPROTO, or if a message block cannot be allocated. If successful, putnextctl calls the put(D2DK) procedure of the queue pointed to by *q->q_next*, passing it the allocated message.

RETURN VALUE

Upon successful completion, putnextctl returns 1. If *type* is a data type, or if a message block cannot be allocated, 0 is returned.

LEVEL

Base or Interrupt.

NOTES

Does not sleep.

The caller cannot have the stream frozen [see freezestr(D3DK)] when calling this function.

Driver defined basic locks, read/write locks, and sleep locks may not be held across calls to this function.

The *q* argument to putctl(D3DK) and putnextctl may not reference q_next (for example, an argument of q->q_next is erroneous on a multiprocessor and is disallowed by the DDI/DKI). putnextctl(q, type) is provided as a multiprocessor-safe equivalent to the common call putctl(q->q_next, type), which is no longer allowed.

SEE ALSO

put(D2DK), put(D3DK), putctl(D3DK), putctl1(D3DK), putnextctl1(D3DK)

EXAMPLE

The send_ctl routine is used to pass control messages downstream. M_BREAK messages are handled with putnextctl (line 9). putnextctl1 (line 11) is used for M_DELAY messages, so that *param* can be used to specify the length of the delay. If an invalid message type is detected, send_ctl returns 0, indicating failure (line 13).

```
1   int
2   send_ctl(wrq, type, param)
3       queue_t *wrq;
4       uchar_t type;
5       uchar_t param;
6   {
```

```
7     switch (type) {
8     case M_BREAK:
9             return(putnextctl(wrq, M_BREAK));

10    case M_DELAY:
11            return(putnextctl1(wrq, M_DELAY, param));

12    default:
13            return(0);
14    }
15 }
```

NAME

putnextctl1 – send a control message with a one byte parameter to a queue

SYNOPSIS

```
#include <sys/stream.h>

int putnextctl1(queue_t *q, int type, int param);
```

ARGUMENTS

q   Pointer to the queue from which the message is to be sent.

type   Message type (must be control type).

param   One byte parameter.

DESCRIPTION

putnextctl1 tests the *type* argument to make sure a data type has not been specified, and then attempts to allocate a message block. putnextctl1 fails if *type* is **M_DATA**, **M_PROTO**, or **M_PCPROTO**, or if a message block cannot be allocated. If successful, putnextctl calls the put(D2DK) procedure of the queue pointed to by *q->q_next*, passing it the allocated message with the one byte parameter specified by *param*.

RETURN VALUE

Upon successful completion, putnextctl1 returns 1. If *type* is a data type, or if a message block cannot be allocated, 0 is returned.

LEVEL

Base or Interrupt.

NOTES

Does not sleep.

The caller cannot have the stream frozen [see **freezestr**(D3DK)] when calling this function.

Driver defined basic locks, read/write locks, and sleep locks may not be held across calls to this function.

The *q* argument to **putctl1**(D3DK) and **putnextctl1** may not reference **q_next** (for example, an argument of **q->q_next** is erroneous on a multiprocessor and is disallowed by the DDI/DKI). **putnextctl1(q, type, param)** is provided as a multiprocessor-safe equivalent to the common call **putctl1(q->q_next, type, param)**, which is no longer allowed.

SEE ALSO

put(D2DK), put(D3DK), putctl(D3DK), putctl1(D3DK), putnextctl(D3DK)

EXAMPLE

See putnextctl(D3DK) for an example of putnextctl1.

NAME

putq – put a message on a queue

SYNOPSIS

```
#include <sys/stream.h>

int putq(queue_t *q, mblk_t *bp);
```

ARGUMENTS

q   Pointer to the queue.

bp   Pointer to the message.

DESCRIPTION

putq is used to put messages on a queue after the put(D2DK) routine has finished processing the message. The message is placed after any other messages of the same priority, and flow control parameters are updated. The queue's service routine is scheduled if it has not been disabled by a previous call to noenable(D3DK).

RETURN VALUE

putq returns 1 on success and 0 on failure.

LEVEL

Base or Interrupt.

NOTES

Does not sleep.

Driver-defined basic locks, read/write locks, and sleep locks may be held across calls to this function.

The caller cannot have the stream frozen [see freezestr(D3DK)] when calling this function.

putq can fail if there is not enough memory to allocate the accounting data structures used with messages whose priority bands are greater than zero.

SEE ALSO

put(D2DK), srv(D2DK), getq(D3DK), insq(D3DK), putbq(D3DK), rmvq(D3DK), msgb(D4DK), queue(D4DK)

EXAMPLE

See datamsg(D3DK) for an example of putq.

NAME

qenable – schedule a queue's service routine to be run

SYNOPSIS

```
#include <sys/stream.h>

void qenable(queue_t *q);
```

ARGUMENTS

q Pointer to the queue.

DESCRIPTION

qenable puts the queue pointed to by q on the linked list of those whose service routines are ready to be called by the STREAMS scheduler. qenable works regardless of whether the service routine has been disabled by a previous call to noenable(D3DK).

RETURN VALUE

None.

LEVEL

Base or Interrupt.

NOTES

Does not sleep.

Driver-defined basic locks, read/write locks, and sleep locks may be held across calls to this function.

The caller cannot have the stream frozen [see freezestr(D3DK)] when calling this function.

SEE ALSO

srv(D2DK), enableok(D3DK), noenable(D3DK), queue(D4DK)

EXAMPLE

See enableok(D3DK) for an example of the qenable.

NAME

qprocsoff – disable put and service routines

SYNOPSIS

```
#include <sys/stream.h>

void qprocsoff(queue_t *rq);
```

ARGUMENTS

rq   Pointer to a read queue.

DESCRIPTION

qprocsoff disables the put and service routines of the driver or module whose read queue is pointed to by *rq*. When the routines are disabled in a module, messages flow around the module as if it were not present in the stream.

qprocsoff must be called by the close(D2DK) routine of a driver or module before deallocating any resources on which the driver/module's put and service routines depend.

qprocsoff will remove the queue's service routines from the list of service routines to be run and waits until any concurrent put or service routines are finished.

RETURN VALUE

None.

LEVEL

Base Level Only.

NOTES

May sleep.

The caller cannot have the stream frozen [see freezestr(D3DK)] when calling this function.

Driver defined basic locks and read/write locks may not be held across calls to this function.

Driver defined sleep locks may be held across calls to this function.

SEE ALSO

close(D2DK), put(D2DK), srv(D2DK), qprocson(D3DK)

EXAMPLE

See unbufcall(D3DK) for an example of qprocsoff.

NAME

qprocson – enable put and service routines

SYNOPSIS

```
#include <sys/stream.h>

void qprocson(queue_t *rq);
```

ARGUMENTS

rq   Pointer to a read queue.

DESCRIPTION

qprocson enables the put and service routines of the driver or module whose read queue is pointed to by *rq*. Prior to the call to qprocson, the put and service routines of a newly pushed module or newly opened driver are disabled. For the module, messages flow around it as if it were not present in the stream.

qprocson must be called by the first open of a module or driver after allocation and initialization of any resources on which the put and service routines depend.

RETURN VALUE

None.

LEVEL

Base Level Only.

NOTES

May sleep.

The caller cannot have the stream frozen [see freezestr(D3DK)] when calling this function.

Driver defined basic locks and read/write locks may not be held across calls to this function.

Driver defined sleep locks may be held across calls to this function.

SEE ALSO

open(D2DK), put(D2DK), srv(D2DK), qprocsoff(D3DK)

NAME

qreply – send a message in the opposite direction in a stream

SYNOPSIS

```
#include <sys/stream.h>

void qreply(queue_t *q, mblk_t *bp);
```

ARGUMENTS

q　　　　　　Pointer to the queue from which the message is being sent.

bp　　　　　Pointer to the message to be sent in the opposite direction.

DESCRIPTION

qreply sends a message in the opposite direction from that which q is pointing. It calls the **OTHERQ**(D3DK) function to find q's partner, and passes the message by calling the **put**(D2DK) routine of the next queue in the stream after q's partner.

RETURN VALUE

None.

LEVEL

Base or Interrupt.

NOTES

Does not sleep.

Driver-defined basic locks, read/write locks, and sleep locks may not be held across calls to this function.

The caller cannot have the stream frozen [see **freezestr**(D3DK)] when calling this function.

SEE ALSO

put(D2DK), **OTHERQ**(D3DK), **putnext**(D3DK)

EXAMPLE

See **put**(D2DK) for an example of **qreply**.

NAME

qsize – find the number of messages on a queue

SYNOPSIS

```
#include <sys/stream.h>

int qsize(queue_t *q);
```

ARGUMENTS

q   Pointer to the queue to be evaluated.

DESCRIPTION

qsize evaluates the queue pointed to by q and returns the number of messages it contains.

RETURN VALUE

If there are no message on the queue, **qsize** returns 0. Otherwise, it returns the number of messages on the queue.

LEVEL

Base or Interrupt.

NOTES

Does not sleep.

Driver-defined basic locks, read/write locks, and sleep locks may be held across calls to this function.

The caller cannot have the stream frozen [see **freezestr**(D3DK)] when calling this function.

SEE ALSO

msgb(D4DK), queue(D4DK)

NAME

    RD – get a pointer to the read queue

SYNOPSIS

    `#include <sys/stream.h>`
    `#include <sys/ddi.h>`

    `queue_t *RD(queue_t *`q`);`

ARGUMENTS

    q Pointer to the queue whose read queue is to be returned.

DESCRIPTION

    The **RD** function accepts a queue pointer as an argument and returns a pointer to the read queue of the same module or driver.

RETURN VALUE

    The pointer to the read queue.

LEVEL

    Base or Interrupt.

NOTES

    Does not sleep.

    Driver-defined basic locks, read/write locks, and sleep locks may be held across calls to this function.

SEE ALSO

    OTHERQ(D3DK), WR(D3DK)

EXAMPLE

    See the **put**(D2DK) function page for an example of **RD**.

NAME

repinsb – read bytes from I/O port to buffer

SYNOPSIS

```
#include <sys/types.h>

void repinsb(int port, uchar_t *addr, int cnt);
```

ARGUMENTS

port   A valid 8 bit I/O port.

addr   The address of the buffer where data is stored after *cnt* reads of the I/O port.

cnt   The number of bytes to be read from the I/O port.

DESCRIPTION

This function provides a C language interface to the machine instructions that read a string of bytes from an 8 bit I/O port using the I/O address space, instead of the memory address space. The data from *cnt* reads of the I/O port is stored in the data buffer pointed to by *addr*. The data buffer should be at least *cnt* bytes in length.

RETURN VALUE

None.

LEVEL

Base or Interrupt.

NOTES

Does not sleep.

Driver-defined basic locks, read/write locks, and sleep locks may be held across calls to this function.

This function may not be meaningful on all implementations because some implementations may not support I/O-mapped I/O.

SEE ALSO

Programmer's Reference Manual

Integrated Software Development Guide

inb(D3D), inl(D3D), inw(D3D), outb(D3D), outl(D3D), outw(D3D),
repinsd(D3D), repinsw(D3D), repoutsb(D3D), repoutsd(D3D), repoutsw(D3D)

NAME

repinsd – read 32 bit words from I/O port to buffer

SYNOPSIS

```
#include <sys/types.h>

void repinsd(int port, ulong_t *addr, int cnt);
```

ARGUMENTS

port   A valid 32 bit I/O port.

addr   The address of the buffer where data is stored after *cnt* reads of the I/O port.

cnt   The number of 32 bit words to be read from the I/O port.

DESCRIPTION

This function provides a C language interface to the machine instructions that read a string of 32 bit words from a 32 bit I/O port using the I/O address space, instead of the memory address space. The data from *cnt* reads of the I/O port is stored in the data buffer pointed to by *addr*. The data buffer should be at least *cnt* 32 bit words in length.

RETURN VALUE

None.

LEVEL

Base or Interrupt.

NOTES

Does not sleep.

Driver-defined basic locks, read/write locks, and sleep locks may be held across calls to this function.

This function may not be meaningful on all implementations because some implementations may not support I/O-mapped I/O.

SEE ALSO

Programmer's Reference Manual

Integrated Software Development Guide

inb(D3D), inl(D3D), inw(D3D), outb(D3D), outl(D3D), outw(D3D), repinsb(D3D), repinsw(D3D), repoutsb(D3D), repoutsd(D3D), repoutsw(D3D)

NAME

repinsw – read 16 bit words from I/O port to buffer

SYNOPSIS

```
#include <sys/types.h>

void repinsw(int port, ushort_t *addr, int cnt);
```

ARGUMENTS

port	A valid 16 bit I/O port.
addr	The address of the buffer where data is stored after *cnt* reads of the I/O port.
cnt	The number of 16 bit words to be read from the I/O port.

DESCRIPTION

This function provides a C language interface to the machine instructions that read a string of 16 bit short words from a 16 bit I/O port using the I/O address space, instead of the memory address space. The data from *cnt* reads of the I/O port is stored in the data buffer pointed to by *addr*. The data buffer should be at least *cnt* 16 bit words in length.

RETURN VALUE

None.

LEVEL

Base or Interrupt.

NOTES

Does not sleep.

Driver-defined basic locks, read/write locks, and sleep locks may be held across calls to this function.

This function may not be meaningful on all implementations because some implementations may not support I/O-mapped I/O.

SEE ALSO

Programmer's Reference Manual

Integrated Software Development Guide

inb(D3D), inl(D3D), inw(D3D), outb(D3D), outl(D3D), outw(D3D), repinsb(D3D), repinsd(D3D), repoutsb(D3D), repoutsd(D3D), repoutsw(D3D)

NAME

repoutsb – write bytes from buffer to an I/O port

SYNOPSIS

```
#include <sys/types.h>

void repoutsb(int port, uchar_t *addr, int cnt);
```

ARGUMENTS

port   A valid 8 bit I/O port.

addr   The address of the buffer from which *cnt* bytes are written to the I/O port.

cnt   The number of bytes to be written to the I/O port.

DESCRIPTION

This function provides a C language interface to the machine instructions that write a string of bytes to an 8 bit I/O port using the I/O address space, instead of the memory address space. *cnt* bytes starting at the address pointed to by *addr* are written to the I/O port in *cnt* write operations. The buffer should be at least *cnt* bytes in length.

RETURN VALUE

None.

LEVEL

Base or Interrupt.

NOTES

Does not sleep.

Driver-defined basic locks, read/write locks, and sleep locks may be held across calls to this function.

This function may not be meaningful on all implementations because some implementations may not support I/O-mapped I/O.

SEE ALSO

Programmer's Reference Manual

Integrated Software Development Guide

inb(D3D), inl(D3D), inw(D3D), outb(D3D), outl(D3D), outw(D3D),
repinsb(D3D), repinsd(D3D), repinsw(D3D), repoutsd(D3D), repoutsw(D3D)

NAME
    repoutsd – write 32 bit words from buffer to an I/O port

SYNOPSIS
    #include <sys/types.h>

    void repoutsd(int *port*, ulong_t **addr*, int *cnt*);

ARGUMENTS
    port   A valid 32 bit I/O port.

    addr   The address of the buffer from which *cnt* 32 bit words are written to
                the I/O port.

    cnt   The number of 32 bit words to be written to the I/O port.

DESCRIPTION
    This function provides a C language interface to the machine instructions that
    write a string of 32 bit long words to a 32 bit I/O port using the I/O address
    space, instead of the memory address space. *cnt* 32 bit words starting at the
    address pointed to by *addr* are written to the I/O port in *cnt* write operations.
    The buffer should be at least *cnt* 32 bit words in length.

RETURN VALUE
    None.

LEVEL
    Base or Interrupt.

NOTES
    Does not sleep.

    Driver-defined basic locks, read/write locks, and sleep locks may be held across
    calls to this function.

    This function may not be meaningful on all implementations because some imple-
    mentations may not support I/O-mapped I/O.

SEE ALSO
    Programmer's Reference Manual

    Integrated Software Development Guide

    inb(D3D), inl(D3D), inw(D3D), outb(D3D), outl(D3D), outw(D3D),
    repinsb(D3D), repinsd(D3D), repinsw(D3D), repoutsb(D3D), repoutsw(D3D)

NAME

repoutsw – write 16 bit words from buffer to an I/O port

SYNOPSIS

```
#include <sys/types.h>

void repoutsw(int port, ushort_t *addr, int cnt);
```

ARGUMENTS

port   A valid 16 bit I/O port.

addr   The address of the buffer from which *cnt* 16 bit words are written to the I/O port.

cnt   The number of 16 bit words to be written to the I/O port.

DESCRIPTION

This function provides a C language interface to the machine instructions that write a string of 16 bit short words to a 16 bit I/O port using the I/O address space, instead of the memory address space. *cnt* 16 bit words starting at the address pointed to by *addr* are written to the I/O port in *cnt* write operations. The buffer should be at least *cnt* 16 bit words in length.

RETURN VALUE

None.

LEVEL

Base or Interrupt.

NOTES

Does not sleep.

Driver-defined basic locks, read/write locks, and sleep locks may be held across calls to this function.

This function may not be meaningful on all implementations because some implementations may not support I/O-mapped I/O.

SEE ALSO

Programmer's Reference Manual

Integrated Software Development Guide

inb(D3D), inl(D3D), inw(D3D), outb(D3D), outl(D3D), outw(D3D), repinsb(D3D), repinsd(D3D), repinsw(D3D), repoutsb(D3D), repoutsd(D3D)

NAME

rmalloc – allocate space from a private space management map

SYNOPSIS

```
#include <sys/types.h>
#include <sys/map.h>
#include <sys/ddi.h>

ulong_t rmalloc(struct map *mp, size_t size);
```

ARGUMENTS

mp Pointer to the map from which space is to be allocated.

$size$ Number of units of space to allocate.

DESCRIPTION

rmalloc allocates space from the private space management map pointed to by mp. The map must have been allocated by a call to rmallocmap(D3DK) and the space managed by the map must have been added using rmfree(D3DK) prior to the first call to rmalloc for the map.

$size$ specifies the amount of space to allocate and is in arbitrary units. The driver using the map places whatever semantics on the units are appropriate for the type of space being managed. For example, units may be byte addresses, pages of memory, or blocks on a device.

The system allocates space from the memory map on a first-fit basis and coalesces adjacent space fragments when space is returned to the map by rmfree.

RETURN VALUE

Upon successful completion, rmalloc returns the base of the allocated space. If $size$ units cannot be allocated, 0 is returned.

LEVEL

Base or Interrupt.

NOTES

Does not sleep.

Driver-defined basic locks, read/write locks, and sleep locks may be held across calls to this function.

SEE ALSO

rmalloc_wait(D3DK), rmallocmap(D3DK), rmfree(D3DK), rmfreemap(D3DK)

NAME

rmallocmap – allocate and initialize a private space management map

SYNOPSIS

```
#include <sys/types.h>
#include <sys/map.h>

struct map *rmallocmap(ulong_t mapsize);
```

ARGUMENTS

mapsize   Number of entries for the map.

DESCRIPTION

rmallocmap allocates and initializes a private map array that can be used for the allocation of space.

Although **rmallocmap** allocates and initializes the map array itself, it does not allocate the space that the map will manage. This space must be allocated separately and must be added to the map using **rmfree**(D3DK) prior to attempting to allocate space from the map using **rmalloc**(D3DK) or **rmalloc_wait**(D3DK).

The system maintains the map list structure by size and index. The caller places whatever semantics on the units of size are appropriate for the type of space being managed. For example, units may be byte addresses, pages of memory, or blocks. The elements of the map are sorted by index.

RETURN VALUE

Upon successful completion, **rmallocmap** returns a pointer to the newly allocated map. Upon failure, a **NULL** pointer is returned.

LEVEL

Base or Interrupt.

NOTES

Does not sleep.

Driver defined basic locks, read/write locks, and sleep locks may be held across calls to this function.

DDI/DKI conforming drivers may only use **map** structures which have been allocated and initialized using **rmallocmap**. Use of **map** structures which have been obtained by any other means is prohibited.

SEE ALSO

rmalloc(D3DK), **rmalloc_wait**(D3DK), **rmfree**(D3DK), **rmfreemap**(D3DK)

NAME

　　rmalloc_wait – allocate space from a private space management map

SYNOPSIS

```
#include <sys/types.h>
#include <sys/map.h>

ulong_t rmalloc_wait(struct map *mp, size_t size);
```

ARGUMENTS

　　mp　　　　　Pointer to map to resource map.

　　size　　　　Number of units to allocate.

DESCRIPTION

　　rmalloc_wait allocates space from a private map previously allocated using
　　rmallocmap(D3DK). **rmalloc_wait** is identical to **rmalloc**(D3DK), except that a
　　caller to **rmalloc_wait** will sleep (uninterruptible by signals), if necessary, until
　　space becomes available.

　　Space allocated using **rmalloc_wait** may be returned to the map using
　　rmfree(D3DK).

RETURN VALUE

　　rmalloc_wait returns the base of the allocated space.

LEVEL

　　Base Level Only.

NOTES

　　May sleep.

　　Driver defined basic locks and read/write locks may not be held across calls to
　　this function.

　　Driver defined sleep locks may be held across calls to this function, but the driver
　　writer must be cautious to avoid deadlock between the process holding the lock
　　and trying to acquire the resource and another process holding the resource and
　　trying to acquire the lock.

SEE ALSO

　　rmalloc(D3DK), **rmallocmap**(D3DK), **rmfree**(D3DK), **rmfreemap**(D3DK)

NAME

rmfree – free space into a private space management map

SYNOPSIS

```
#include <sys/types.h>
#include <sys/map.h>
#include <sys/ddi.h>

void rmfree(struct map *mp, size_t size, ulong_t index);
```

ARGUMENTS

mp   Pointer to the map.

size   Number of units to free into the map.

index   Index of the first unit of the space being freed.

DESCRIPTION

rmfree releases space into the private space management map pointed to by *mp* and wakes up any processes that are waiting for space using **rmalloc_wait**(D3DK). **rmfree** should be called to return space that had been allocated by a previous call to **rmalloc**(D3DK), in which case *index* is the value returned from the corresponding call to **rmalloc**. **rmfree** should also be called to add space to a newly allocated map prior to the first call to **rmalloc**, in which case *index* specifies the base of the space being added.

Both size and index are in arbitrary units. The driver using the map places whatever semantics on the units are appropriate for the type of space being managed. For example, units may be byte addresses, pages of memory, or blocks on a device.

If the space being returned is adjacent to other space in the map, **rmfree** will coalesce the adjacent fragments.

RETURN VALUE

None.

LEVEL

Base or Interrupt.

NOTES

Does not sleep.

Driver-defined basic locks, read/write locks, and sleep locks may be held across calls to this function.

If the **rmfree** call causes the number of fragments in the map to exceed the number of map entries allocated by **rmallocmap**(D3DK), the following warning message is displayed on the console:

> **WARNING: rmfree map overflow** *mp* **lost** *size* **items at** *index*

This implies that the driver should specify a larger number of map entries when allocating the map with **rmallocmap**.

SEE ALSO

rmalloc(D3DK), **rmalloc_wait**(D3DK), **rmallocmap**(D3DK), **rmfreemap**(D3DK)

NAME

rmfreemap – free a private space management map

SYNOPSIS

`#include <sys/map.h>`

`void rmfreemap(struct map *`*mp*`);`

ARGUMENTS

mp   Pointer to the map to be freed. The **map** structure array pointed to by *mp* must have been previously allocated by a call to `rmallocmap`(D3DK).

DESCRIPTION

rmfreemap frees the map pointed to by *mp*.

RETURN VALUE

None.

LEVEL

Base or Interrupt.

NOTES

Does not sleep.

Driver defined basic locks, read/write locks, and sleep locks may be held across calls to this function.

DDI/DKI conforming drivers may only use **map** structures which have been allocated and initialized using **rmallocmap**. Use of **map** structures which have been obtained by any other means is prohibited.

Before freeing the map, the caller must ensure that nobody is using space managed by the map, and that nobody is waiting for space in the map.

SEE ALSO

`rmalloc`(D3DK), `rmalloc_wait`(D3DK), `rmallocmap`(D3DK), `rmfree`(D3DK)

NAME

rmvb – remove a message block from a message

SYNOPSIS

```
#include <sys/stream.h>

mblk_t *rmvb(mblk_t *mp, mblk_t *bp);
```

ARGUMENTS

mp   Message from which a message block is to be removed.

bp   Message block to be removed.

DESCRIPTION

rmvb removes a message block (*bp*) from a message (*mp*), and returns a pointer to the altered message. The message block is not freed, merely removed from the message. It is the caller's responsibility to free the message block.

RETURN VALUE

If successful, a pointer to the message (minus the removed block) is returned. If *bp* was the only block in the message before rmvb was called, NULL is returned. If the designated message block (*bp*) was not in the message, −1 is returned.

LEVEL

Base or Interrupt.

NOTES

Does not sleep.

Driver-defined basic locks, read/write locks, and sleep locks may be held across calls to this function.

EXAMPLE

This routine removes all zero-length M_DATA message blocks from the given message. For each message block in the message, we save the next message block (line 9). If the current message block is of type M_DATA and has no data in its buffer (lines 10-11), then we remove the message block from the message (line 12) and free it (line 13). In either case, we continue with the next message block (line 15), until we have checked every message block in the message.

```
1   void
2   xxclean(mp)
3       mblk_t *mp;
4   {
5       mblk_t *tmp;
6       mblk_t *nmp;

7       tmp = mp;
8       while (tmp) {
9               nmp = tmp->b_next;
10              if ((tmp->b_datap->db_type == M_DATA) &&
11                  (tmp->b_rptr == tmp->b_wptr)) {
12                      mp = rmvb(mp, tmp);
13                      freeb(tmp);
14              }
15              tmp = nmp;
16      }
17  }
```

NAME

rmvq – remove a message from a queue

SYNOPSIS

```
#include <sys/stream.h>
void rmvq(queue_t *q, mblk_t *mp);
```

ARGUMENTS

q Pointer to the queue containing the message to be removed.

mp Pointer to the message to remove.

DESCRIPTION

rmvq removes a message from a queue. A message can be removed from any-where in a queue. To prevent modules and drivers from having to deal with the internals of message linkage on a queue, either rmvq or getq(D3DK) should be used to remove a message from a queue.

RETURN VALUE

None.

LEVEL

Base or Interrupt.

NOTES

Does not sleep.

Driver-defined basic locks, read/write locks, and sleep locks may be held across calls to this function.

The caller must have the stream frozen [see freezestr(D3DK)] when calling this function.

mp must point to an existing message in the queue pointed to by q, or a system panic will occur.

SEE ALSO

freezestr(D3DK), getq(D3DK), insq(D3DK), unfreezestr(D3DK)

EXAMPLE

See insq(D3DK) for an example of rmvq.

NAME

RW_ALLOC – allocate and initialize a read/write lock

SYNOPSIS

```
#include <sys/types.h>
#include <sys/kmem.h>
#include <sys/ksynch.h>
```

rwlock_t *RW_ALLOC(uchar_t *hierarchy*, pl_t *min_pl*, lkinfo_t **lkinfop*, int *flag*);

ARGUMENTS

hierarchy   Hierarchy value which asserts the order in which this lock will be acquired relative to other basic and read/write locks. This assertion is enforced by the system when the driver is compiled with the **DEBUG** and **_LOCKTEST** compilation options defined. *hierarchy* must be within the range 1 through 32 inclusive and must be chosen such that locks are normally acquired in order of increasing *hierarchy* number. In other words, when acquiring a read/write lock using any function other than **RW_TRYRDLOCK**(D3DK) or **RW_TRYWRLOCK**(D3DK), the lock being acquired must have a *hierarchy* value that is strictly greater than the *hierarchy* values associated with all locks currently held by the calling context.

Implementations of lock testing may differ in whether they assume a separate range of *hierarchy* values for each interrupt priority level or a single range that spans all interrupt priority levels. In order to be portable across different implementations, drivers which may acquire locks at more than one interrupt priority level should define the *hierarchy* among those locks such that the *hierarchy* is strictly increasing with increasing priority level (e.g. if M is the maximum *hierarchy* value defined for any lock that may be acquired at priority level N, then M + 1 should be the minimum hierarchy value defined for any lock that may be acquired at any priority level greater than N).

min_pl   Minimum priority level argument which asserts the minimum priority level that will be passed in with any attempt to acquire this lock [see **RW_RDLOCK**(D3DK) and **RW_WRLOCK**(D3DK)]. This assertion may be enforced by the system when the driver is compiled with the **DEBUG** and **_LOCKTEST** compilation options defined. Implementations which do not require that the interrupt priority level be raised during lock acquisition may choose not to enforce the *min_pl* assertion, even when the appropriate compilation options have been defined. The valid values for this argument are as follows:

plbase	Block no interrupts
pltimeout	Block functions scheduled by itimeout and dtimeout
pldisk	Block disk device interrupts
plstr	Block STREAMS interrupts
plhi	Block all interrupts

The notion of a *min_pl* assumes a defined order of priority levels. The following partial order is defined:

```
plbase < pltimeout <= pldisk,plstr <= plhi
```

The ordering of **pldisk** and **plstr** relative to each other is not defined.

Setting a given priority level will block interrupts associated with that level as well as any levels that are defined to be less than or equal to the specified level. In order to be portable a driver should not acquire locks at different priority levels where the relative order of those priority levels is not defined above.

The *min_pl* argument should specify a priority level that would be sufficient to block out any interrupt handler that might attempt to acquire this lock. In addition, potential deadlock problems involving multiple locks should be considered when defining the *min_pl* value. For example, if the normal order of acquisition of locks A and B (as defined by the lock hierarchy) is to acquire A first and then B, lock B should never be acquired at a priority level less than the *min_pl* for lock A. Therefore, the *min_pl* for lock B should be greater than or equal to the *min_pl* for lock A.

Note that the specification of *min_pl* with a **RW_ALLOC** call does not actually cause any interrupts to be blocked upon lock acquisition, it simply asserts that subsequent **RW_RDLOCK/RW_WRLOCK** calls to acquire this lock will pass in a priority level at least as great as *min_pl*.

lkinfop Pointer to a **lkinfo**(D4DK) structure. The **lk_name** member of the **lkinfo** structure points to a character string defining a name that will be associated with the lock for the purpose of statistics gathering. The name should begin with the driver prefix and should be unique to the lock or group of locks for which the driver wishes to collect a uniquely identifiable set of statistics (i.e. if a given name is shared by a group of locks, the statistics of individual locks within the group will not be uniquely identifiable). There are no flags defined within the **lk_flags** member of the **lkinfo** structure for use with **RW_ALLOC**.

The *lkinfop* pointer is recorded in a statistics buffer along with the lock statistics when the driver is compiled with the **DEBUG** and **_MPSTATS** compilation options defined. A given **lkinfo** structure may be shared among multiple read/write locks and basic locks but a **lkinfo** structure may not be shared between a read/write lock and a sleep lock. The caller must ensure that the **lk_flags** and **lk_pad** members of the **lkinfo** structure are zeroed out before passing it to **RW_ALLOC**.

flag Specifies whether the caller is willing to sleep waiting for memory. If *flag* is set to **KM_SLEEP**, the caller will sleep if necessary until sufficient memory is available. If *flag* is set to **KM_NOSLEEP**, the caller will not sleep, but **RW_ALLOC** will return **NULL** if sufficient memory is not immediately available. Under the **_MPSTATS** compilation option, if **KM_NOSLEEP** is specified and sufficient memory can be immediately allocated for the lock itself but not for an accompanying statistics buffer, **RW_ALLOC** will return a pointer to the allocated lock but individual statistics will not be collected for the lock.

DESCRIPTION

RW_ALLOC dynamically allocates and initializes an instance of a read/write lock. The lock is initialized to the unlocked state.

RETURN VALUE

Upon successful completion, RW_ALLOC returns a pointer to the newly allocated lock. If KM_NOSLEEP is specified and sufficient memory is not immediately available, RW_ALLOC returns a NULL pointer.

LEVEL

Base only if *flag* is set to KM_SLEEP. Base or interrupt if *flag* is set to KM_NOSLEEP.

NOTES

May sleep if flag is set to KM_SLEEP.

Driver defined basic locks and read/write locks may be held across calls to this function if *flag* is KM_NOSLEEP but may not be held if *flag* is KM_SLEEP.

Driver defined sleep locks may be held across calls to this function regardless of the value of *flag*.

SEE ALSO

RW_DEALLOC(D3DK), RW_RDLOCK(D3DK), RW_TRYRDLOCK(D3DK), RW_TRYWRLOCK(D3DK), RW_UNLOCK(D3DK), RW_WRLOCK(D3DK), lkinfo(D4DK)

NAME

RW_DEALLOC – deallocate an instance of a read/write lock

SYNOPSIS

```
#include <sys/types.h>
#include <sys/ksynch.h>

void RW_DEALLOC(rwlock_t *lockp);
```

ARGUMENTS

lockp   Pointer to the read/write lock to be deallocated.

DESCRIPTION

RW_DEALLOC deallocates the read/write lock specified by *lockp*.

RETURN VALUE

None.

LEVEL

Base or Interrupt.

NOTES

Does not sleep.

Attempting to deallocate a lock that is currently locked or is being waited for is an error and will result in undefined behavior.

Driver defined locks, read/write locks (other than the one being deallocated), and sleep locks may be held across calls to this function.

SEE ALSO

RW_ALLOC(D3DK), RW_RDLOCK(D3DK), RW_TRYRDLOCK(D3DK),
RW_TRYWRLOCK(D3DK), RW_UNLOCK(D3DK), RW_WRLOCK(D3DK)

NAME

RW_RDLOCK – acquire a read/write lock in read mode

SYNOPSIS

```
#include <sys/types.h>
#include <sys/ksynch.h>

pl_t RW_RDLOCK(rwlock_t *lockp, pl_t pl);
```

ARGUMENTS

lockp   Pointer to the read/write lock to be acquired.

pl   The interrupt priority level to be set while the lock is held by the caller. Because some implementations require that interrupts that might attempt to acquire the lock be blocked on the processor on which the lock is held, portable drivers must specify a *pl* value that is sufficient to block out any interrupt handler that might attempt to acquire this lock. See the description of the *min_pl* argument to RW_ALLOC(D3DK) for additional discussion and a list of the valid values for *pl*. Implementations which do not require that the interrupt priority level be raised during lock acquisition may choose to ignore this argument.

DESCRIPTION

RW_RDLOCK sets the interrupt priority level in accordance with the value specified by *pl* (if required by the implementation) and acquires the lock specified by *lockp* in read mode. If the lock cannot be acquired immediately in read mode, the caller will wait until the lock is available in read mode. (A read/write lock is available in read mode when the lock is not held by any context or when the lock is held by one or more readers and there are no waiting writers). It is implementation defined whether the caller will block during the wait. Some implementations may cause the caller to spin for the duration of the wait, while on others the caller may block at some point.

RETURN VALUE

Upon acquiring the lock, RW_RDLOCK returns the previous interrupt priority level (plbase - plhi).

LEVEL

Base or Interrupt.

NOTES

Read/write locks are not recursive. A call to LOCK attempting to acquire a lock that is currently held by the calling context may result in deadlock.

Calls to RW_RDLOCK should honor the ordering defined by the lock hierarchy [see RW_ALLOC(D3DK)] in order to avoid deadlock.

Driver defined sleep locks may be held across calls to this function.

Driver defined basic locks and read/write locks may be held across calls to this function subject to the hierarchy and recursion restrictions described above.

When called from interrupt level, the *pl* argument must not specify a priority level below the level at which the interrupt handler is running.

SEE ALSO

RW_ALLOC(D3DK), RW_DEALLOC(D3DK), RW_TRYRDLOCK(D3DK),
RW_TRYWRLOCK(D3DK), RW_UNLOCK(D3DK), RW_WRLOCK(D3DK)

NAME

RW_TRYRDLOCK – try to acquire a read/write lock in read mode

SYNOPSIS

```
#include <sys/types.h>
#include <sys/ksynch.h>

pl_t RW_TRYRDLOCK(rwlock_t *lockp, pl_t pl);
```

ARGUMENTS

lockp   Pointer to the read/write lock to be acquired.

pl   The interrupt priority level to be set while the lock is held by the caller. Because some implementations require that interrupts that might attempt to acquire the lock be blocked on the processor on which the lock is held, portable drivers must specify a *pl* value that is sufficient to block out any interrupt handler that might attempt to acquire this lock. See the description of the *min_pl* argument to RW_ALLOC(D3DK) for additional discussion and a list of the valid values for *pl*. Implementations which do not require that the interrupt priority level be raised during lock acquisition may choose to ignore this argument.

DESCRIPTION

If the lock specified by *lockp* is immediately available in read mode (there is not a writer holding the lock and there are no waiting writers), RW_TRYRDLOCK sets the interrupt priority level in accordance with the value specified by *pl* (if required by the implementation) and acquires the lock in read mode. If the lock is not immediately available in read mode, the function returns without acquiring the lock.

RETURN VALUE

If the lock is acquired, RW_TRYRDLOCK returns the previous interrupt priority level (plbase - plhi). If the lock is not acquired the value invpl is returned.

LEVEL

Base or Interrupt.

NOTES

Does not sleep.

RW_TRYRDLOCK may be used to acquire a lock in a different order from the order defined by the lock hierarchy.

Driver defined basic locks, read/write locks, and sleep locks may be held across calls to this function.

When called from interrupt level, the *pl* argument must not specify a priority level below the level at which the interrupt handler is running.

SEE ALSO

RW_ALLOC(D3DK), RW_DEALLOC(D3DK), RW_RDLOCK(D3DK),
RW_TRYWRLOCK(D3DK), RW_UNLOCK(D3DK), RW_WRLOCK(D3DK)

NAME

RW_TRYWRLOCK – try to acquire a read/write lock in write mode

SYNOPSIS

```
#include <sys/types.h>
#include <sys/ksynch.h>

pl_t RW_TRYWRLOCK(rwlock_t *lockp, pl_t pl);
```

ARGUMENTS

lockp   Pointer to the read/write lock to be acquired.

pl   The interrupt priority level to be set while the lock is held by the caller. Because some implementations require that interrupts that might attempt to acquire the lock be blocked on the processor on which the lock is held, portable drivers must specify a *pl* value that is sufficient to block out any interrupt handler that might attempt to acquire this lock. See the description of the *min_pl* argument to **RW_ALLOC**(D3DK) for additional discussion and a list of the valid values for *pl*. Implementations which do not require that the interrupt priority level be raised during lock acquisition may choose to ignore this argument.

DESCRIPTION

If the lock specified by *lockp* is immediately available in write mode (no context is holding the lock in read mode or write mode), **RW_TRYWRLOCK** sets the interrupt priority level in accordance with the value specified by *pl* (if required by the implementation) and acquires the lock in write mode. If the lock is not immediately available in write mode, the function returns without acquiring the lock.

RETURN VALUE

If the lock is acquired, **RW_TRYWRLOCK** returns the previous interrupt priority level (**plbase - plhi**). If the lock is not acquired the value **invpl** is returned.

LEVEL

Base or Interrupt.

NOTES

Does not sleep.

RW_TRYWRLOCK may be used to acquire a lock in a different order from the order defined by the lock hierarchy.

Driver defined basic locks, read/write locks, and sleep locks may be held across calls to this function.

When called from interrupt level, the *pl* argument must not specify a priority level below the level at which the interrupt handler is running.

SEE ALSO

RW_ALLOC(D3DK), RW_DEALLOC(D3DK), RW_RDLOCK(D3DK), RW_TRYRDLOCK(D3DK), RW_UNLOCK(D3DK), RW_WRLOCK(D3DK)

NAME

RW_UNLOCK – release a read/write lock

SYNOPSIS

```
#include <sys/types.h>
#include <sys/ksynch.h>

void RW_UNLOCK(rwlock_t *lockp, pl_t pl);
```

ARGUMENTS

lockp　　　　Pointer to the read/write lock to be released.

pl　　　　The interrupt priority level to be set after releasing the lock. See the description of the *min_pl* argument to **RW_ALLOC**(D3DK) for a list of the valid values for *pl*. If lock calls are not being nested or if the caller is unlocking in the reverse order that locks were acquired, the *pl* argument will typically be the value that was returned from the corresponding call to acquire the lock. The caller may need to specify a different value for *pl* if nested locks are released in some order other than the reverse order of acquisition, so as to ensure that the interrupt priority level is kept sufficiently high to block interrupt code that might attempt to acquire locks which are still held. Although portable drivers must always specify an appropriate *pl* argument, implementations which do not require that the interrupt priority level be raised during lock acquisition may choose to ignore this argument.

DESCRIPTION

RW_UNLOCK releases the read/write lock specified by *lockp* and then sets the interrupt priority level in accordance with the value specified by *pl* (if required by the implementation). If the lock is held in read mode by multiple contexts, **RW_UNLOCK** releases the lock in the calling context but does not cause the lock to be released in any other context.

RETURN VALUE

None.

LEVEL

Base or Interrupt.

NOTES

Does not sleep.

Driver defined basic locks, read/write locks, and sleep locks may be held across calls to this function.

SEE ALSO

RW_ALLOC(D3DK), RW_DEALLOC(D3DK), RW_RDLOCK(D3DK), RW_TRYRDLOCK(D3DK), RW_TRYWRLOCK(D3DK), RW_WRLOCK(D3DK)

NAME

RW_WRLOCK – acquire a read/write lock in write mode

SYNOPSIS

```
#include <sys/types.h>
#include <sys/ksynch.h>

pl_t RW_WRLOCK(rwlock_t *lockp, pl_t pl);
```

ARGUMENTS

lockp　　　Pointer to the read/write lock to be acquired.

pl　　　The interrupt priority level to be set while the lock is held by the caller. Because some implementations require that interrupts that might attempt to acquire the lock be blocked on the processor on which the lock is held, portable drivers must specify a *pl* value that is sufficient to block out any interrupt handler that might attempt to acquire this lock. See the description of the *min_pl* argument to RW_ALLOC(D3DK) for additional discussion and a list of the valid values for *pl*. Implementations which do not require that the interrupt priority level be raised during lock acquisition may choose to ignore this argument.

DESCRIPTION

RW_WRLOCK sets the interrupt priority level in accordance with the value specified by *pl* (if required by the implementation) and acquires the lock specified by *lockp* in write mode. If the lock cannot be acquired immediately in write mode, the caller will wait until the lock is available in write mode. (A read/write lock is available in write mode when the lock is not held by any context). It is implementation defined whether the caller will block during the wait. Some implementations may cause the caller to spin for the duration of the wait, while on others the caller may block at some point.

RETURN VALUE

Upon acquiring the lock, RW_WRLOCK returns the previous interrupt priority level (`plbase - plhi`).

LEVEL

Base or Interrupt.

NOTES

Read/write locks are not recursive. A call to LOCK attempting to acquire a lock that is currently held by the calling context may result in deadlock.

Calls to RW_WRLOCK should honor the ordering defined by the lock hierarchy [see RW_ALLOC(D3DK)] in order to avoid deadlock.

Driver defined sleep locks may be held across calls to this function.

Driver defined basic locks and read/write locks may be held across calls to this function subject to the hierarchy and recursion restrictions described above.

When called from interrupt level, the *pl* argument must not specify a priority level below the level at which the interrupt handler is running.

SEE ALSO

RW_ALLOC(D3DK), RW_DEALLOC(D3DK), RW_RDLOCK(D3DK),
RW_TRYRDLOCK(D3DK), RW_TRYWRLOCK(D3DK), RW_UNLOCK(D3DK)

NAME

SAMESTR – test if next queue is same type

SYNOPSIS

```
#include <sys/stream.h>

int SAMESTR(queue_t *q);
```

ARGUMENTS

q   Pointer to the queue.

DESCRIPTION

The **SAMESTR** function is used to see if the next queue in a stream (if it exists) is the same type as the current queue (that is, both are read queues or both are write queues). This can be used to determine the point in a STREAMS-based pipe where a read queue is linked to a write queue.

RETURN VALUE

SAMESTR returns 1 if the next queue is the same type as the current queue. It returns 0 if the next queue does not exist or if it is not the same type.

LEVEL

Base or Interrupt.

NOTES

Does not sleep.

The caller cannot have the stream frozen [see **freezestr**(D3DK)] when calling this function.

Driver-defined basic locks, read/write locks, and sleep locks may be held across calls to this function.

The argument *q* may not reference **q_next** (for example, an argument of **q->q_next** is erroneous on a multiprocessor and is disallowed by the DDI/DKI).

SEE ALSO

OTHERQ(D3DK)

EXAMPLE

See the **put**(D2DK) manual page for an example of **SAMESTR**.

NAME
    SLEEP_ALLOC – allocate and initialize a sleep lock

SYNOPSIS
    #include <sys/types.h>
    #include <sys/kmem.h>
    #include <sys/ksynch.h>

    sleep_t *SLEEP_ALLOC(int *arg*, lkinfo_t *lkinfop*, int *flag*);

ARGUMENTS
    arg   Placeholder for future use. *arg* must be equal to zero.

    lkinfop   Pointer to a lkinfo(D4DK) structure. The lk_name member of the
                   lkinfo structure points to a character string defining a name that will
                   be associated with the lock for the purpose of statistics gathering. The
                   name should begin with the driver prefix and should be unique to the
                   lock or group of locks for which the driver wishes to collect a
                   uniquely identifiable set of statistics (i.e. if a given name is shared by a
                   group of locks, the statistics of individual locks within the group will
                   not be uniquely identifiable). The only bit flag currently specified
                   within the lk_flags member of the lkinfo structure is the
                   LK_NOSTATS flag, which specifies that statistics are not to be collected
                   for this particular lock under the _MPSTATS compilation option. If the
                   LK_NOSTATS flag is not specified, statistics will be collected for this
                   lock under the _MPSTATS compilation option, and the *lkinfop* pointer
                   will be recorded in the statistics buffer along with the lock statistics.

                   A given lkinfo structure may be shared among multiple sleep locks
                   but a lkinfo structure may not be shared between a sleep lock and a
                   basic or read/write lock. The caller must ensure that the lk_pad
                   member of the lkinfo structure is zeroed out before passing it to
                   SLEEP_ALLOC.

    flag   Specifies whether the caller is willing to sleep waiting for memory. If
                   flag is set to KM_SLEEP, the caller will sleep if necessary until sufficient
                   memory is available. If *flag* is set to KM_NOSLEEP, the caller will not
                   sleep, but SLEEP_ALLOC will return NULL if sufficient memory is not
                   immediately available. Under the _MPSTATS compilation option, if
                   KM_NOSLEEP is specified and sufficient memory can be immediately
                   allocated for the lock itself but not for an accompanying statistics
                   buffer, SLEEP_ALLOC will return a pointer to the allocated lock but
                   individual statistics will not be collected for the lock.

DESCRIPTION
    SLEEP_ALLOC dynamically allocates and initializes an instance of a sleep lock.
    The lock is initialized to the unlocked state.

RETURN VALUE
    Upon successful completion, SLEEP_ALLOC returns a pointer to the newly allo-
    cated lock. If KM_NOSLEEP is specified and sufficient memory is not immediately
    available, SLEEP_ALLOC returns a NULL pointer.

LEVEL

Base only if *flag* is set to **KM_SLEEP**. Base or interrupt if *flag* is set to **KM_NOSLEEP**.

NOTES

May sleep if flag is set to **KM_SLEEP**.

Driver defined basic locks and read/write locks may be held across calls to this function if *flag* is **KM_NOSLEEP** but may not be held if *flag* is **KM_SLEEP**.

Driver defined sleep locks may be held across calls to this function regardless of the value of *flag*.

SEE ALSO

SLEEP_DEALLOC(D3DK), SLEEP_LOCK(D3DK), SLEEP_LOCK_SIG(D3DK), SLEEP_LOCKAVAIL(D3DK), SLEEP_LOCKOWNED(D3DK), SLEEP_TRYLOCK(D3DK), SLEEP_UNLOCK(D3DK), lkinfo(D4DK)

NAME

SLEEP_DEALLOC – deallocate an instance of a sleep lock

SYNOPSIS

#include <sys/ksynch.h>

void SLEEP_DEALLOC(sleep_t *lockp);

ARGUMENTS

lockp　　　　Pointer to the sleep lock to be deallocated.

DESCRIPTION

SLEEP_DEALLOC deallocates the lock specified by lockp.

RETURN VALUE

None.

LEVEL

Base or Interrupt.

NOTES

Does not sleep.

Attempting to deallocate a lock that is currently locked or is being waited for is an error and results in undefined behavior.

Driver defined basic locks, read/write locks, and sleep locks (other than the one being deallocated), may be held across calls to this function.

SEE ALSO

SLEEP_ALLOC(D3DK), SLEEP_LOCK(D3DK), SLEEP_LOCK_SIG(D3DK), SLEEP_LOCKAVAIL(D3DK), SLEEP_LOCKOWNED(D3DK) SLEEP_TRYLOCK(D3DK), SLEEP_UNLOCK(D3DK)

NAME
SLEEP_LOCK – acquire a sleep lock

SYNOPSIS
#include <sys/ksynch.h>

void SLEEP_LOCK(sleep_t *lockp, int priority);

ARGUMENTS
lockp   Pointer to the sleep lock to be acquired.

priority   A hint to the the scheduling policy as to the relative priority the caller
            wishes to be assigned while running in the kernel after waking up.
            The valid values for this argument are as follows:

pridisk   Priority appropriate for disk driver.
prinet   Priority appropriate for network driver.
pritty   Priority appropriate for terminal driver.
pritape   Priority appropriate for tape driver.
prihi   High priority.
primed   Medium priority.
prilo   Low priority.

Drivers may use these values to request a priority appropriate to a
given type of device or to request a priority that is high, medium or
low relative to other activities within the kernel.

It is also permissible to specify positive or negative offsets from the
values defined above. Positive offsets result in more favorable priority. The maximum allowable offset in all cases is 3 (e.g. **pridisk+3**
and **pridisk-3** are valid values but **pridisk+4** and **pridisk-4** are
not valid). Offsets can be useful in defining the relative importance of
different locks or resources that may be held by a given driver. In
general, a higher relative priority should be used when the caller is attempting to acquire a highly contended lock or resource, or when the
caller is already holding one or more locks or kernel resources upon
entry to **SLEEP_LOCK**.

The exact semantic of the *priority* argument is specific to the scheduling class of the caller, and some scheduling classes may choose to ignore the argument for the purposes of assigning a scheduling priority.

DESCRIPTION
SLEEP_LOCK acquires the sleep lock specified by *lockp*. If the lock is not immediately available, the caller is put to sleep (the caller's execution is suspended and
other processes may be scheduled) until the lock becomes available to the caller,
at which point the caller wakes up and returns with the lock held.

The caller will not be interrupted by signals while sleeping inside **SLEEP_LOCK**.

RETURN VALUE
None.

LEVEL

Base Level Only.

NOTES

May sleep.

Sleep locks are not recursive. A call to **SLEEP_LOCK** attempting to acquire a lock that is currently held by the calling context will result in deadlock.

Driver defined basic locks and read/write locks may not be held across calls to this function.

Driver defined sleep locks may be held across calls to this function subject to the recursion restrictions described above.

SEE ALSO

SLEEP_ALLOC(D3DK), SLEEP_DEALLOC(D3DK), SLEEP_LOCK_SIG(D3DK), SLEEP_LOCKAVAIL(D3DK), SLEEP_LOCKOWNED(D3DK), SLEEP_TRYLOCK(D3DK), SLEEP_UNLOCK(D3DK)

NAME

SLEEP_LOCKAVAIL – query whether a sleep lock is available

SYNOPSIS

```
#include <sys/types.h>
#include <sys/ksynch.h>

bool_t SLEEP_LOCKAVAIL(sleep_t *lockp);
```

ARGUMENTS

lockp   Pointer to the sleep lock to be queried.

DESCRIPTION

SLEEP_LOCKAVAIL returns an indication of whether the sleep lock specified by *lockp* is currently available.

The state of the lock may change and the value returned may no longer be valid by the time the caller sees it. The caller is expected to understand that this is "stale data" and is either using it as a heuristic or has arranged for the return value to be meaningful by other means.

RETURN VALUE

SLEEP_LOCKAVAIL returns TRUE (a non-zero value) if the lock was available or FALSE (zero) if the lock was not available.

LEVEL

Base or Interrupt.

NOTES

Does not sleep.

Driver defined basic locks, read/write locks, and sleep locks may be held across calls to this function.

SEE ALSO

SLEEP_ALLOC(D3DK), SLEEP_DEALLOC(D3DK), SLEEP_LOCK(D3DK), SLEEP_LOCK_SIG(D3DK), SLEEP_LOCKOWNED(D3DK), SLEEP_TRYLOCK(D3DK), SLEEP_UNLOCK(D3DK)

NAME

SLEEP_LOCKOWNED – query whether a sleep lock is held by the caller

SYNOPSIS

```
#include <sys/types.h>
#include <sys/ksynch.h>

bool_t SLEEP_LOCKOWNED(sleep_t *lockp);
```

ARGUMENTS

lockp   Pointer to the sleep lock to be queried.

DESCRIPTION

SLEEP_LOCKOWNED returns an indication of whether the sleep lock specified by *lockp* is currently held by the calling context.

SLEEP_LOCKOWNED is intended for use only within ASSERT expressions [see ASSERT(D3DK)] and other code that is conditionally compiled under the DEBUG compilation option. The SLEEP_LOCKOWNED function is only defined under the DEBUG compilation option, and therefore calls to SLEEP_LOCKOWNED will not compile when DEBUG is not defined.

RETURN VALUE

SLEEP_LOCKOWNED returns TRUE (a non-zero value) if the lock is currently held by the calling context or FALSE (zero) if the lock is not currently held by the calling context.

LEVEL

Base Level Only.

NOTES

Does not sleep.

Driver defined basic locks, read/write locks, and sleep locks may be held across calls to this function.

SEE ALSO

SLEEP_ALLOC(D3DK), SLEEP_DEALLOC(D3DK), SLEEP_LOCK(D3DK), SLEEP_LOCK_SIG(D3DK), SLEEP_LOCKAVAIL(D3DK), SLEEP_TRYLOCK(D3DK), SLEEP_UNLOCK(D3DK)

NAME

SLEEP_LOCK_SIG – acquire a sleep lock

SYNOPSIS

```
#include <sys/types.h>
#include <sys/ksynch.h>

bool_t SLEEP_LOCK_SIG(sleep_t *lockp, int priority);
```

ARGUMENTS

lockp   Pointer to the sleep lock to be acquired.

priority   A hint to the the scheduling policy as to the relative priority the caller wishes to be assigned while running in the kernel after waking up. The valid values for this argument are as follows:

pridisk	Priority appropriate for disk driver.
prinet	Priority appropriate for network driver.
pritty	Priority appropriate for terminal driver.
pritape	Priority appropriate for tape driver.
prihi	High priority.
primed	Medium priority.
prilo	Low priority.

Drivers may use these values to request a priority appropriate to a given type of device or to request a priority that is high, medium or low relative to other activities within the kernel.

It is also permissible to specify positive or negative offsets from the values defined above. Positive offsets result in more favorable priority. The maximum allowable offset in all cases is 3 (e.g. **pridisk+3** and **pridisk-3** are valid values but **pridisk+4** and **pridisk-4** are not valid). Offsets can be useful in defining the relative importance of different locks or resources that may be held by a given driver. In general, a higher relative priority should be used when the caller is attempting to acquire a highly contended lock or resource, or when the caller is already holding one or more locks or kernel resources upon entry to **SLEEP_LOCK_SIG**.

The exact semantic of the *priority* argument is specific to the scheduling class of the caller, and some scheduling classes may choose to ignore the argument for the purposes of assigning a scheduling priority.

DESCRIPTION

SLEEP_LOCK_SIG acquires the sleep lock specified by *lockp*. If the lock is not immediately available, the caller is put to sleep (the caller's execution is suspended and other processes may be scheduled) until the lock becomes available to the caller, at which point the caller wakes up and returns with the lock held.

SLEEP_LOCK_SIG may be interrupted by a signal, in which case it may return early without acquiring the lock.

If the function is interrupted by a job control stop signal (e.g. **SIGSTOP**, **SIGTSTP**, **SIGTTIN**, **SIGTTOU**) which results in the caller entering a stopped state, the **SLEEP_LOCK_SIG** function will transparently retry the lock operation upon continuing (the call will not return without the lock).

If the function is interrupted by a signal other than a job control stop signal, or by a job control stop signal that does not result in the caller stopping (because the signal has a non-default disposition), the **SLEEP_LOCK_SIG** call will return early without acquiring the lock.

RETURN VALUE

SLEEP_LOCK_SIG returns **TRUE** (a non-zero value) if the lock is successfully acquired or **FALSE** (zero) if the function returned early because of a signal.

LEVEL

Base Level Only.

NOTES

May sleep.

Sleep locks are not recursive. A call to **SLEEP_LOCK_SIG** attempting to acquire a lock that is currently held by the calling context will result in deadlock.

Driver defined basic locks and read/write locks may not be held across calls to this function.

Driver defined sleep locks may be held across calls to this function subject to the recursion restrictions described above.

SEE ALSO

SLEEP_ALLOC(D3DK), SLEEP_DEALLOC(D3DK), SLEEP_LOCK(D3DK),
SLEEP_LOCKAVAIL(D3DK), SLEEP_LOCKOWNED(D3DK), SLEEP_TRYLOCK(D3DK),
SLEEP_UNLOCK(D3DK), signals(D5DK)

NAME

SLEEP_TRYLOCK – try to acquire a sleep lock

SYNOPSIS

```
#include <sys/types.h>
#include <sys/ksynch.h>

bool_t SLEEP_TRYLOCK(sleep_t *lockp);
```

ARGUMENTS

lockp   Pointer to the sleep lock to be acquired.

DESCRIPTION

If the lock specified by *lockp* is immediately available (can be acquired without sleeping) SLEEP_TRYLOCK acquires the lock. If the lock is not immediately available, the function returns without acquiring the lock.

RETURN VALUE

SLEEP_TRYLOCK returns TRUE (a non-zero value) if the lock is successfully acquired or FALSE (zero) if the lock is not acquired.

LEVEL

Base Level Only.

NOTES

Does not sleep.

Driver defined basic locks, read/write locks, and sleep locks may be held across calls to this function.

SEE ALSO

SLEEP_ALLOC(D3DK), SLEEP_DEALLOC(D3DK), SLEEP_LOCK(D3DK), SLEEP_LOCK_SIG(D3DK), SLEEP_LOCKAVAIL(D3DK), SLEEP_LOCKOWNED(D3DK), SLEEP_UNLOCK(D3DK)

NAME

SLEEP_UNLOCK – release a sleep lock

SYNOPSIS

`#include <sys/ksynch.h>`

`void SLEEP_UNLOCK(sleep_t *`*lockp*`);`

ARGUMENTS

lockp   Pointer to the sleep lock to be released.

DESCRIPTION

SLEEP_UNLOCK releases the sleep lock specified by *lockp*. If there are processes waiting for the lock, one of the waiting processes is awakened.

RETURN VALUE

None.

LEVEL

Base or Interrupt.

NOTES

Does not sleep.

Driver defined basic locks, read/write locks, and sleep locks may be held across calls to this function.

SEE ALSO

SLEEP_ALLOC(D3DK), SLEEP_DEALLOC(D3DK), SLEEP_LOCK(D3DK), SLEEP_LOCK_SIG(D3DK), SLEEP_LOCKAVAIL(D3DK), SLEEP_LOCKOWNED(D3DK), SLEEP_TRYLOCK(D3DK)

NAME

      spl – block/allow interrupts on a processor

SYNOPSIS

      `pl_t splbase();`
      `pl_t spltimeout();`
      `pl_t spldisk();`
      `pl_t splstr();`
      `pl_t splhi();`

      `pl_t splx(pl_t` *oldlevel*`);`

ARGUMENTS

      oldlevel   Last set priority value (only **splx** has an input argument).

DESCRIPTION

The **spl** functions block or allow servicing of interrupts on the processor on which the function is called. Hardware devices are assigned to interrupt priority levels depending on the type of device. Each **spl** function which blocks interrupts is associated with some machine dependent interrupt priority level and will prevent interrupts occurring at or below this priority level from being serviced on the processor on which the **spl** function is called.

On a multiprocessor system, interrupts may be serviced by more than one processor and, therefore, use of a **spl** function alone is not sufficient to prevent interrupt code from executing and manipulating driver data structures during a critical section. Drivers that must prevent execution of interrupt-level code in order to protect the integrity of their data should use basic locks or read/write locks for this purpose [see **LOCK_ALLOC**(D3DK) or **RW_ALLOC**(D3DK)].

The **spl** functions include the following:

    splbase   Block no interrupts.
    spltimeout   Block functions scheduled by **itimeout** and **dtimeout**.
    spldisk   Block disk device interrupts.
    splstr   Block STREAMS interrupts.
    splhi   Block all interrupts.

Calling a given **spl** function will block interrupts specified for that function as well as interrupts at equal and lower levels. The notion of low vs. high levels assumes a defined order of priority levels. The following partial order is defined:

      `splbase <= spltimeout <= spldisk, splstr <= splhi`

The ordering of **spldisk** and **splstr** relative to each other is not defined.

RETURN VALUE

All **spl** functions return the previous priority level.

NOTES

All **spl** functions do not sleep.

Driver defined basic locks and read/write locks may be held across calls to these functions, but the **spl** call must not cause the priority level to be lowered below the level associated with the lock.

Driver defined sleep locks may be held across calls to these functions.

When setting a given priority level, the previous level returned should be saved and **splx**, **UNLOCK**(D3DK), or **RW_UNLOCK**(D3DK) should be used as appropriate to restore this level.

Interrupt-level code must never lower the interrupt priority level below the level at which the interrupt handler was entered. For example, if an interrupt handler is entered at the priority level associated with **spldisk**, the handler must not call **spltimeout**.

SEE ALSO

LOCK(D3DK), LOCK_ALLOC(D3DK), RW_RDLOCK(D3DK), RW_UNLOCK(D3DK), RW_WRLOCK(D3DK), RW_ALLOC(D3DK)

NAME

strlog – submit messages to the **log** driver

SYNOPSIS

```
#include <sys/types.h>
#include <sys/stream.h>
#include <sys/strlog.h>
#include <sys/log.h>
```

int **strlog**(short *mid,* short *sid,* char *level,* ushort_t *flags,*
　　char **fmt,* ... /* *args* */);

ARGUMENTS

mid　　　　Identification number of the module or driver submitting the message.

sid　　　　Identification number for a particular minor device.

level　　　Tracing level for selective screening of low priority messages.

flags　　　Bitmask of flags indicating message purpose. Valid flags are:

SL_ERROR	Message is for error logger.
SL_TRACE	Message is for tracing.
SL_CONSOLE	Message is for console logger.
SL_NOTIFY	If **SL_ERROR** is also set, mail copy of message to system administrator.
SL_FATAL	Modifier indicating error is fatal.
SL_WARN	Modifier indicating error is a warning.
SL_NOTE	Modifier indicating error is a notice.

fmt　　　　**printf**(3S) style format string. **%s**, **%e**, **%g**, and **%G** formats are not allowed.

args　　　Zero or more arguments to **printf** (maximum of **NLOGARGS**, currently three).

DESCRIPTION

strlog submits formatted messages to the **log**(7) driver. The messages can be retrieved with the **getmsg**(2) system call. The *flags* argument specifies the type of the message and where it is to be sent. **strace**(1M) receives messages from the **log** driver and sends them to the standard output. **strerr**(1M) receives error messages from the **log** driver and appends them to a file called **/var/adm/streams/error.***mm-dd*, where *mm-dd* identifies the date of the error message.

RETURN VALUE

strlog returns 0 if the message is not seen by all the readers, 1 otherwise.

LEVEL

Base or Interrupt.

NOTES

Does not sleep.

Driver-defined basic locks, read/write locks, and sleep locks may be held across calls to this function.

SEE ALSO

    log(7) in the *Programmer's Guide: STREAMS*

    strace(1M), **strerr**(1M) in the *System Administrator's Reference Manual*

NAME

strqget – get information about a queue or band of the queue

SYNOPSIS

```
#include <sys/types.h>
#include <sys/stream.h>

int strqget(queue_t *q, qfields_t what, uchar_t pri, long *valp);
```

ARGUMENTS

q   Pointer to the queue.

what The field of the queue about which to return information. Valid values are:

    QHIWAT High water mark of the specified priority band.

    QLOWAT Low water mark of the specified priority band.

    QMAXPSZ Maximum packet size of the specified priority band.

    QMINPSZ Minimum packet size of the specified priority band.

    QCOUNT Number of bytes of data in messages in the specified priority band.

    QFIRST Pointer to the first message in the specified priority band.

    QLAST Pointer to the last message in the specified priority band.

    QFLAG Flags for the specified priority band [see queue(D4DK)].

pri   Priority band of the queue about which to obtain information.

valp Pointer to the memory location where the value is to be stored.

DESCRIPTION

strqget gives drivers and modules a way to get information about a queue or a particular priority band of a queue without directly accessing STREAMS data structures.

RETURN VALUE

On success, 0 is returned. An error number is returned on failure. The actual value of the requested field is returned through the reference parameter, *valp*.

LEVEL

Base or Interrupt.

NOTES

Does not sleep.

Driver-defined basic locks, read/write locks, and sleep locks may be held across calls to this function.

The caller must have the stream frozen [see freezestr(D3DK)] when calling this function.

SEE ALSO

freezestr(D3DK), strqset(D3DK), unfreezestr(D3DK), queue(D4DK)

NAME

strqset – change information about a queue or band of the queue

SYNOPSIS

```
#include <sys/types.h>
#include <sys/stream.h>

int strqset(queue_t *q, qfields_t what, uchar_t pri, long val);
```

ARGUMENTS

q	Pointer to the queue.
what	The field of the queue to change. Valid values are:

	QHIWAT	High water mark of the specified priority band.
	QLOWAT	Low water mark of the specified priority band.
	QMAXPSZ	Maximum packet size of the specified priority band.
	QMINPSZ	Minimum packet size of the specified priority band.

pri	Priority band of the queue to be changed.
val	New value for the field to be changed.

DESCRIPTION

strqset gives drivers and modules a way to change information about a queue or a particular priority band of a queue without directly accessing STREAMS data structures.

RETURN VALUE

On success, 0 is returned. An error number is returned on failure.

LEVEL

Base or Interrupt.

NOTES

Does not sleep.

Driver-defined basic locks, read/write locks, and sleep locks may be held across calls to this function.

The caller must have the stream frozen [see freezestr(D3DK)] when calling this function.

SEE ALSO

freezestr(D3DK), strqget(D3DK), unfreezestr(D3DK), queue(D4DK)

NAME

SV_ALLOC – allocate and initialize a synchronization variable

SYNOPSIS

```
#include <sys/kmem.h>
#include <sys/ksynch.h>

sv_t *SV_ALLOC(int flag);
```

ARGUMENTS

flag   Specifies whether the caller is willing to sleep waiting for memory. If *flag* is set to **KM_SLEEP**, the caller will sleep if necessary until sufficient memory is available. If *flag* is set to **KM_NOSLEEP**, the caller will not sleep, but **SV_ALLOC** will return **NULL** if sufficient memory is not immediately available.

DESCRIPTION

SV_ALLOC dynamically allocates and initializes an instance of a synchronization variable.

RETURN VALUE

Upon successful completion, **SV_ALLOC** returns a pointer to the newly allocated synchronization variable. If **KM_NOSLEEP** is specified and sufficient memory is not immediately available, **SV_ALLOC** returns a **NULL** pointer.

LEVEL

Base only if *flag* is set to **KM_SLEEP**. Base or interrupt if *flag* is set to **KM_NOSLEEP**.

NOTES

May sleep if flag is set to **KM_SLEEP**.

Driver defined basic locks and read/write locks may be held across calls to this function if *flag* is **KM_NOSLEEP** but may not be held if *flag* is **KM_SLEEP**.

Driver defined sleep locks may be held across calls to this function regardless of the value of *flag*.

SEE ALSO

SV_BROADCAST(D3DK), **SV_DEALLOC**(D3DK), **SV_SIGNAL**(D3DK), **SV_WAIT**(D3DK), **SV_WAIT_SIG**(D3DK)

NAME

SV_BROADCAST – wake up all processes sleeping on a synchronization variable

SYNOPSIS

```
#include <sys/ksynch.h>
```

void SV_BROADCAST(sv_t *svp, int flags);

ARGUMENTS

svp   Pointer to the synchronization variable to be broadcast signaled.

flags   Bit field for flags. No flags are currently defined for use in drivers and the *flags* argument must be set to zero.

DESCRIPTION

If one or more processes are blocked on the synchronization variable specified by *svp*, **SV_BROADCAST** wakes up all of the blocked processes. Note that synchronization variables are stateless, and therefore calls to **SV_BROADCAST** only affect processes currently blocked on the synchronization variable and have no effect on processes that block on the synchronization variable at a later time.

RETURN VALUE

None.

LEVEL

Base or Interrupt.

NOTES

Does not sleep.

Driver defined basic locks, read/write locks, and sleep locks may be held across calls to this function.

SEE ALSO

SV_ALLOC(D3DK), SV_DEALLOC(D3DK), SV_SIGNAL(D3DK), SV_WAIT(D3DK), SV_WAIT_SIG(D3DK)

NAME

SV_DEALLOC – deallocate an instance of a synchronization variable

SYNOPSIS

#include <sys/ksynch.h>

void SV_DEALLOC(sv_t *svp);

ARGUMENTS

lockp   Pointer to the synchronization variable to be deallocated.

DESCRIPTION

SV_DEALLOC deallocates the synchronization variable specified by *svp*.

RETURN VALUE

None.

LEVEL

Base or Interrupt.

NOTES

Does not sleep.

Driver defined basic locks, read/write locks, and sleep locks may be held across calls to this function.

SEE ALSO

SV_ALLOC(D3DK), SV_BROADCAST(D3DK), SV_SIGNAL(D3DK), SV_WAIT(D3DK), SV_WAIT_SIG(D3DK)

NAME

SV_SIGNAL – wake up one process sleeping on a synchronization variable

SYNOPSIS

#include <sys/ksynch.h>

void SV_SIGNAL(sv_t *svp, int flags);

ARGUMENTS

svp   Pointer to the synchronization variable to be signaled.

flags   Bit field for flags. No flags are currently defined for use in drivers
           and the flags argument must be set to zero.

DESCRIPTION

If one or more processes are blocked on the synchronization variable specified by
svp, SV_SIGNAL wakes up a single blocked process. Note that synchronization
variables are stateless, and therefore calls to SV_SIGNAL only affect processes
currently blocked on the synchronization variable and have no effect on processes
that block on the synchronization variable at a later time.

RETURN VALUE

None.

LEVEL

Base or Interrupt.

NOTES

Does not sleep.

Driver defined basic locks, read/write locks, and sleep locks may be held across
calls to this function.

SEE ALSO

SV_ALLOC(D3DK), SV_BROADCAST(D3DK), SV_DEALLOC(D3DK), SV_WAIT(D3DK),
SV_WAIT_SIG(D3DK)

NAME

SV_WAIT – sleep on a synchronization variable

SYNOPSIS

```
#include <sys/types.h>
#include <sys/ksynch.h>

void SV_WAIT(sv_t *svp, int priority, lock_t *lkp);
```

ARGUMENTS

svp   Pointer to the synchronization variable on which to sleep.

priority   A hint to the the scheduling policy as to the relative priority the caller wishes to be assigned while running in the kernel after waking up. The valid values for this argument are as follows:

pridisk   Priority appropriate for disk driver.
prinet   Priority appropriate for network driver.
pritty   Priority appropriate for terminal driver.
pritape   Priority appropriate for tape driver.
prihi   High priority.
primed   Medium priority.
prilo   Low priority.

Drivers may use these values to request a priority appropriate to a given type of device or to request a priority that is high, medium or low relative to other activities within the kernel.

It is also permissible to specify positive or negative offsets from the values defined above. Positive offsets result in more favorable priority. The maximum allowable offset in all cases is 3 (e.g. **pridisk+3** and **pridisk-3** are valid values but **pridisk+4** and **pridisk-4** are not valid). Offsets can be useful in defining the relative importance of different locks or resources that may be held by a given driver. In general, a higher relative priority should be used when the caller is sleeping waiting for a highly contended kernel resource, or when the caller is already holding one or more locks or kernel resources upon entry to **SV_WAIT**.

The exact semantic of the *priority* argument is specific to the scheduling class of the caller, and some scheduling classes may choose to ignore the argument for the purposes of assigning a scheduling priority.

lkp   Pointer to a basic lock which must be locked when **SV_WAIT** is called. The basic lock is released when the calling process goes to sleep, as described below.

DESCRIPTION

SV_WAIT causes the calling process to go to sleep (the caller's execution is suspended and other processes may be scheduled) waiting for a call to **SV_SIGNAL**(D3DK) or **SV_BROADCAST**(D3DK) for the synchronization variable specified by *svp*.

The basic lock specified by *lkp* must be held by the caller upon entry. The lock is released and the interrupt priority level is set to **pl0** after the process is queued on the synchronization variable but prior to context switching to another process. When the caller returns from **SV_WAIT** the basic lock is not held and the interrupt priority level is equal to **pl0**.

The caller will not be interrupted by signals while sleeping inside **SV_WAIT**.

RETURN VALUE

None.

LEVEL

Base Level Only.

NOTES

May sleep.

Driver defined basic locks (with the exception of the lock specified by *lkp*) and read/write locks may not be held across calls to this function.

Driver defined sleep locks may be held across calls to this function.

SEE ALSO

SV_ALLOC(D3DK), SV_BROADCAST(D3DK), SV_DEALLOC(D3DK),
SV_SIGNAL(D3DK), SV_WAIT_SIG(D3DK)

NAME

SV_WAIT_SIG – sleep on a synchronization variable

SYNOPSIS

```
#include <sys/types.h>
#include <sys/ksynch.h>

bool_t SV_WAIT_SIG(sv_t *svp, int priority, lock_t *lkp);
```

ARGUMENTS

svp   Pointer to the synchronization variable on which to sleep.

priority   A hint to the the scheduling policy as to the relative priority the caller
               wishes to be assigned while running in the kernel after waking up.
               The valid values for this argument are as follows:

  pridisk   Priority appropriate for disk driver.
  prinet   Priority appropriate for network driver.
  pritty   Priority appropriate for terminal driver.
  pritape   Priority appropriate for tape driver.
  prihi   High priority.
  primed   Medium priority.
  prilo   Low priority.

               Drivers may use these values to request a priority appropriate to a
               given type of device or to request a priority that is high, medium or
               low relative to other activities within the kernel.

               It is also permissible to specify positive or negative offsets from the
               values defined above. Positive offsets result in more favorable prior-
               ity. The maximum allowable offset in all cases is 3 (e.g. **pridisk+3**
               and **pridisk-3** are valid values but **pridisk+4** and **pridisk-4** are
               not valid). Offsets can be useful in defining the relative importance of
               different locks or resources that may be held by a given driver. In
               general, a higher relative priority should be used when the caller is
               sleeping waiting for a highly contended kernel resource, or when the
               caller is already holding one or more locks or kernel resources upon
               entry to SV_WAIT_SIG.

               The exact semantic of the *priority* argument is specific to the schedul-
               ing class of the caller, and some scheduling classes may choose to ig-
               nore the argument for the purposes of assigning a scheduling priority.

lkp   Pointer to a basic lock which must be locked when SV_WAIT_SIG is
               called. The basic lock is released when the calling process goes to
               sleep, as described below.

DESCRIPTION

SV_WAIT_SIG causes the calling process to go to sleep (the caller's execution is
suspended and other processes may be scheduled) waiting for a call to
SV_SIGNAL(D3DK) or SV_BROADCAST(D3DK) for the synchronization variable
specified by *svp*.

The basic lock specified by *lkp* must be held upon entry. The lock is released and the interrupt priority level is set to **pl0** after the process is queued on the synchronization variable but prior to context switching to another process. When the caller returns from **SV_WAIT_SIG** the basic lock is not held and the interrupt priority level is equal to **pl0**.

SV_WAIT_SIG may be interrupted by a signal, in which case it will return early without waiting for a call to **SV_SIGNAL** or **SV_BROADCAST**.

If the function is interrupted by a job control stop signal (e.g. **SIGSTOP**, **SIGTSTP**, **SIGTTIN**, **SIGTTOU**) which results in the caller entering a stopped state, when continued, the **SV_WAIT_SIG** function will return **TRUE** as if the process had been awakened by a call to **SV_SIGNAL** or **SV_BROADCAST**.

If the function is interrupted by a signal other than a job control stop signal, or by a job control stop signal that does not result in the caller stopping (because the signal has a non-default disposition), the **SV_WAIT_SIG** call will return **FALSE**.

RETURN VALUE

SV_WAIT_SIG returns **TRUE** (a non-zero value) if the caller woke up because of a call to **SV_SIGNAL** or **SV_BROADCAST**, or if the caller was stopped and subsequently continued. **SV_WAIT_SIG** returns **FALSE** (zero) if the caller woke up and returned early because of a signal other than a job control stop signal, or by a job control stop signal that did not result in the caller stopping because the signal had a non-default disposition.

LEVEL

Base Level Only.

NOTES

May sleep.

Driver defined basic locks (with the exception of the lock specified by *lkp*) and read/write locks may not be held across calls to this function.

Driver defined sleep locks may be held across calls to this function.

SEE ALSO

SV_ALLOC(D3DK), **SV_BROADCAST**(D3DK), **SV_DEALLOC**(D3DK), **SV_SIGNAL**(D3DK), **SV_WAIT**(D3DK), **signals**(D5DK)

NAME

TRYLOCK – try to acquire a basic lock

SYNOPSIS

```
#include <sys/types.h>
#include <sys/ksynch.h>

pl_t TRYLOCK(lock_t *lockp, pl_t pl);
```

ARGUMENTS

lockp   Pointer to the basic lock to be acquired.

pl   The interrupt priority level to be set while the lock is held by the caller. Because some implementations require that interrupts that might attempt to acquire the lock be blocked on the processor on which the lock is held, portable drivers must specify a *pl* value that is sufficient to block out any interrupt handler that might attempt to acquire this lock. See the description of the *min_pl* argument to LOCK_ALLOC(D3DK) for additional discussion and a list of the valid values for *pl*. Implementations which do not require that the interrupt priority level be raised during lock acquisition may choose to ignore this argument.

DESCRIPTION

If the lock specified by *lockp* is immediately available (can be acquired without waiting) TRYLOCK sets the interrupt priority level in accordance with the value specified by *pl* (if required by the implementation) and acquires the lock. If the lock is not immediately available, the function returns without acquiring the lock.

RETURN VALUE

If the lock is acquired, TRYLOCK returns the previous interrupt priority level (plbase - plhi). If the lock is not acquired the value invpl is returned.

LEVEL

Base or Interrupt.

NOTES

Does not sleep.

TRYLOCK may be used to acquire a lock in a different order from the order defined by the lock hierarchy.

Driver defined basic locks, read/write locks, and sleep locks may be held across calls to this function.

When called from interrupt level, the *pl* argument must not specify a priority level below the level at which the interrupt handler is running.

SEE ALSO

LOCK(D3DK), LOCK_ALLOC(D3DK), LOCK_DEALLOC(D3DK), UNLOCK(D3DK)

NAME

uiomove – copy data using uio(D4DK) structure

SYNOPSIS

```
#include <sys/types.h>
#include <sys/uio.h>

int uiomove(caddr_t addr, long nbytes, uio_rw_t rwflag, uio_t * uiop);
```

ARGUMENTS

addr   Source/destination kernel address of the copy.

nbytes   Number of bytes to copy.

rwflag   Flag indicating read or write operation. Possible values are **UIO_READ** and **UIO_WRITE**.

uiop   Pointer to the **uio** structure for the copy.

DESCRIPTION

The **uiomove** function copies *nbytes* of data between the kernel address *addr* and the space defined by the **uio** structure pointed to by *uiop*. If *rwflag* is **UIO_READ**, the data is copied from *addr* to the space described by the **uio** structure. If *rwflag* is **UIO_WRITE**, the data is copied from the space described by the **uio** structure to *addr*.

The **uio_segflg** member of the **uio** structure specifies the type of space described by the **uio** structure. If **uio_segflg** is set to **UIO_SYSSPACE** the **uio** structure describes a portion of the kernel address space. If **uio_segflg** is set to **UIO_USERSPACE** the **uio** structure describes a portion of the user address space.

If the copy is successful, **uiomove** updates the appropriate members of the **uio** and **iovec**(D4DK) structures to reflect the copy (**uio_offset** and **iov_base** are increased by *nbytes* and **uio_resid** and **iov_len** are decrease by *nbytes*).

RETURN VALUE

uiomove returns 0 on success or an error number on failure. If a partial transfer occurs, the **uio** structure is updated to indicate the amount not transferred and an error is returned.

LEVEL

Base only if **uio_segflg** is set to **UIO_USERSPACE**. Base or interrupt if **uio_segflg** is set to **UIO_SYSSPACE**.

NOTES

May sleep if **uio_segflg** is set to **UIO_USERSPACE**.

Driver-defined basic locks and read/write locks may be held across calls to this function if **uio_segflg** is **UIO_SYSSPACE** but may not be held if **uio_segflg** is **UIO_USERSPACE**.

Driver-defined sleep locks may be held across calls to this function regardless of the value of **uio_segflg**.

When holding locks across calls to this function, drivers must be careful to avoid creating a deadlock. During the data transfer, page fault resolution might result in another I/O to the same device. For example, this could occur if the driver controls the disk drive used as the swap device.

If *addr* specifies an address in user space, or if the value of `uio_segflg` is not consistent with the type of address space described by the `uio` structure, the system can panic.

SEE ALSO

bcopy(D3DK), copyin(D3DK), copyout(D3DK), ureadc(D3DK), uwritec(D3DK), iovec(D4DK), uio(D4DK)

NAME

unbufcall – cancel a pending **bufcall** request

SYNOPSIS

#include <sys/stream.h>

void unbufcall(toid_t *id*);

ARGUMENTS

id   Identifier returned from **bufcall**(D3DK) or **esbbcall**(D3DK).

DESCRIPTION

unbufcall cancels a pending **bufcall** or **esbbcall** request. The argument *id* is a non-zero identifier for the request to be canceled. *id* is returned from the **bufcall** or **esbbcall** function used to issue the request.

RETURN VALUE

None.

LEVEL

Base or Interrupt.

NOTES

Does not sleep.

Driver-defined basic locks, read/write locks, and sleep locks may not be held across calls to this function.

SEE ALSO

bufcall(D3DK), **esbbcall**(D3DK)

EXAMPLE

See **bufcall** for the other half of this example.

In the module close routine, the **put**(D2DK) and **srv**(D2DK) routines are disabled by calling **qprocsoff**(D3DK) (line 16). This will prevent any further **bufcall** or **timeout** requests from being issued by the service routine. If a **bufcall** request is pending (line 17), we cancel it (line 18). Otherwise, if a **timeout** request is pending (line 19), we cancel it (line 20). Then the **m_type** field of the module's private data structure is set to 0, indicating no pending **bufcall** or **timeout**.

```
 1  struct mod {
 2      toid_t m_id;
 3      char    m_type;
 4      lock_t *m_lock;
        . . .
 5  };
 6  #define TIMEOUT   1
 7  #define BUFCALL   2
        . . .
 8  modclose(q, flag, crp)
 9      queue_t *q;
10      int flag;
11      cred_t *crp;
12  {
13      struct mod *modp;

14      modp = (struct mod *)q->q_ptr;
```

```
15      qprocsoff(q);
16      if (modp->m_type == BUFCALL)
17              unbufcall(modp->m_id);
18      else if (modp->m_type == TIMEOUT)
19              untimeout(modp->m_id);
20      modp->m_type = 0;
        . . .
```

NAME

unfreezestr – unfreeze the state of a stream

SYNOPSIS

```
#include <sys/types.h>
#include <sys/stream.h>

void unfreezestr(queue_t *q, pl_t pl);
```

ARGUMENTS

q   Pointer to a message queue.

pl   The interrupt priority level to be set (if the implementation requires that interrupts be blocked in order to prevent deadlock) after unfreezing the stream. See **LOCK_ALLOC**(D3DK) for a list of valid values for *pl*. *pl* should be the value that was returned from the corresponding call to **freezestr**(D3DK) unless the caller has a specific need to set some other interrupt priority level. Although portable drivers must always specify an appropriate *pl* argument, implementations which do not require that the interrupt priority level be raised while the stream is frozen may choose to ignore this argument.

DESCRIPTION

unfreezestr unfreezes the state of the stream containing the queue specified by *q* and sets the interrupt priority level to the value specified by *pl*. Unfreezing the stream allows continuation of all activities that were forced to wait while the stream was frozen.

RETURN VALUE

None.

LEVEL

Base or Interrupt.

NOTES

Does not sleep.

Driver defined basic locks, read/write locks, and sleep locks may be held across calls to this function.

SEE ALSO

freezestr(D3DK)

EXAMPLE

See **insq**(D3DK) for an example of **unfreezestr**.

NAME

unlinkb – remove a message block from the head of a message

SYNOPSIS

```
#include <sys/stream.h>

mblk_t *unlinkb(mblk_t *mp);
```

ARGUMENTS

mp   Pointer to the message.

DESCRIPTION

unlinkb removes the first message block from the message pointed to by *mp*. The removed message block is not freed. It is the caller's responsibility to free it.

RETURN VALUE

unlinkb returns a pointer to the remainder of the message after the first message block has been removed. If there is only one message block in the message, **NULL** is returned.

LEVEL

Base or Interrupt.

NOTES

Does not sleep.

Driver-defined basic locks, read/write locks, and sleep locks may be held across calls to this function.

SEE ALSO

linkb(D3DK)

EXAMPLE

The routine expects to get passed an **M_PROTO T_DATA_IND** message. It will remove and free the **M_PROTO** header and return the remaining **M_DATA** portion of the message.

```
1  mblk_t *
2  makedata(mp)
3      mblk_t *mp;
4  {
5      mblk_t *nmp;

6      nmp = unlinkb(mp);
7      freeb(mp);
8      return(nmp);
9  }
```

NAME

UNLOCK – release a basic lock

SYNOPSIS

```
#include <sys/types.h>
#include <sys/ksynch.h>

void UNLOCK(lock_t *lockp, pl_t pl);
```

ARGUMENTS

lockp   Pointer to the basic lock to be released.

pl   The interrupt priority level to be set after releasing the lock. See the description of the *min_pl* argument to LOCK_ALLOC(D3DK) for a list of the valid values for *pl*. If lock calls are not being nested or if the caller is unlocking in the reverse order that locks were acquired, the *pl* argument will typically be the value that was returned from the corresponding call to acquire the lock. The caller may need to specify a different value for *pl* if nested locks are released in some order other than the reverse order of acquisition, so as to ensure that the interrupt priority level is kept sufficiently high to block interrupt code that might attempt to acquire locks which are still held. Although portable drivers must always specify an appropriate *pl* argument, implementations which do not require that the interrupt priority level be raised during lock acquisition may choose to ignore this argument.

DESCRIPTION

UNLOCK releases the basic lock specified by *lockp* and then sets the interrupt priority level in accordance with the value specified by *pl* (if required by the implementation).

RETURN VALUE

None.

LEVEL

Base or Interrupt.

NOTES

Does not sleep.

Driver defined basic locks, read/write locks, and sleep locks may be held across calls to this function.

SEE ALSO

LOCK(D3DK), LOCK_ALLOC(D3DK), LOCK_DEALLOC(D3DK), TRYLOCK(D3DK)

NAME

untimeout – cancel previous **timeout** request

SYNOPSIS

#include <sys/types.h>

void untimeout(toid_t *id*);

ARGUMENTS

id　　　　　　Identifier returned from a previous call to **dtimeout**(D3D) or **itimeout**(D3DK).

DESCRIPTION

untimeout cancels a pending **timeout** request. If the **untimeout** is called while the function is running, then **untimeout** will not return until the function has completed. The function that runs as a result of a call to **dtimeout** or **itimeout** cannot use **untimeout** to cancel itself.

RETURN VALUE

None.

LEVEL

Base or Interrupt, with the following exception: The **untimeout** can only be performed from interrupt levels less than, or equal to, the level specified when the function was scheduled.

NOTES

Does not sleep.

Driver-defined basic locks, read/write locks, and sleep locks may not be held across calls to this function if these locks are contended by the function being canceled.

SEE ALSO

delay(D3DK), **dtimeout**(D3D), **itimeout**(D3DK), **unbufcall**(D3DK)

EXAMPLE

See **unbufcall**(D3DK) for an example of **untimeout**.

NAME

ureadc – copy a character to space described by uio(D4DK) structure

SYNOPSIS

```
#include <sys/uio.h>

int ureadc(int c, uio_t *uiop);
```

ARGUMENTS

c   The character to be copied.

uiop   Pointer to the **uio** structure.

DESCRIPTION

ureadc copies the character *c* into the space described by the **uio** structure pointed to by *uiop*.

The **uio_segflg** member of the **uio** structure specifies the type of space to which the copy is made. If **uio_segflg** is set to **UIO_SYSSPACE** the character is copied to a kernel address. If **uio_segflg** is set to **UIO_USERSPACE** the character is copied to a user address.

If the character is successfully copied, **ureadc** updates the appropriate members of the **uio** and **iovec**(D4DK) structures to reflect the copy (**uio_offset** and **iov_base** are incremented and **uio_resid** and **iov_len** are decremented).

RETURN VALUE

ureadc returns **0** on success or an error number on failure.

LEVEL

Base only if **uio_segflg** is set to **UIO_USERSPACE**. Base or interrupt if **uio_segflg** is set to **UIO_SYSSPACE**.

NOTES

May sleep if **uio_segflg** is set to **UIO_USERSPACE**.

Driver-defined basic locks and read/write locks may be held across calls to this function if **uio_segflg** is **UIO_SYSSPACE** but may not be held if **uio_segflg** is **UIO_USERSPACE**.

Driver-defined sleep locks may be held across calls to this function regardless of the value of **uio_segflg**.

When holding locks across calls to this function, drivers must be careful to avoid creating a deadlock. During the data transfer, page fault resolution might result in another I/O to the same device. For example, this could occur if the driver controls the disk drive used as the swap device.

SEE ALSO

uiomove(D3DK), **uwritec**(D3DK), **iovec**(D4DK), **uio**(D4DK)

NAME

uwritec – return a character from space described by **uio**(D4DK) structure

SYNOPSIS

```
#include <sys/uio.h>

int uwritec(uio_t *uiop);
```

ARGUMENTS

uiop   Pointer to the **uio** structure.

DESCRIPTION

uwritec copies a character from the space described by the **uio** structure pointed to by *uiop* and returns the character to the caller.

The **uio_segflg** member of the **uio** structure specifies the type of space from which the copy is made. If **uio_segflg** is set to **UIO_SYSSPACE** the character is copied from a kernel address. If **uio_segflg** is set to **UIO_USERSPACE** the character is copied from a user address.

If the character is successfully copied, **uwritec** updates the appropriate members of the **uio** and **iovec**(D4DK) structures to reflect the copy (**uio_offset** and **iov_base** are incremented and **uio_resid** and **iov_len** are decremented) and returns the character to the caller.

RETURN VALUE

If successful, **uwritec** returns the character. **-1** is returned if the space described by the **uio** structure is empty or there is an error.

LEVEL

Base only if **uio_segflg** is set to **UIO_USERSPACE**. Base or interrupt if **uio_segflg** is set to **UIO_SYSSPACE**.

NOTES

May sleep if **uio_segflg** is set to **UIO_USERSPACE**.

Driver-defined basic locks and read/write locks may be held across calls to this function if **uio_segflg** is **UIO_SYSSPACE** but may not be held if **uio_segflg** is **UIO_USERSPACE**.

Driver-defined sleep locks may be held across calls to this function regardless of the value of **uio_segflg**.

When holding locks across calls to this function, drivers must be careful to avoid creating a deadlock. During the data transfer, page fault resolution might result in another I/O to the same device. For example, this could occur if the driver controls the disk drive used as the swap device.

SEE ALSO

uiomove(D3DK), ureadc(D3DK), iovec(D4DK), uio(D4DK)

NAME

   vtop – convert virtual address to physical address

SYNOPSIS

   #include <sys/types.h>

   paddr_t vtop(caddr_t *vaddr*, proc_t *p);

ARGUMENTS

   vaddr   Virtual address to convert.

   p   Pointer to the process structure used by **vtop** to locate the information
               tables used for memory management. To indicate that the address is
               in kernel virtual space, *p* must be set to **NULL**. Block drivers that can
               transfer data directly in and out of user memory space must set *p* to
               the **b_proc** member of the **buf**(D4DK) structure. A pointer to the
               currently running process can be obtained by calling
               drv_getparm(D3DK) with the **UPROCP** parameter.

DESCRIPTION

   vtop converts a virtual address to a physical address. When a driver receives a
   memory address from the kernel, that address is virtual. Generally, memory
   management is performed by the MMU. However, devices that access memory
   directly using physical DMA deal only with physical memory addresses. In such
   cases, the driver must provide the device with physical memory addresses.

   The only addresses that are safe to pass to **vtop** are those provided to drivers
   from the kernel through driver entry points, DDI/DKI kernel routines, DDI/DKI
   kernel data structures, or statically-allocated global driver variables.

RETURN VALUE

   On success, the physical address is returned. Otherwise, if there is no physical
   memory mapped to the virtual address, 0 is returned. If *vaddr* specifies an
   invalid kernel address, a system panic will occur.

LEVEL

   Base or Interrupt.

NOTES

   Does not sleep.

   Driver-defined basic locks, read/write locks, and sleep locks may be held across
   calls to this function.

SEE ALSO

   btop(D3DK), **btopr**(D3DK), **drv_getparm**(D3DK), **ptob**(D3DK), **buf**(D4DK)

NAME

WR – get a pointer to the write queue

SYNOPSIS

```
#include <sys/stream.h>
#include <sys/ddi.h>

queue_t *WR(queue_t *q);
```

ARGUMENTS

q   Pointer to the queue whose write queue is to be returned.

DESCRIPTION

The **WR** function accepts a queue pointer as an argument and returns a pointer to the write queue of the same module.

RETURN VALUE

The pointer to the write queue.

LEVEL

Base or Interrupt.

NOTES

Does not sleep.

Driver-defined basic locks, read/write locks, and sleep locks may be held across calls to this function.

SEE ALSO

OTHERQ(D3DK), RD(D3DK)

EXAMPLE

In a STREAMS **open**(D2DK) routine, the driver or module is passed a pointer to the read queue. The driver or module can store a pointer to a private data structure in the **q_ptr** field of both the read and write queues if it needs to identify the data structures from its **put**(D2DK) or **srv**(D2DK) routines.

```
1   extern struct xxx_dev[];
    ...
2   xxxopen(queue_t *q, dev_t *devp, int flag, int sflag, cred_t *crp)
3   {
      ...
3     q->q_ptr = (caddr_t)&xxx_dev[getminor(*devp)];
4     WR(q)->q_ptr = (caddr_t)&xxx_dev[getminor(*devp)];
      ...
5   }
```

NAME

    `intro` – introduction to DMA utility routines

SYNOPSIS

    `#include <sys/types.h>`
    `#include <sys/dma.h>`
    `#include <sys/ddi.h>`

DESCRIPTION

This section describes the kernel utility functions available for use by device drivers that directly program DMA controllers. Intel 80x86-based implementations that support DMA by having drivers directly program DMA controllers support these functions.

Unless otherwise stated, any kernel utility routine that sleeps will do so such that signals will not interrupt the sleep.

NAME

dma_disable – disable recognition of hardware requests on a DMA channel

SYNOPSIS

    #include <sys/dma.h>

    void dma_disable(int *chan*);

ARGUMENTS

chan   Channel to be disabled.

DESCRIPTION

dma_disable disables recognition of hardware requests on the DMA channel *chan*. The channel is then released and made available for other use.

RETURN VALUE

None.

LEVEL

Base or Interrupt.

NOTES

Does not sleep.

The caller must ensure that it is acting on behalf of the channel owner, and that it makes sense to release the channel.

The caller must ensure that the channel is in use for hardware-initiated DMA transfers and not software-initiated transfers.

SEE ALSO

dma_enable(D3X), dma_prog(D3X), dma_cb(D4X)

DMA UTILITY ROUTINES (D3X)

NAME

dma_enable – enable recognition of hardware requests on a DMA channel

SYNOPSIS

```
#include <sys/dma.h>

void dma_enable(int chan);
```

ARGUMENTS

chan   Channel to be enabled.

DESCRIPTION

dma_enable enables recognition of hardware requests on the DMA channel *chan*. The channel should have been programmed previously by dma_prog(D3X).

RETURN VALUE

None.

LEVEL

Base or Interrupt.

NOTES

Does not sleep.

SEE ALSO

dma_disable(D3X), dma_prog(D3X), dma_cb(D4X)

NAME

dma_free_buf – free a previously allocated DMA buffer descriptor

SYNOPSIS

```
#include <sys/dma.h>

void dma_free_buf(struct dma_buf *dmabufptr);
```

ARGUMENTS

dmabufptr Address of the allocated DMA buffer descriptor to be returned.

DESCRIPTION

dma_free_buf frees a DMA buffer descriptor. The *dmabufptr* argument must specify the address of a DMA buffer descriptor previously allocated by dma_get_buf(D3X).

RETURN VALUE

None.

LEVEL

Base or Interrupt.

NOTES

Does not sleep.

SEE ALSO

dma_get_buf(D3X), dma_buf(D4X)

NAME

dma_free_cb – free a previously allocated DMA command block

SYNOPSIS

#include <sys/dma.h>

void dma_free_cb(struct dma_cb *dmacbptr);

ARGUMENTS

dmacbptr   Address of the allocated DMA command block to be returned.

DESCRIPTION

dma_free_cb frees a DMA command block. The *dmacbptr* argument must specify the address of a DMA command block previously allocated by dma_get_cb(D3X).

RETURN VALUE

None.

LEVEL

Base or Interrupt.

NOTES

Does not sleep.

SEE ALSO

dma_get_cb(D3X), dma_cb(D4X)

NAME

dma_get_buf – allocate a DMA buffer descriptor

SYNOPSIS

```
#include <sys/types.h>
#include <sys/dma.h>

struct dma_buf *dma_get_buf(uchar_t mode);
```

ARGUMENTS

mode   Specifies whether the caller is willing to sleep waiting for memory. If *mode* is set to **DMA_SLEEP**, the caller will sleep if necessary until the memory for a **dma_buf** is available. If *mode* is set to **DMA_NOSLEEP**, the caller will not sleep, but **dma_get_buf** will return **NULL** if memory for a **dma_buf** is not immediately available.

DESCRIPTION

dma_get_buf allocates memory for a DMA command block structure [see **dma_buf**(D4X)], zeroes it out, and returns a pointer to the structure.

RETURN VALUE

dma_get_buf returns a pointer to the allocated DMA control block. If **DMA_NOSLEEP** is specified and memory for a **dma_buf** is not immediately available, **dma_get_buf** returns a **NULL** pointer.

LEVEL

Base only if *mode* is set to **DMA_SLEEP**. Base or Interrupt if *mode* is set to **DMA_NOSLEEP**.

NOTES

Can sleep if *mode* is set to **DMA_SLEEP**.

SEE ALSO

dma_free_buf(D3X), **dma_buf**(D4X)

NAME

　　dma_get_best_mode – determine best transfer mode for DMA command

SYNOPSIS

　　`#include <sys/types.h>`
　　`#include <sys/dma.h>`

　　`uchar_t dma_get_best_mode(struct dma_cb` *dmacbptr*`);`

ARGUMENTS

　　dmacbptr　　Pointer to a DMA command block.

DESCRIPTION

　　dma_get_best_mode determines the best DMA transfer mode to use with the DMA operation specified in the command block whose address is given by *dmacbptr*. Prior to the call to **dma_get_best_mode**, all fields of the command block should have been initialized except for **cycles**. The **cycles** field should be initialized using the return value from **dma_get_best_mode**.

RETURN VALUE

　　dma_get_best_mode returns a value that specifies the transfer mode. This value should be used to set the **cycles** field of the **dma_cb**(D4X) structure.

LEVEL

　　Base or Interrupt.

NOTES

　　Does not sleep.

SEE ALSO

　　dma_cb(D4X)

NAME
    dma_get_cb – allocate a DMA command block

SYNOPSIS
    #include <sys/types.h>
    #include <sys/dma.h>

    struct dma_cb *dma_get_cb(uchar_t *mode*);

ARGUMENTS
    mode　　　Specifies whether the caller is willing to sleep waiting for memory. If
    mode is set to **DMA_SLEEP**, the caller will sleep if necessary until the
    memory for a **dma_cb** is available. If *mode* is set to **DMA_NOSLEEP**, the
    caller will not sleep, but **dma_get_cb** will return **NULL** if memory for a
    dma_cb is not immediately available.

DESCRIPTION
    dma_get_cb allocates memory for a DMA command block structure [see
    dma_cb(D4X)], zeroes it out, and returns a pointer to the structure.

RETURN VALUE
    dma_get_cb returns a pointer to the allocated DMA control block. If
    DMA_NOSLEEP is specified and memory for a **dma_cb** is not immediately available,
    dma_get_cb returns a **NULL** pointer.

LEVEL
    Base only if *mode* is set to **DMA_SLEEP**. Base or Interrupt if *mode* is set to
    DMA_NOSLEEP.

NOTES
    Can sleep if *mode* is set to **DMA_SLEEP**.

SEE ALSO
    dma_free_cb(D3X), **dma_cb**(D4X)

NAME

dma_prog – program a DMA operation for a subsequent hardware request

SYNOPSIS

```
#include <sys/types.h>
#include <sys/dma.h>

int dma_prog(struct dma_cb *dmacbptr, int chan, uchar_t mode);
```

ARGUMENTS

dmacbptr Pointer to the DMA command block specifying the DMA operation.

chan   DMA channel over which the operation is to take place.

mode   Specifies whether the caller is willing to sleep waiting to allocate desired DMA channel. If *mode* is set to **DMA_SLEEP**, the caller will sleep if necessary until the requested channel becomes available for its use. If *mode* is set to **DMA_NOSLEEP**, the caller will not sleep, but **dma_prog** will return **FALSE** if the requested DMA channel is not immediately available.

DESCRIPTION

dma_prog programs the DMA channel *chan* for the operation specified by the DMA command block whose address is given by *dmacbptr*. Note that **dma_prog** does not initiate the DMA transfer. Instead, the transfer will be initiated by a subsequent request from hardware. The hardware request will be recognized only if the channel has been enabled via **dma_enable**(D3X) following the call to **dma_prog**.

In order to program the operation, **dma_prog** requires exclusive use of the specified DMA channel. The caller may specify, via the *mode* argument, whether or not **dma_prog** should sleep waiting for a busy channel to become available. If the specified channel is in use, and *mode* is set to **DMA_SLEEP**, then **dma_prog** will sleep until the channel becomes available for its use. Otherwise, if **DMA_NOSLEEP** is specified and the requested channel is not immediately available, **dma_prog** will not program the channel, but will simply return a value of **FALSE**.

RETURN VALUE

dma_prog returns the value **TRUE** upon successful completion and returns the value **FALSE** otherwise.

LEVEL

Base only if *mode* is set to **DMA_SLEEP**. Base or Interrupt if *mode* is set to **DMA_NOSLEEP**.

NOTES

May sleep if *mode* is set to **DMA_SLEEP**.

SEE ALSO

dma_disable(D3X), dma_enable(D3X), dma_cb(D4X)

NAME

dma_stop – stop software-initiated DMA operation on a channel and release it

SYNOPSIS

```
#include <sys/dma.h>

void dma_stop(int chan);
```

ARGUMENTS

chan   Channel on which DMA operation is to be stopped.

DESCRIPTION

dma_stop stops a software-initiated DMA operation in progress on the channel *chan*. The channel is then released and made available for other use.

RETURN VALUE

None.

LEVEL

Base or Interrupt.

NOTES

Does not sleep.

The caller must ensure that it is acting on behalf of the channel owner, and that it makes sense to release the channel.

The caller must ensure that the channel is currently in use for software-initiated DMA transfers rather than hardware-initiated transfers.

SEE ALSO

dma_swsetup(D3X), dma_swstart(D3X), dma_cb(D4X)

NAME

dma_swstart – initiate a DMA operation via software request

SYNOPSIS

```
#include <sys/types.h>
#include <sys/dma.h>
```

void dma_swstart(struct dma_cb *dmacbptr, int chan, uchar_t mode);

ARGUMENTS

dmacbptr   Pointer to a DMA command block specifying the DMA operation.

chan   Channel over which the operation is to take place.

mode   Specifies whether the caller should sleep waiting for the operation to complete. If *mode* is set to **DMA_NOSLEEP**, then **dma_swstart** simply starts the operation but does not wait for the operation to complete and instead returns to the caller immediately. If *mode* is set to **DMA_SLEEP**, then **dma_swstart** starts the operation and then waits for the operation to complete, and returns to the caller after the operation has finished.

DESCRIPTION

dma_swstart initiates a DMA operation previously programmed by **dma_swsetup**(D3X). If *mode* is **DMA_SLEEP**, then **dma_swstart** returns to the caller after the operation completes. If *mode* is **DMA_NOSLEEP**, then **dma_swstart** returns to the caller immediately after starting the operation.

RETURN VALUE

None.

LEVEL

Base only if *mode* is set to **DMA_SLEEP**. Base or Interrupt if *mode* is set to **DMA_NOSLEEP**.

NOTES

The operation being initiated must have already been programmed on the specified channel by **dma_swsetup**.

Will sleep if *mode* is set to **DMA_SLEEP**.

SEE ALSO

dma_stop(D3X), dma_swsetup(D3X), dma_cb(D4X)

NAME

dma_swsetup – program a DMA operation for a subsequent software request

SYNOPSIS

```
#include <sys/types.h>
#include <sys/dma.h>

int dma_swsetup(struct dma_cb *dmacbptr, int chan, uchar_t mode);
```

ARGUMENTS

dmacbptr   Pointer to the DMA command block specifying the DMA operation.

chan   DMA channel over which the operation is to take place.

mode   Specifies whether the caller is willing to sleep waiting to allocate desired DMA channel. If *mode* is set to **DMA_SLEEP**, the caller will sleep if necessary until the requested channel becomes available for its use. If *mode* is set to **DMA_NOSLEEP**, the caller will not sleep, but dma_swsetup will return **FALSE** if the requested DMA channel is not immediately available.

DESCRIPTION

dma_swsetup programs the DMA channel *chan* for the operation specified by the DMA command block whose address is given by *dmacbptr*. Note that dma_swsetup does not initiate the DMA transfer. Instead, the transfer will be initiated by a subsequent request initiated via software by **dma_swstart**(D3X).

If dma_swsetup programs the operation successfully, it then calls the procedure specified by the **proc** field of the **dma_cb**(D4X) structure. It passes as an argument the value in the **procparms** field. If **proc** is set to **NULL**, then no routine is called.

To program the operation, dma_swsetup requires exclusive use of the specified DMA channel. The caller may specify, via the *mode* argument, whether dma_swsetup should sleep waiting for a busy channel to become available. If the specified channel is in use and *mode* is set to **DMA_SLEEP**, then dma_swsetup will sleep until the channel becomes available for its use. Otherwise, if **DMA_NOSLEEP** is specified and the requested channel is not immediately available, dma_swsetup will not program the channel, but will simply return a value of **FALSE**.

RETURN VALUE

dma_swsetup returns the value **TRUE** on success and returns the value **FALSE** otherwise.

LEVEL

Base only if either (1) *mode* is set to **DMA_SLEEP** or (2) the routine specified by the **proc** field of the **dma_cb** structure sleeps. Base or Interrupt otherwise.

NOTES

Can sleep if *mode* is set to **DMA_SLEEP** or if the routine specified by the **proc** field of the **dma_cb** structure sleeps.

SEE ALSO

dma_swstart(D3X), dma_stop(D3X), dma_cb(D4X)

NAME

intro – introduction to kernel data structures

SYNOPSIS

```
#include <sys/types.h>
#include <sys/ddi.h>
```

DESCRIPTION

This section describes the kernel data structures a developer might need to use in a device driver. Driver developers should not declare arrays of these structures, as the size of any structure might change between releases. Two exceptions to this are the **iovec**(D4DK) and **uio**(D4DK) structures.

Drivers can only reference those structure members described on the manual page. The actual data structures may have additional structure members beyond those described, but drivers must not reference them.

Some structure members are flags fields that consist of a bitmask of flags. Drivers must never directly assign values to these structure members. Drivers should only set and clear flags they are interested in, since the actual implementation may contain unlisted flags.

Data structures that are "black boxes" to drivers are not described in this section. These structures are referenced on the manual pages where they are used. Drivers should not be written to use any of their structure members. Their only valid use is passing pointers to the structures to the particular kernel routines.

KERNEL DATA STRUCTURES (D4)

NAME

buf – block I/O data transfer structure

SYNOPSIS

```
#include <sys/types.h>
#include <sys/page.h>
#include <sys/proc.h>
#include <sys/buf.h>
```

DESCRIPTION

The **buf** structure is the basic data structure for block I/O transfers. Each block I/O transfer has an associated buffer header. The header contains all the buffer control and status information. For drivers, the buffer header pointer is the sole argument to a block driver **strategy**(D2DK) routine. Do not depend on the size of the **buf** structure when writing a driver.

It is important to note that a buffer header may be linked in multiple lists simultaneously. Because of this, most of the members in the buffer header cannot be changed by the driver, even when the buffer header is in one of the drivers' work lists.

Buffer headers may be used by the system to describe a portion of the kernel data space for I/O for block drivers. Buffer headers are also used by the system for physical I/O for block drivers. In this case, the buffer describes a portion of user data space that is locked into memory [see **physiock**(D3DK)].

Block drivers often chain block requests so that overall throughput for the device is maximized. The **av_forw** and the **av_back** members of the **buf** structure can serve as link pointers for chaining block requests.

STRUCTURE MEMBERS

```
int             b_flags;        /* Buffer status */
struct buf      *b_forw;        /* Kernel/driver list link */
struct buf      *b_back;        /* Kernel/driver list link */
struct buf      *av_forw;       /* Driver work list link */
struct buf      *av_back;       /* Driver work list link */
uint_t          b_bcount;       /* # of bytes to transfer */
union {
        caddr_t b_addr;         /* Buffer's virtual address */
} b_un;
daddr_t         b_blkno;        /* Block number on device */
uint_t          b_resid;        /* # of bytes not transferred */
clock_t         b_start;        /* Request start time */
struct proc     *b_proc;        /* Process structure address */
long            b_bufsize;      /* Size of allocated buffer */
int             (*b_iodone)();  /* Function called by biodone */
dev_t           b_edev;         /* Expanded dev field */
void            *b_private;     /* For driver's use */
```

The members of the buffer header available to test or set by a driver are described below:

b_flags is a bitmask that stores the buffer status and tells the driver whether to read from or write to the device. The driver must never clear the **b_flags** member. If this is done, unpredictable results can occur.

Valid flags are as follows:

B_PAGEIO   The buffer is being used in a paged I/O request. If **B_PAGEIO** is set, the the buffer header will refer to a list of page structures sorted by block location on the device. Also, the **b_un.b_addr** field of the buffer header will be the offset into the first page of the page list. If **B_PAGEIO** is not set, the **b_un.b_addr** field of the buffer header will contain the starting virtual address of the I/O request (in user address space if **B_PHYS** is set or kernel address space otherwise). The driver must not set or clear the **B_PAGEIO** flag.

B_PHYS   The buffer header is being used for physical (direct) I/O to a user data area. The **b_un.b_addr** member contains the starting virtual address of the user data area. NOTE: **B_PHYS** and **B_PAGEIO** are never set simultaneously and must not be changed by the driver.

B_READ   Data are to be read from the peripheral device into main memory. The driver should not change this flag unless the driver acquired the buffer with **getrbuf**(D3DK), **geteblk**(D3DK), or **ngeteblk**(D3DK).

B_WRITE   Data are to be transferred from main memory to the peripheral device. **B_WRITE** is a pseudo-flag that occupies the same bit location as **B_READ**. **B_WRITE** cannot be directly tested; it is only detected as the absence of **B_READ** (`!(bp->b_flags&B_READ)`.)

b_forw and **b_back** may only be used by the driver if the buffer was acquired by the driver with the **getrbuf** routine. In that case, these members can be used to link the buffer into driver work lists.

av_forw and **av_back** can be used by the driver to link the buffer into driver work lists.

b_bcount specifies the number of bytes to be transferred in both a paged and a non-paged I/O request. The driver may change this member.

b_un.b_addr is either the virtual address of the I/O request, or an offset into the first page of a page list depending on whether **B_PAGEIO** is set. If it is set, the buffer header will refer to a sorted list of page structures and **b_un.b_addr** will be the offset into the first page. If **B_PAGEIO** is not set, **b_un.b_addr** is the virtual address from which data are read or to which data are written. It represents a user virtual address if **B_PHYS** is set, or a kernel virtual address otherwise. The driver may change this member if the driver allocated the buffer header via **getrbuf**.

b_blkno identifies which logical block on the device is to be accessed. The driver may have to convert this logical block number to a physical location such as a cylinder, track, and sector of a disk. The driver may change this member if the driver allocated the buffer via **geteblk**, **ngeteblk**, or **getrbuf**.

b_resid indicates the number of bytes not transferred because of an error. The driver may change this member.

b_start holds the time the I/O request was started. It is provided for the driver's use in calculating response time and is set by the driver. Its type, **clock_t**, is an integral type upon which direct integer calculations can be performed. It represents clock ticks.

b_proc contains the process structure address for the process requesting an unbuffered (direct) data transfer to or from a user data area (this member is set to **NULL** when the transfer is buffered). The process table entry is used to perform proper virtual to physical address translation of the **b_un.b_addr** member [see **vtop**(D3D)]. The driver may not change this member.

b_bufsize contains the size in bytes of the allocated buffer. The driver may not change this member unless the driver acquired the buffer with **getrbuf**.

(*b_iodone) identifies a specific driver routine to be called by the system when the I/O is complete. If one is specified, the **biodone**(D3DK) routine does not return the buffer to the system. The driver may change this member.

b_edev contains the external device number of the device.

b_private is a private field for use by the driver. The system does not interpret it. The driver is free to use it in whatever manner it chooses. For example, the driver could use it as part of a disk block sorting algorithm.

NOTES

Buffers are a shared resource within the kernel. Drivers should only read or write the members listed in this section in accordance with the rules given above. Drivers that attempt to use undocumented members of the **buf** structure risk corrupting data in the kernel and on the device.

DDI/DKI conforming drivers may only use buffer headers that have been allocated using **geteblk**, **ngeteblk** or **getrbuf**, or have been passed to the driver **strategy** routine.

SEE ALSO

strategy(D2DK), **biodone**(D3DK), **bioerror**(D3DK), **biowait**(D3DK), **brelse**(D3DK), **clrbuf**(D3DK), **freerbuf**(D3DK), **geteblk**(D3DK), **geterror**(D3DK), **getrbuf**(D3DK), **ngeteblk**(D3DK), **physiock**(D3DK), **iovec**(D4DK), **uio**(D4DK)

NAME

copyreq – STREAMS transparent ioctl copy request structure

SYNOPSIS

```
#include <sys/stream.h>
```

DESCRIPTION

The **copyreq** structure contains the information necessary to process transparent ioctls. It is used in **M_COPYIN** and **M_COPYOUT** messages. The module or driver usually converts an **M_IOCTL** or **M_IOCDATA** message into an **M_COPYIN** or **M_COPYOUT** message. The **copyreq** structure is thus overlaid on top of the iocblk(D4DK) or **copyresp**(D4DK) structure. The stream head guarantees that the message is large enough to contain the different structures.

STRUCTURE MEMBERS

```
int      cq_cmd;        /* ioctl command */
cred_t   *cq_cr;        /* user credentials */
uint_t   cq_id;         /* ioctl ID */
caddr_t  cq_addr;       /* copy buffer address */
uint_t   cq_size;       /* number of bytes to copy */
int      cq_flag;       /* for future use */
mblk_t   *cq_private;   /* module private data */
```

The **cq_cmd** field is the **ioctl** command, copied from the **ioc_cmd** field of the **iocblk** structure. If the same message is used, then the **cq_cmd** field directly overlays the **ioc_cmd** field (that is, it need not be copied.)

The **cq_cr** field contains a pointer to the user credentials. It is copied from the **ioc_cr** field of the **iocblk** structure. If the same message is used, then the **cq_cr** field directly overlays the **ioc_cr** field (that is, it need not be copied.)

The **cq_id** field is the **ioctl** ID, copied from the **ioc_id** field of the **iocblk** structure. It is used to uniquely identify the **ioctl** request in the stream. If the same message is used, then the **cq_id** field directly overlays the **ioc_id** field (that is, it need not be copied.)

For an **M_COPYIN** message, the **cq_addr** field contains the user address from which the data are to be copied. For an **M_COPYOUT** message, the **cq_addr** field contains the user address to which the data are to be copied. In both cases, the **cq_size** field contains the number of bytes to copy.

The **cq_flag** field is reserved for future use and should be set to 0 by the module or driver.

The **cq_private** field is a field set aside for use by the driver. It can be used to hold whatever state information is necessary to process the **ioctl**. It is copied to the **cp_private** field in the resultant **M_IOCDATA** message.

NOTES

When the **M_COPYIN** or **M_COPYOUT** message is freed, any message that **cq_private** refers to is not freed by the STREAMS subsystem. It is the responsibility of the module or driver to free it.

SEE ALSO
Programmer's Guide: STREAMS

datab(D4DK), msgb(D4DK), copyresp(D4DK), iocblk(D4DK), messages(D5DK)

NAME

copyresp – STREAMS transparent **ioctl** copy response structure

SYNOPSIS

#include <sys/stream.h>

DESCRIPTION

The **copyresp** structure contains information in response to a prior copy request necessary to continue processing transparent **ioctl**s. **M_IOCDATA** messages, generated by the stream head, contain the **copyresp** structure.

STRUCTURE MEMBERS

```
int       cp_cmd;      /* ioctl command */
cred_t    *cp_cr;      /* user credentials */
uint_t    cp_id;       /* ioctl ID */
caddr_t   cp_rval;     /* status of request */
mblk_t    *cp_private; /* module private data */
```

The **cp_cmd** field is the **ioctl** command, copied from the **cq_cmd** field of the **copyreq** structure.

The **cp_cr** field contains a pointer to the user credentials. It is copied from the **cq_cr** field of the **copyreq** structure.

The **cp_id** field is the **ioctl** ID, copied from the **cq_id** field of the **copyreq** structure. It is used to uniquely identify the **ioctl** request in the stream.

The **cq_rval** field contains the return value from the last copy request. If the request succeeded, it is set to 0. Otherwise, if it is non-zero, the request failed. On success, the module or driver should continue processing the **ioctl**. On failure, the module or driver should abort **ioctl** processing and free the message. No **M_IOCNAK** message need be generated.

The **cp_private** field is copied from the **cq_private** field of the **copyreq** structure. It is available so that the module or driver can regain enough state information to continue processing the **ioctl** request.

NOTES

If an **M_IOCDATA** message is reused, any unused fields in the new message should be cleared.

When the **M_IOCDATA** message is freed, any message that **cp_private** refers to is not freed by the STREAMS subsystem. It is the responsibility of the module or driver to free it.

SEE ALSO

Programmer's Guide: STREAMS

datab(D4DK), **msgb**(D4DK), **copyreq**(D4DK), **iocblk**(D4DK), **messages**(D5DK)

NAME

datab – STREAMS data block structure

SYNOPSIS

```
#include <sys/types.h>
#include <sys/stream.h>
```

DESCRIPTION

The **datab** structure describes the data of a STREAMS message. The actual data contained in a STREAMS message is stored in a data buffer pointed to by this structure. A message block structure [**msgb**(D4DK)] includes a field that points to a **datab** structure.

A data block can have more than one message block pointing to it at one time, so the **db_ref** member keeps track of a data block's references, preventing it from being deallocated until all message blocks are finished with it.

STRUCTURE MEMBERS

```
uchar_t  *db_base;   /* first byte of buffer */
uchar_t  *db_lim;    /* last byte (+1) of buffer */
uchar_t  db_ref;     /* # of message pointers to this data */
uchar_t  db_type;    /* message type */
```

The **db_base** field points to the beginning of the data buffer. Drivers and modules should not change this field.

The **db_lim** field points to one byte past the end of the data buffer. Drivers and modules should not change this field.

The **db_ref** field contains a count of the number of message blocks sharing the data buffer. If it is greater than 1, drivers and modules should not change the contents of the data buffer. Drivers and modules should not change this field.

The **db_type** field contains the message type associated with the data buffer. This field can be changed by the driver. However, if the **db_ref** field is greater than 1, this field should not be changed.

NOTES

The **datab** structure is defined as type **dblk_t**.

SEE ALSO

Programmer's Guide: STREAMS

free_rtn(D4DK), **msgb**(D4DK), **messages**(D5DK)

NAME

free_rtn – STREAMS driver's message free routine structure

SYNOPSIS

```
#include <sys/stream.h>
```

DESCRIPTION

A **free_rtn** structure is needed for messages allocated via **esballoc**(D3DK). Since the driver is providing the memory for the data buffer, a way is needed to notify the driver when the buffer is no longer in use. **esballoc** associates the free routine structure with the message when it is allocated. When **freeb**(D3DK) is called to free the message and the reference count goes to zero, the driver's message free routine is called, with the argument specified, to free the data buffer.

STRUCTURE MEMBERS

```
void  (*free_func)()  /* driver's free routine */
char  *free_arg       /* argument to free_func() */
```

The **free_func** field specifies the driver's function to be called when the message has been freed. It is called with interrupts from STREAMS devices blocked on the processor on which the function is running.

The **free_arg** field is the only argument to the driver's free routine.

The **free_rtn** structure is defined as type **frtn_t**.

SEE ALSO

Programmer's Guide: STREAMS

esballoc(D3DK), **freeb**(D3DK)

NAME

iocblk – STREAMS ioctl structure

SYNOPSIS

#include <sys/stream.h>

DESCRIPTION

The **iocblk** structure describes a user's **ioctl**(2) request. It is used in **M_IOCTL**, **M_IOCACK**, and **M_IOCNAK** messages. Modules and drivers usually convert **M_IOCTL** messages into **M_IOCACK** or **M_IOCNAK** messages by changing the type and updating the relevant fields in the **iocblk** structure. When processing a transparent **ioctl**, the **iocblk** structure is usually overlaid with a **copyreq**(D4DK) structure. The stream head guarantees that the message is large enough to contain either structure.

STRUCTURE MEMBERS

```
int     ioc_cmd;    /* ioctl command */
cred_t  *ioc_cr;    /* user credentials */
uint_t  ioc_id;     /* ioctl ID */
uint_t  ioc_count;  /* number of bytes of data */
int     ioc_error;  /* error code for M_IOCACK or M_IOCNAK */
int     ioc_rval;   /* return value for M_IOCACK */
```

The **ioc_cmd** field is the **ioctl** command request specified by the user.

The **ioc_cr** field contains a pointer to the user credentials.

The **ioc_id** field is the **ioctl** ID, used to uniquely identify the **ioctl** request in the stream.

The **ioc_count** field specifies the amount of user data contained in the **M_IOCTL** message. User data will appear in **M_DATA** message blocks linked to the **M_IOCTL** message block. If **ioc_count** is set to the special value **TRANSPARENT**, then the **ioctl** request is "transparent." This means that the user did not use the **I_STR** format of STREAMS **ioctl**s and the module or driver will have to obtain any user data with **M_COPYIN** messages, and change any user data with **M_COPYOUT** messages. In this case, the **M_DATA** message block linked to the **M_IOCTL** message block contains the value of the *arg* parameter in the **ioctl** system call. For an **M_IOCACK** message, the **ioc_count** field specifies the amount of data to copy back to the user's buffer.

The **ioc_error** field can be used to set an error for either an **M_IOCACK** or an **M_IOCNAK** message.

The **ioc_rval** field can be used to set the return value in an **M_IOCACK** message. This will be returned to the user as the return value for the **ioctl** system call that generated the request.

NOTES

Data cannot be copied to the user's buffer with an **M_IOCACK** message if the **ioctl** is transparent.

No data can be copied to the user's buffer with an **M_IOCNAK** message.

SEE ALSO

Programmer's Guide: STREAMS

datab(D4DK), **msgb**(D4DK), **copyreq**(D4DK), **copyresp**(D4DK), **messages**(D5DK)

NAME
iovec – data storage structure for I/O using **uio**(D4DK)

SYNOPSIS
```
#include <sys/types.h>
#include <sys/uio.h>
```

DESCRIPTION
An **iovec** structure describes a data storage area for transfer in a **uio** structure. Conceptually, it may be thought of as a base address and length specification.

STRUCTURE MEMBERS
```
caddr_t  iov_base;  /* base address of the data storage area */
int      iov_len;   /* size of the data storage area in bytes */
```

The driver may only set **iovec** structure members to initialize them for a data transfer for which the driver created the **iovec** structure. The driver must not otherwise change **iovec** structure members. However, drivers may read them. The **iovec** structure members available to the driver are:

iov_base contains the address for a range of memory to or from which data are transferred.

iov_len contains the number of bytes of data to be transferred to or from the range of memory starting at **iov_base**.

NOTES
A separate interface does not currently exist for allocating **iovec**(D4DK) structures when the driver needs to create them itself. Therefore, the driver may either use **kmem_zalloc**(D3DK) to allocate them, or allocate them statically.

SEE ALSO
physiock(D3DK), **uiomove**(D3DK), **ureadc**(D3DK), **uwritec**(D3DK), **uio**(D4DK)

NAME

linkblk – STREAMS multiplexor link structure

SYNOPSIS

```
#include <sys/stream.h>
```

DESCRIPTION

The **linkblk** structure contains the information needed by a multiplexing driver to set up or take down a multiplexor link. The structure is embedded in the **M_DATA** portion of the **M_IOCTL** messages generated from the following **ioctl**(2) calls: **I_LINK**, **I_UNLINK**, **I_PLINK**, and **I_PUNLINK** [see **streamio**(7)].

STRUCTURE MEMBERS

```
queue_t  *l_qtop;   /* lower queue of top stream */
queue_t  *l_qbot;   /* upper queue of bottom stream */
int      l_index;   /* unique ID */
```

The **l_qtop** field is a pointer to the lowest write queue in the upper stream. In other words, it is the write queue of the multiplexing driver. If the link is persistent across closes of the driver, then this field is set to **NULL**.

The **l_qbot** field is a pointer to the upper write queue in the lower stream. The lower stream is the stream being linked under the multiplexor. The topmost read and write queues in the lower stream are given to the multiplexing driver to use for the lower half of its multiplexor processing. The **qinit**(D4DK) structures associated with these queues are those specified for the lower processing in the multiplexing driver's **streamtab**(D4DK) structure.

The **l_index** field is a unique ID that identifies the multiplexing link in the system. The driver can use this as a key on which it can multiplex or de-multiplex.

SEE ALSO

streamio(7) in the *Programmer's Guide: STREAMS*

datab(D4DK), **iocblk**(D4DK), **msgb**(D4DK), **qinit**(D4DK), **streamtab**(D4DK), **messages**(D5DK)

ioctl(2) in the *Programmer's Reference Manual*

NAME

module_info – STREAMS driver and module information structure

SYNOPSIS

```
#include <sys/types.h>
#include <sys/conf.h>
#include <sys/stream.h>
```

DESCRIPTION

When a module or driver is declared, several identification and limit values can be set. These values are stored in the **module_info** structure. These values are used to initialize the module's or driver's queues when they are created.

After the initial declaration, the **module_info** structure is intended to be read-only. However, the flow control limits (**mi_hiwat** and **mi_lowat**) and the packet size limits (**mi_minpsz** and **mi_maxpsz**) are copied to the **queue**(D4DK) structure, where they may be modified.

STRUCTURE MEMBERS

```
ushort_t  mi_idnum;      /* module ID number */
char      *mi_idname;    /* module name */
long      mi_minpsz;     /* minimum packet size */
long      mi_maxpsz;     /* maximum packet size */
ulong_t   mi_hiwat;      /* high water mark */
ulong_t   mi_lowat;      /* low water mark */
```

The **mi_idnum** field is a unique identifier for the driver or module that distinguishes the driver or module from the other drivers and modules in the system.

The **mi_idname** field points to the driver or module name. The constant **FMNAMESZ** limits the length of the name, not including the terminating **NULL**. It is currently set to eight characters.

The **mi_minpsz** field is the default minimum packet size for the driver or module queues. This is an advisory limit specifying the smallest message that can be accepted by the driver or module.

The **mi_maxpsz** field is the default maximum packet size for the driver or module queues. This is an advisory limit specifying the largest message that can be accepted by the driver or module.

The **mi_hiwat** field is the default high water mark for the driver or module queues. This specifies the number of bytes of data contained in messages on the queue such that the queue is considered full and hence flow-controlled.

The **mi_lowat** field is the default low water mark for the driver or module queues. This specifies the number of bytes of data contained in messages on the queue such that the queue is no longer flow-controlled.

NOTES

There may be one **module_info** structure per read and write queue, or the driver or module may use the same **module_info** structure for both the read and write queues.

SEE ALSO
   queue(D4DK)

NAME

msgb – STREAMS message block structure

SYNOPSIS

```
#include <sys/types.h>
#include <sys/stream.h>
```

DESCRIPTION

A STREAMS message is made up of one or more message blocks, referenced by a pointer to a **msgb** structure. When a message is on a queue, all fields are read-only to drivers and modules.

STRUCTURE MEMBERS

```
struct msgb    *b_next;    /* next message on queue */
struct msgb    *b_prev;    /* previous message on queue */
struct msgb    *b_cont;    /* next block in message */
uchar_t        *b_rptr;    /* 1st unread data byte of buffer */
uchar_t        *b_wptr;    /* 1st unwritten data byte of buffer */
struct datab   *b_datap;   /* pointer to data block */
uchar_t        b_band;     /* message priority  */
ushort_t       b_flag;     /* used by stream head  */
```

The **b_next** and **b_prev** pointers are used to link messages together on a **queue**(D4DK). These fields can be used by drivers and modules to create linked lists of messages.

The **b_cont** pointer links message blocks together when a message is composed of more than one block. Drivers and modules can use this field to create complex messages from single message blocks.

The **b_rptr** and **b_wptr** pointers describe the valid data region in the associated data buffer. The **b_rptr** field points to the first unread byte in the buffer and the **b_wptr** field points to the next byte to be written in the buffer.

The **b_datap** field points to the data block [see **datab**(D4DK)] associated with the message block. This field should never be changed by modules or drivers.

The **b_band** field contains the priority band associated with the message. Normal priority messages and high priority messages have **b_band** set to zero. High priority messages are high priority by virtue of their message type. This field can be used to alter the queueing priority of the message. The higher the priority band, the closer to the head of the queue the message is placed.

The **b_flag** field contains a bitmask of flags that can be set to alter the way the stream head will process the message. Valid flags are:

MSGMARK   The last byte in the message is "marked." This condition is testable from user level via the **I_ATMARK ioctl**(2).

NOTES

The **msgb** structure is defined as type **mblk_t**.

SEE ALSO

Programmer's Guide: STREAMS
allocb(D3DK), **esballoc**(D3DK), **freeb**(D3DK), **datab**(D4DK),
free_rtn(D4DK), **messages**(D5DK)

NAME

qinit – STREAMS queue initialization structure

SYNOPSIS

```
#include <sys/stream.h>
```

DESCRIPTION

The **qinit** structure contains pointers to processing procedures and default values for a **queue**(D4DK). Drivers and modules declare **qinit** structure for their read and write queues, and place the addresses of the structures in their **streamtab**(D4DK) structure. After the initial declaration, all fields are intended to be read-only.

STRUCTURE MEMBERS

```
int               (*qi_putp)();     /* put procedure */
int               (*qi_srvp)();     /* service procedure */
int               (*qi_qopen)();    /* open procedure */
int               (*qi_qclose)();   /* close procedure */
int               (*qi_qadmin)();   /* for future use */
struct module_info *qi_minfo;       /* module parameters */
struct module_stat *qi_mstat;       /* module statistics */
```

The **qi_putp** field contains the address of the **put**(D2DK) routine for the **queue**.

The **qi_srvp** field contains the address of the service [**srv**(D2DK)] routine for the **queue**. If there is no service routine, this field should be set to NULL.

The **qi_qopen** field contains the address of the **open**(D2DK) routine for the driver or module. Only the read-side **qinit** structure need define contain the routine address. The write-side value should be set to NULL.

The **qi_qclose** field contains the address of the **close**(D2DK) routine for the driver or module. Only the read-side **qinit** structure need define contain the routine address. The write-side value should be set to NULL.

The **qi_qadmin** field is intended for future use and should be set to NULL.

The **qi_minfo** field contains the address of the **module_info**(D4DK) structure for the driver or module.

The **qi_mstat** field contains the address of the **module_stat** structure for the driver or module. The **module_stat** structure is defined in **/usr/include/sys/strstat.h**. This field should be set to NULL if the driver or module does not keep statistics.

NOTES

There is usually one **qinit** structure for the read side of a module or driver, and one **qinit** structure for the write side.

SEE ALSO

Programmer's Guide: STREAMS

queue(D4DK), **module_info**(D4DK), **streamtab**(D4DK)

NAME

queue – STREAMS queue structure

SYNOPSIS

```
#include <sys/types.h>
#include <sys/stream.h>
```

DESCRIPTION

A instance of a STREAMS driver or module consists of two **queue** structures, one for upstream (read-side) processing and one for downstream (write-side) processing. This structure is the major building block of a stream. It contains pointers to the processing procedures, pointers to the next queue in the stream, flow control parameters, and a list of messages to be processed.

STRUCTURE MEMBERS

```
struct qinit  *q_qinfo;   /* module or driver entry points */
struct msgb   *q_first;   /* first message in queue */
struct msgb   *q_last;    /* last message in queue */
struct queue  *q_next;    /* next queue in stream */
void          *q_ptr;     /* pointer to private data structure */
ulong_t       q_count;    /* approximate size of message queue */
ulong_t       q_flag;     /* status of queue */
long          q_minpsz;   /* smallest packet accepted by QUEUE */
long          q_maxpsz;   /* largest packet accepted by QUEUE */
ulong_t       q_hiwat;    /* high water mark */
ulong_t       q_lowat;    /* low water mark */
```

The **q_qinfo** field contains a pointer to the **qinit**(D4DK) structure specifying the processing routines and default values for the queue. This field should not be changed by drivers or modules.

The **q_first** field points to the first message on the queue, or is **NULL** if the queue is empty. This field should not be changed by drivers or modules.

The **q_last** field points to the last message on the queue, or is **NULL** if the queue is empty. This field should not be changed by drivers or modules.

The **q_next** field points to the next queue in the stream. This field should not be changed by drivers or modules.

The **q_ptr** field is a private field for use by drivers and modules. It provides a way to associate the driver's per-minor data structure with the queue.

The **q_count** field contains the number of bytes in messages on the queue in priority band 0. This includes normal messages and high priority messages.

The **q_flag** field contains a bitmask of flags that indicate different queue characteristics. No flags may be set or cleared by drivers or modules. However, the following flags may be tested:

QREADR   The queue is the read queue. Absence of this flag implies a write queue.

The **q_minpsz** field is the minimum packet size for the queue. This is an advisory limit specifying the smallest message that can be accepted by the queue. It is initially set to the value specified by the **mi_minpsz** field in the **module_info**(D4DK) structure. This field can be changed by drivers or modules.

The **q_maxpsz** field is the maximum packet size for the queue. This is an advisory limit specifying the largest message that can be accepted by the queue. It is initially set to the value specified by the **mi_maxpsz** field in the **module_info** structure. This field can be changed by drivers or modules.

The **q_hiwat** field is the high water mark for the queue. This specifies the number of bytes of data contained in messages on the queue such that the queue is considered full, and hence flow-controlled. It is initially set to the value specified by the **mi_hiwat** field in the **module_info** structure. This field can be changed by drivers or modules.

The **q_lowat** field is the low water mark for the queue. This specifies the number of bytes of data contained in messages on the queue such that the queue is no longer flow-controlled. It is initially set to the value specified by the **mi_lowat** field in the **module_info** structure. This field can be changed by drivers or modules.

NOTES
The **queue** structure is defined as type **queue_t**.

SEE ALSO
getq(D3DK), **putq**(D3DK), **strqget**(D3DK), **strqset**(D3DK), **module_info**(D4DK), **msgb**(D4DK), **qinit**(D4DK)

NAME

streamtab – STREAMS driver and module declaration structure

SYNOPSIS

```
#include <sys/stream.h>
```

DESCRIPTION

Each STREAMS driver or module must have a **streamtab** structure. The stream-tab structure must be named *prefix***info**, where *prefix* is the driver prefix.

The **streamtab** structure is made up of pointers to **qinit** structures for both the read and write queue portions of each module or driver. (Multiplexing drivers require both upper and lower **qinit** structures.) The **qinit** structure contains the entry points through which the module or driver routines are called.

STRUCTURE MEMBERS

```
struct qinit   *st_rdinit;    /* read queue */
struct qinit   *st_wrinit;    /* write queue */
struct qinit   *st_muxrinit;  /* lower read queue*/
struct qinit   *st_muxwinit;  /* lower write queue*/
```

The **st_rdinit** field contains a pointer to the read-side **qinit** structure. For a multiplexing driver, this is the **qinit** structure for the upper read side.

The **st_wrinit** field contains a pointer to the write-side **qinit** structure. For a multiplexing driver, this is the **qinit** structure for the upper write side.

The **st_muxrinit** field contains a pointer to the lower read-side **qinit** structure for multiplexing drivers. For modules and non-multiplexing drivers, this field should be set to **NULL**.

The **st_muxwinit** field contains a pointer to the lower write-side **qinit** structure for multiplexing drivers. For modules and non-multiplexing drivers, this field should be set to **NULL**.

SEE ALSO

qinit(D4DK)

NAME

    `stroptions` – stream head option structure

SYNOPSIS

```
#include <sys/stream.h>
#include <sys/stropts.h>
```

DESCRIPTION

    The **stroptions** structure, used in an **M_SETOPTS** or **M_PCSETOPTS** message, contains options for the stream head. The message is sent upstream by drivers and modules when they want to change stream head options for their stream.

STRUCTURE MEMBERS

```
ulong_t   so_flags;    /* options to set */
short     so_readopt;  /* read option */
ushort_t  so_wroff;    /* write offset */
long      so_minpsz;   /* minimum read packet size */
long      so_maxpsz;   /* maximum read packet size */
ulong_t   so_hiwat;    /* read queue high water mark */
ulong_t   so_lowat;    /* read queue low water mark */
uchar_t   so_band;     /* band for water marks */
```

    The **so_flags** field determines which options are to be set, and which of the other fields in the structure are used. This field is a bitmask and is comprised of the bit-wise OR of the following flags:

SO_READOPT   Set the read option to that specified by the **so_readopt** field.

SO_WROFF   Set the write offset to that specified by the **so_wroff** field.

SO_MINPSZ   Set the minimum packet size on the stream head read queue to that specified by the **so_minpsz** field.

SO_MAXPSZ   Set the maximum packet size on the stream head read queue to that specified by the **so_maxpsz** field.

SO_HIWAT   Set the high water mark on the stream head read queue to that specified by the **so_hiwat** field.

SO_LOWAT   Set the low water mark on the stream head read queue to that specified by the **so_lowat** field.

SO_ALL   Set all of the above options (SO_READOPT | SO_WROFF | SO_MINPSZ | SO_MAXPSZ | SO_HIWAT | SO_LOWAT).

SO_MREADON   Turn on generation of **M_READ** messages by the stream head.

SO_MREADOFF   Turn off generation of **M_READ** messages by the stream head.

SO_NDELON   Use old TTY semantics for no-delay reads and writes.

SO_NDELOFF   Use STREAMS semantics for no-delay reads and writes.

SO_ISTTY   The stream is acting as a terminal.

SO_ISNTTY   The stream is no longer acting as a terminal.

SO_TOSTOP   Stop processes on background writes to this stream.

SO_TONSTOP   Don't stop processes on background writes to this stream.

SO_BAND   The water marks changes affect the priority band specified by the **so_band** field.

The **so_readopt** field specifies options for the stream head that alter the way it handles **read**(2) calls. This field is a bitmask whose flags are grouped in sets. Within a set, the flags are mutually exclusive. The first set of flags determines how data messages are treated when they are read:

RNORM   Normal (byte stream) mode. **read** returns the lesser of the number of bytes asked for and the number of bytes available. Messages with partially read data are placed back on the head of the stream head read queue. This is the default behavior.

RMSGD   Message discard mode. **read** returns the lesser of the number of bytes asked for and the number of bytes in the first message on the stream head read queue. Messages with partially read data are freed.

RMSGN   Message non-discard mode. **read** returns the lesser of the number of bytes asked for and the number of bytes in the first message on the stream head read queue. Messages with partially read data are placed back on the head of the stream head read queue.

The second set of flags determines how protocol messages (**M_PROTO** and **M_PCPROTO**) are treated during a **read**:

RPROTNORM   Normal mode. **read** fails with the error code **EBADMSG** if there is a protocol message at the front of the stream head read queue. This is the default behavior.

RPROTDIS   Protocol discard mode. **read** discards the **M_PROTO** or **M_PCPROTO** portions of the message and return any **M_DATA** portions that may be present. **M_PASSFP** messages are also freed in this mode.

RPROTDAT   Protocol data mode. **read** treats the **M_PROTO** or **M_PCPROTO** portions of the message as if they were normal data (that is, they are delivered to the user.)

The **so_wroff** field specifies a byte offset to be included in the first message block of every **M_DATA** message created by a **write**(2) and the first **M_DATA** message block created by each call to **putmsg**(2).

The **so_minpsz** field specifies the minimum packet size for the stream head read queue.

The **so_maxpsz** field specifies the maximum packet size for the stream head read queue.

The **so_hiwat** field specifies the high water mark for the stream head read queue.

The **so_lowat** field specifies the low water mark for the stream head read queue.

The **so_band** field specifies the priority band to which the high and/or low water mark changes should be applied.

SEE ALSO

streamio(7) in the *Programmer's Guide: STREAMS*

datab(D4DK), **msgb**(D4DK), **messages**(D5DK)

read(2) in the *Programmer's Reference Manual*

NAME

uio – scatter/gather I/O request structure

SYNOPSIS

```
#include <sys/types.h>
#include <sys/file.h>
#include <sys/uio.h>
```

DESCRIPTION

The **uio** structure describes an I/O request that can be broken up into different data storage areas (scatter/gather I/O). A request is a list of **iovec**(D4DK) structures (base/length pairs) indicating where in user space or kernel space the data are to be read/written.

The contents of the **uio** structure passed to the driver through the entry points in section D2 should not be changed directly by the driver. The **uiomove**(D3DK), **ureadc**(D3DK), and **uwritec**(D3DK) functions take care of maintaining the the **uio** structure. A block driver may also use the **physiock**(D3DK) function to perform unbuffered I/O. **physiock** also takes care of maintaining the **uio** structure.

A driver that creates its own **uio** structures for a data transfer is responsible for zeroing it prior to initializing members accessible to the driver. The driver must not change the **uio** structure afterwards; the functions take care of maintaining the **uio** structure.

STRUCTURE MEMBERS

```
iovec_t  *uio_iov;    /* Pointer to the start of the iovec */
                      /* array for the uio structure */
int      uio_iovcnt;  /* The number of iovecs in the array */
off_t    uio_offset;  /* Offset into file where data are */
                      /* transferred from or to */
short    uio_segflg;  /* Identifies the type of I/O transfer */
short    uio_fmode;   /* File mode flags */
int      uio_resid;   /* Residual count */
```

The driver may only set **uio** structure members to initialize them for a data transfer for which the driver created the **uio** structure. The driver must not otherwise change **uio** structure members. However, drivers may read them. The **uio** structure members available for the driver to test or set are described below:

uio_iov contains a pointer to the **iovec** array for the **uio** structure. If the driver creates a **uio** structure for a data transfer, an associated **iovec** array must also be created by the driver.

uio_iovcnt contains the number of elements in the **iovec** array for the **uio** structure.

uio_offset contains the starting logical byte address on the device where the data transfer is to occur. Applicability of this field to the the driver is device-dependent. It applies to randomly accessed devices, but may not apply to all sequentially accessed devices.

uio_segflg identifies the virtual address space in which the transfer data areas reside. The value **UIO_SYSSPACE** indicates the data areas are within kernel space. The value **UIO_USERSPACE** indicates one data area is within kernel space and the other is within the user space of the current process context.

uio_fmode contains flags describing the file access mode for which the data transfer is to occur. Valid flags are:

FNDELAY   The driver should not wait if the requested data transfer cannot occur immediately; it should terminate the request without indicating an error occurred. The driver's implementation of this flag's implied semantics are subject to device-dependent interpretation.

FNONBLOCK   The driver should not wait if the requested data transfer cannot occur immediately; it should terminate the request, returning the **EAGAIN** error code as the completion status [see **errnos**(D5DK)]. The driver's implementation of the implied semantics of this flag are subject to device-dependent interpretation.

If the driver creates a **uio** structure for a data transfer, it may set the flags described above in **uio_fmode**.

uio_resid indicates the number of bytes that have not been transferred to or from the data area. If the driver creates a **uio** structure for a data transfer, **uio_resid** is initialized by the driver as the number of bytes to be transferred.

NOTES

A separate interface does not currently exist for allocating **uio**(D4DK) and **iovec**(D4DK) structures when the driver needs to create them itself. Therefore, the driver may either use **kmem_zalloc**(D3DK) to allocate them, or allocate them statically.

SEE ALSO

read(D2DK), **write**(D2DK), **physiock**(D3DK), **uiomove**(D3DK), **ureadc**(D3DK), **uwritec**(D3DK), **iovec**(D4DK)

NAME

    intro – introduction to DMA data structures

SYNOPSIS

    #include <sys/types.h>
    #include <sys/dma.h>
    #include <sys/ddi.h>

DESCRIPTION

This section describes the data structures available for use by device drivers that directly program DMA controllers. Intel 80x86-based implementations that support DMA by having drivers directly program DMA controllers define these structures in **sys/dma.h**.

Driver developers should not declare arrays of these structures, as the size of any structure might change between releases. Drivers can only reference those structure members described on the manual page. The actual data structures may have additional structure members beyond those described, but drivers must not reference them.

DMA DATA STRUCTURES (D4X)

NAME

dma_buf – DMA buffer descriptor structure

SYNOPSIS

```
#include <sys/types.h>
#include <sys/dma.h>
```

DESCRIPTION

The DMA buffer descriptor structure is used to specify the data to be transferred by a DMA operation. Each DMA operation is controlled by a DMA command block [see dma_cb(D4X)] structure that includes pointers to two dma_buf structures.

Each dma_buf structure provides the physical address and size of a data block involved in a DMA transfer. Scatter/gather operations involving multiple data blocks may be implemented by linking together multiple dma_bufs in a singly-linked list. Each dma_buf includes both the virtual and physical address of the next DMA buffer descriptor in the list.

DMA buffer descriptor structures should only be allocated via dma_get_buf(D3X). Although drivers may access the members listed below, they should not make any assumptions about the size of the structure or the contents of other fields in the structure.

STRUCTURE MEMBERS

```
ushort_t        count;        /* size of block*/
paddr_t         address;      /* physical address of data block */
paddr_t         physical;     /* physical address of next dma_buf */
struct dma_buf  *next_buf;    /* next buffer descriptor */
ushort_t        count_hi;     /* for big blocks */
```

The members of the dma_buf structure are:

count specifies the low-order 16 bits of the size of the data block in bytes.

address specifies the physical address of the data block.

physical specifies the physical address of the next dma_buf in a linked list of DMA buffers descriptors. It should be NULL if the buffer descriptor is the last one in the list. Note that a DMA buffer descriptor allocated by dma_get_buf will be zeroed out initially, thus no explicit initialization is required for this field if a value of NULL is desired.

next_buf specifies the virtual address of the next dma_buf in a linked list of DMA buffer descriptors. It should be NULL if the buffer descriptor is the last one in the list. Note that a DMA buffer descriptor allocated by dma_get_buf will be zeroed out initially, thus no explicit initialization is required for this field if a value of NULL is desired.

count_hi specifies the high-order 16 bits of the size of the data block in bytes. Since a dma_buf allocated by dma_get_buf is initially zeroed out, no explicit initialization is required for this field if the size of the data block may be specified by a ushort_t.

SEE ALSO
    dma_free_buf(D3X), dma_get_buf(D3X), dma_cb(D4X)

NAME
>   dma_cb – DMA command block structure

SYNOPSIS
>   #include <sys/types.h>
>   #include <sys/dma.h>

DESCRIPTION
>   The DMA command block structure is used to control a DMA operation. Each
>   DMA operation requested by a driver is controlled by a command block structure
>   whose fields specify the operation to occur.

>   A number of fields of the DMA control block come in pairs: one for the requestor
>   and one for the target. The requestor is the hardware device that is requesting
>   the DMA operation, while the target is the target of the operation. The typical
>   case is one in which the requestor is an I/O device and the target is memory.

>   DMA command block structures should only be allocated via dma_get_cb(D3X).
>   Although drivers may access the structure members listed below, they should not
>   make any assumptions about the size of the structure or the contents of other
>   fields in the structure.

STRUCTURE MEMBERS

```
struct dma_buf  *targbufs;   /* list of target data buffers */
struct dma_buf  *reqrbufs;   /* list of requestor data buffers */
uchar_t         command;     /* Read/Write/Translate/Verify */
uchar_t         targ_type;   /* Memory/IO */
uchar_t         reqr_type;   /* Memory/IO  */
uchar_t         targ_step;   /* Inc/Dec/Hold  */
uchar_t         reqr_step;   /* Inc/Dec/Hold  */
uchar_t         trans_type;  /* Single/Demand/Block/Cascade */
uchar_t         targ_path;   /* 8/16/32 */
uchar_t         reqr_path;   /* 8/16/32 */
uchar_t         cycles;      /* 1 or 2 */
uchar_t         bufprocess;  /* Single/Chain/Auto-Init */
char            *procparam;  /* parameter buffer for appl call */
int             (*proc)();   /* address of application call routines */
```

>   The members of the dma_cb structure are:

>   targbufs is a pointer to a list of DMA buffer structures [see dma_buf(D4X)] that
>   describes the target of the DMA operation.

>   reqrbufs is a pointer to a list of DMA buffer structures [see dma_buf(D4X)] that
>   describes the requestor of the DMA operation.

>   command specifies the command for the DMA operation. It may be one of the fol-
>   lowing:

>   DMA_CMD_READ   Specifies a DMA read from the target to the requestor.

>   DMA_CMD_WRITE   Specifies a DMA write from the requestor to the target.

targ_type and reqr_type specify the type of the target and requestor, respectively. They each may have one of the following values:

DMA_TYPE_MEM   Specifies that the target (or requestor) is memory.

DMA_TYPE_IO   Specifies that the target (or requestor) is an I/O device.

targ_step and reqr_step specify how the target and requestor addresses are to be modified after each transfer. They each may have one of the following values:

DMA_STEP_INC   Specifies that the target (or requestor) address is to be incremented following each data transfer.

DMA_STEP_DEC   Specifies that the target (or requestor) address is to be decremented following each data transfer

DMA_STEP_HOLD   Specifies that the target (or requestor) address is to remain the same following each data transfer.

trans_type specifies the transfer type of the operation. It can have one of the following values:

DMA_TRANS_SNGL   Specifies that a single transfer is to occur.

DMA_TRANS_BLCK   Specifies that a block transfer is to occur. This is the only acceptable value for software-initiated transfers.

DMA_TRANS_DMND   Specifies demand transfer mode, which is a variation on block transfer in which the requestor may provide additional control flow on the transfer.

targ_path and reqr_path specify the size of the data path for the target and requestor, respectively. They each may have one of the following values:

DMA_PATH_8   Specifies that the target (or requestor) uses an eight-bit data path.

DMA_PATH_16   Specifies that the target (or requestor) uses a 16-bit data path.

DMA_PATH_32   Specifies that the target (or requestor) uses a 32-bit data path.

DMA_PATH_64   Specifies that the target (or requestor) uses a 64-bit data path.

cycles is an integer that specifies the number of cycles required for each transfer. Its value should be taken from the result of dma_get_best_mode(D3X).

bufprocess specifies how the DMA target buffer structures are to be processed. It may have the following values:

DMA_BUF_SNGL   Specifies that the target consists of a single DMA Buffer.

DMA_BUF_CHAIN   Specifies that the target consists of a chain of DMA Buffers.

procparam is the parameter to be passed to the subroutine specified by the proc field.

proc specifies the address of a routine to be called when a DMA operation is successfully set up by dma_swsetup(D3X). The value in the procparam field is passed as an argument to this routine. This field may be set to NULL if no procedure is to be called.

SEE ALSO
  dma_free_cb(D3X), dma_get_best_mode(D3X), dma_get_cb(D3X),
  dma_prog(D3X), dma_swsetup(D3X), dma_swstart(D3X), dma_buf(D4X)

NAME

intro – introduction to kernel **#define**'s

SYNOPSIS

```
#include <sys/types.h>
#include <sys/ddi.h>
```

DESCRIPTION

This section describes the kernel **#define**'s a developer may need to use in a device driver. Most **#define**'s are specified on the manual page in which they are used. However, some **#define**'s are too general or numerous to include in another manual page. Instead, they have been given a separate page in this section.

NOTE

`#include <sys/ddi.h>` must always be the last header file included.

KERNEL DEFINES (D5)

KERNEL DEFINES (D5)

NAME
errnos – error numbers

SYNOPSIS
#include <sys/errno.h>

DESCRIPTION
The following is a list of the error codes that drivers may return from their entry points, or include in STREAMS messages (for example, **M_ERROR** messages).

EACCES	Permission denied. An attempt was made to access a file in a way forbidden by its file access permissions.
EADDRINUSE	The address requested is already in use.
EADDRNOTAVAIL	The address requested cannot be assigned.
EAFNOSUPPORT	The address family specified is not installed or supported on the host.
EAGAIN	Temporary resource allocation failure; try again later. Drivers can return this error when resource allocation fails, for example, **kmem_alloc**(D3DK) or **allocb**(D3DK).
EALREADY	The operation requested is already being performed.
EBUSY	Device is busy. This can be used for devices that require exclusive access.
ECONNABORTED	A received connect request was aborted when the peer closed its endpoint.
ECONNREFUSED	The connection was refused.
ECONNRESET	The connection was reset by the peer entity.
EDESTADDRREQ	The requested operation required a destination address but none was supplied.
EFAULT	Bad address. Drivers should return this error whenever a call to **copyin**(D3DK) or **copyout**(D3DK) fails.
EHOSTDOWN	Host is down.
EHOSTUNREACH	No route to host.
EINPROGRESS	The operation requested is now in progress.
EINTR	Interrupted operation. Drivers can return this error whenever an interruptible operation is interrupted by receipt of an asynchronous signal.
EINVAL	Invalid argument. Drivers can return this error for operations that have invalid parameters specified.
EIO	An I/O error has occurred. Drivers can return this error when an input or output request has failed.
EISCONN	The endpoint is already connected.

EMSGSIZE	Message too long. The protocol is such that there is a limit to the size of a message and that limit has been exceeded.
ENETDOWN	The network trying to be reached is down.
ENETRESET	The network dropped the connection because of a reset.
ENETUNREACH	The network trying to be reached is unreachable.
ENOBUFS	No buffer space available.
ENODEV	No such device. Drivers can return this error when an attempt is made to apply an inappropriate function to a device; for example, trying to write a write-protected medium.
ENOMEM	Not enough memory. Drivers can return this error when resource allocation fails and it is either inconvenient or impossible for a retry to occur.
ENOPROTOOPT	The protocol option requested is not available at the level indicated.
ENOSPC	The device is out of free space.
ENOTCONN	The requested operation requires the endpoint to be connected but it is not.
ENXIO	No such device or address. Drivers can return this error when trying to open an invalid minor device, or when trying to perform I/O past the end of a device.
EOPNOTSUPP	The operation requested is not supported.
EPERM	Permission denied. Drivers can return this error when a operation is attempted that requires more privilege than the current process has.
EPROTO	Protocol error. Drivers can return this error when they incur a protocol error, such as not being able to generate the proper protocol message because of resource exhaustion, and not being able to recover gracefully.
ETIMEDOUT	The connection timed out.

NOTES

The above examples are not exhaustive.

SEE ALSO

bioerror(D3DK), geterror(D3DK)

NAME

messages – STREAMS messages

SYNOPSIS

```
#include <sys/stream.h>
```

DESCRIPTION

The following is a list of the STREAMS messages types that can be used by drivers and modules.

M_DATA	Data message.
M_PROTO	Protocol control message.
M_BREAK	Control message used to generate a line break.
M_SIG	Control message used to send a signal to processes.
M_DELAY	Control message used to generate a real-time delay.
M_CTL	Control message used between neighboring modules and drivers.
M_IOCTL	Control message used to indicate a user **ioctl**(2) request.
M_SETOPTS	Control message used to set stream head options.
M_IOCACK	High priority control message used to indicate success of an **ioctl** request.
M_IOCNAK	High priority control message used to indicate failure of an **ioctl** request.
M_PCPROTO	High priority protocol control message.
M_PCSIG	High priority control message used to send a signal to processes.
M_READ	High priority control message used to indicate the occurrence of a **read**(2) when there are no data on the stream head read queue.
M_FLUSH	High priority control message used to indicate that queues should be flushed.
M_STOP	High priority control message used to indicate that output should be stopped immediately.
M_START	High priority control message used to indicate that output can be restarted.
M_HANGUP	High priority control message used to indicate that the device has been disconnected.
M_ERROR	High priority control message used to indicate that the stream has incurred a fatal error.
M_COPYIN	High priority control message used during transparent **ioctl** processing to copy data from the user to a STREAMS message.

M_COPYOUT　　　High priority control message used during transparent `ioctl` processing to copy data from a STREAMS message to the user.

M_IOCDATA　　　High priority control message used during transparent `ioctl` processing to return the status and data of a previous **M_COPYIN** or **M_COPYOUT** request.

M_STOPI　　　High priority control message used to indicate that input should be stopped immediately.

M_STARTI　　　High priority control message used to indicate that input can be restarted.

M_PCCTL　　　High priority control message used between neighboring modules and drivers.

M_PCSETOPTS　　　High priority control message used to set stream head options.

SEE ALSO

put(D2DK), srv(D2DK), allocb(D3DK), copyreq(D4DK), copyresp(D4DK), datab(D4DK), iocblk(D4DK), linkblk(D4DK), msgb(D4DK), stroptions(D4DK)

NAME

signals – signal numbers

SYNOPSIS

#include <sys/signal.h>

DESCRIPTION

There are two ways to send a signal to a process. The first, **proc_signal**(D3DK), can be used by non-STREAMS drivers. The second, by using an **M_SIG** or **M_PCSIG** message, can be used by STREAMS drivers and modules. The following is a list of the signals that drivers may send to processes.

SIGHUP   The device has been disconnected.

SIGINT   The interrupt character has been received.

SIGQUIT   The quit character has been received.

SIGWINCH   The window size has changed.

SIGURG   Urgent data are available.

SIGPOLL   A pollable event has occurred.

SIGTSTP   Interactive stop of the process.

NOTES

The signal **SIGTSTP** cannot be generated with **proc_signal**. It is only valid when generated from a stream.

SEE ALSO

proc_ref(D3DK), **proc_signal**(D3DK), **proc_unref**(D3DK)

A Appendix A: Migration from Release 3.2 to Release 4 Multi-Processor

Appendix A: Migration from Release 3.2 to Release 4 Multi-Processor

The *UNIX System V Block and Character Interface (BCI) Reference Manual* defined the functions, routines, and structures appropriate for use by drivers in the UNIX System V Release 3.2 environment. Many, but not all, of the routines in the BCI have been incorporated into the Device Driver Interface as is or, in the case of macros, reimplemented as procedures.

The functionality of some other BCI routines has been incorporated into the DDI/DKI either by renaming the BCI routine, but otherwise providing the identical interface, or by replacing the BCI routine with a different, but similar, interface. Still other BCI routines provide functionality that is obsolete; these routines have been dropped, and there are no DDI/DKI routines that provide similar functionality.

Because compatibility for BCI routines is not provided, drivers must be converted to use the DDI/DKI. Table A-1 is intended to assist developers in this task by summarizing the correspondence between routines in the BCI and routines in the DDI/DKI.

Each entry in the table lists the name of the BCI routine, some comments about changes made to the routine in the DDI/DKI, and the name of the corresponding Release 4 Multi-Processor DDI/DKI routine. Routines are categorized as follows:

- No change. The BCI routine has been retained in the DDI/DKI with the same name, interface, and functionality.

- Macro reimplemented as procedure. A BCI macro has been retained in the DDI/DKI, but has been implemented as a procedure with the identical calling and return syntax.

- New restrictions. The routine remains in the DDI/DKI with the same interface and functionality, but new restrictions are placed on its use.

- Extended. The interface to the routine remains the same, but the semantics have been changed in a compatible manner.

- Renamed. The BCI routine has been retained in the DDI/DKI with a different name, but otherwise provides the same interface and functionality.

■ Replaced. The BCI routine has been removed from the DDI/DKI. The DDI/DKI provides a new interface that provides a similar function.

■ Obsolete interface. The BCI routine has been removed from the DDI/DKI. The DDI/DKI does not provide a new interface; the interface itself is obsolete. For instance, the DDI/DKI does not support clist-based drivers; thus any routines dealing with clists have been removed from the DDI/DKI.

Again, please note that this table is a guide for programmers attempting to convert old driver source from BCI to DDI/DKI.

Table A-1: 3.2 to Release 4 Multi-Processor Migration

BCI	Comments	Release 4 Multi-Processor DDI/DKI
`adjmsg`	No change	`adjmsg`
`allocb`	No change; for memory-mapped I/O, use `esballoc`	`allocb`
`backq`	Obsolete interface.	—
`bcopy`	No change	`bcopy`
`brelse`	No change	`brelse`
`btoc`	Replaced	`btop`, `btopr`
`bufcall`	No change; don't use with `esballoc`	`bufcall`
`bzero`	Word alignment no longer required	`bzero`
`canon`	Obsolete interface.	—
`canput`	New restrictions; use `canputnext(q)` instead of `canput(q->q_next)`; stream cannot be frozen; use `bcanput` to test specific priority band	`canput`
`clrbuf`	No change	`clrbuf`
`cmn_err`	New restrictions; cannot hold locks if *level* is `CE_PANIC`	`cmn_err`
`copyb`	No change	`copyb`
`copyin`	New restrictions; cannot hold basic locks or read/write locks	`copyin` or `uiomove`
`copymsg`	No change	`copymsg`

Table A-1: 3.2 to Release 4 Multi-Processor Migration (continued)

BCI	Comments	Release 4 Multi-Processor DDI/DKI
copyout	New restrictions; cannot hold basic locks or read/write locks	copyout or uiomove
ctob	Replaced	ptob
datamsg	No change	datamsg
delay	New restrictions; cannot hold basic locks or read/write locks	delay
dma_alloc	Obsolete interface.	—
dma_breakup	Replaced	dma_pageio
dma_enable	No change	dma_enable
dma_param	Replaced	dma_prog
dma_relse	Obsolete interface.	—
dma_resid	Obsolete interface.	—
dma_start	Replaced	dma_swstart
dupb	No change	dupb
dupmsg	No change	dupmsg
enableok	Macro reimplemented as function and new restrictions; stream cannot be frozen	enableok
flushq	New restrictions; stream cannot be frozen; use **flushband** to flush specific priority band	flushq
freeb	No change	freeb
freemsg	No change	freemsg
fubyte	Replaced	copyin, uiomove, or uwritec
fuword	Replaced	copyin, uiomove, or uwritec
getc	Obsolete interface.	—
getcb	Obsolete interface.	—
getcf	Obsolete interface.	—
geteblk	New restrictions; cannot hold basic locks or	geteblk

Table A-1: 3.2 to Release 4 Multi-Processor Migration (continued)

BCI	Comments	Release 4 Multi-Processor DDI/DKI
	read/write locks; use **ngeteblk** or **getrbuf** for alternate buffer sizes	
getq	New restrictions; stream cannot be frozen	getq
inb	No change	inb
ind	Renamed only	inl
insq	New restrictions; stream must be frozen	insq
inw	No change	inw
iodone	Renamed only	biodone
iomove	Replaced	uiomove
iowait	Renamed and new restrictions; cannot hold basic locks or read/write locks	biowait
kseg	Obsolete interface.	kmem_alloc
linkb	No change	linkb
longjmp	Obsolete interface.	—
major	Renamed; macro reimplemented as function	getmajor
makedev	Renamed; macro reimplemented as function	makedevice
malloc	Renamed only	rmalloc
mapinit	Replaced	rmallocmap
mapwant	Replaced	rmalloc_wait
max	No change	max
mfree	Renamed only	rmfree
min	No change	min
minor	Renamed; macro reimplemented as function	getminor
msgdsize	No change	msgdsize
noenable	Macro reimplemented as function and new restrictions; stream cannot be frozen	noenable
OTHERQ	Macro reimplemented as function	OTHERQ
outb	No change	outb
outd	Renamed only	outl
outw	No change	outw
physck	Replaced; functionality included in **physiock**	physiock

Table A-1: 3.2 to Release 4 Multi-Processor Migration (continued)

BCI	Comments	Release 4 Multi-Processor DDI/DKI
physio	Replaced; functionality included in **physiock**	physiock
psignal	Replaced	proc_signal
pullupmsg	Replaced	msgpullup
putbq	New restrictions; stream cannot be frozen	putbq
putc	Obsolete interface.	—
putcb	Obsolete interface.	—
putcf	Obsolete interface.	—
putctl	New restrictions; use **putnextctl(q, type)** instead of **putctl(q->q_next, type)**; cannot hold locks; stream cannot be frozen	putctl
putctl1	New restrictions; use **putnextctl1(q, type, param)** instead of **putctl1(q->q_next, type, param)**; cannot hold locks; stream cannot be frozen	putctl1
putnext	Macro reimplemented as function and new restrictions; cannot hold locks; stream cannot be frozen	putnext
putq	New restrictions; stream cannot be frozen	putq
qenable	New restrictions; stream cannot be frozen	qenable
qreply	New restrictions; cannot hold locks; stream cannot be frozen	qreply
qsize	New restrictions; stream cannot be frozen	qsize
RD	Macro reimplemented as function and extended. Accepts both read and write queue pointers	RD
repinsb	No change	repinsb
repinsd	No change	repinsd
repinsw	No change	repinsw
repoutsb	No change	repoutsb
repoutsd	No change	repoutsd
repoutsw	No change	repoutsw

Table A-1: 3.2 to Release 4 Multi-Processor Migration (continued)

BCI	Comments	Release 4 Multi-Processor DDI/DKI
`rmvb`	No change	`rmvb`
`rmvq`	New restrictions; stream must be frozen	`rmvq`
`signal`	Obsolete interface.	—
`sleep`	Replaced	`SV_WAIT_SIG`
`spl`	Replaced; `spl0`, `spl1`, `spl4`, `spl5`, `spl6`, `spl7` functions eliminated; `splbase`, `spltimeout`, `spldisk` added	`spl`
`splx`	No change	`splx`
`sptalloc`	Obsolete interface.	`kmem_alloc` or `physmap`
`sptfree`	Obsolete interface.	`kmem_free`
`strlog`	No change	`strlog`
`subyte`	Replaced	`copyout`, `uiomove`, or `ureadc`
`suser`	Replaced	`drv_priv`
`suword`	Replaced	`copyout`, `uiomove`, or `ureadc`
`testb`	Obsolete interface.	—
`timeout`	Replaced	`itimeout`
`ttclose`	Obsolete interface.	—
`ttin`	Obsolete interface.	—
`ttinit`	Obsolete interface.	—
`ttiocom`	Obsolete interface.	—
`ttioctl`	Obsolete interface.	—
`ttopen`	Obsolete interface.	—
`ttout`	Obsolete interface.	—
`ttread`	Obsolete interface.	—
`ttrstrt`	Obsolete interface.	—
`tttimeo`	Obsolete interface.	—

Table A-1: 3.2 to Release 4 Multi-Processor Migration (continued)

BCI	Comments	Release 4 Multi-Processor DDI/DKI
ttwrite	Obsolete interface.	—
ttxput	Obsolete interface.	—
ttyflush	Obsolete interface.	—
ttywait	Obsolete interface.	—
unkseg	Obsolete interface.	kmem_free
unlinkb	No change	unlinkb
untimeout	Interface changed and new restrictions; argument type changed from **int** to **toid_t**; cannot hold locks	untimeout
useracc	Replaced; functionality included in **physiock**	physiock
vtop	No change	vtop
wakeup	Replaced	SV_BROADCAST
WR	Macro reimplemented as function and extended. Accepts both read and write queue pointers	WR

The **size**(D2DK) entry point was not defined in Release 3.2. Drivers without a **size** routine have the following peculiarities:

- They may not be able to use the last few sectors on the device partition. (The number of unusable sectors is *disk_sectors_in_partition* % *disk_sectors_per_logical_block*. Typically this is zero; it must be smaller than the logical block size.)

- They pay a performance penalty because the kernel avoids some pre-fetches on devices without a **size** routine.

B   Appendix B: Migration from Release 4 to Release 4 Multi-Processor

Appendix B: Migration from Release 4 to Release 4 Multi-Processor

To make the UNIX System V Release 4 DDI/DKI more amenable to a multiprocessing environment, some Release 4 DDI/DKI kernel utility routines have been changed or removed. In addition, many new routines have been added. This appendix contains two tables: one shows how existing routines have been changed or removed, and the other lists new routines.

Changes to Release 4 DDI/DKI Routines

The functionality of some Release 4 DDI/DKI routines has been incorporated into the Release 4 Multi-Processor DDI/DKI by providing a new routine with a different, but similar, interface. Still other routines provided functionality that was obsolete; these routines have been dropped, and there are no DDI/DKI routines that provide similar functionality. In all cases the Release 4 routine is provided in Release 4 Multi-Processor for compatibility.

While compatibility with Release 4 routines is provided, it is still desirable to convert drivers to use the Release 4 Multi-Processor DDI/DKI if possible because the older routines will not be supported in future releases. Table B-1 is intended to assist developers in this task by summarizing the correspondence between routines in Release 4 and routines in Release 4 Multi-Processor.

Each entry in the table lists the name of the routine, some comments about changes made to the routine in the DDI/DKI, and the name of the corresponding Release 4 Multi-Processor DDI/DKI routine. Routines are categorized as follows:

- Replaced. The routine has been removed from the Release 4 DDI/DKI. The Release 4 Multi-Processor DDI/DKI provides a new interface that provides a similar function.

- New restrictions. The routine remains in the DDI/DKI with the same interface and functionality, but new restrictions are placed on its use.

- Extended. The interface to the routine remains the same, but the semantics have been changed in a compatible manner.

- Interface changed. The interface to the routine has changed, but the semantics remain the same.

Again, please note that this table is a guide for programmers attempting to convert old driver source from Release 4 to Release 4 Multi-Processor. All routines in the Release 4 DDI/DKI, regardless of their status in the Release 4 Multi-Processor DDI/DKI, are provided in System V Release 4 Multi-Processor for Intel Processors for compatibility.

Table B-1: Release 4 to Release 4 Multi-Processor Migration

Release 4 DDI/DKI	Comments	Release 4 Multi-Processor DDI/DKI
bcanput	New restrictions; use **bcanputnext(q, pri)** instead of **bcanput(q->q_next, pri)**; stream cannot be frozen	bcanput
biowait	New restrictions; cannot hold basic locks or read/write locks	biowait
bp_mapin	New restrictions; cannot hold basic locks or read/write locks	bp_mapin
canput	New restrictions; use **canputnext(q)** instead of **canput(q->q_next)**; stream cannot be frozen	canput
chpoll	New restrictions; size of **pollhead** structure is not guaranteed; may not call any function that sleeps	chpoll
cmn_err	New restrictions; cannot hold locks if *level* is **CE_PANIC**	cmn_err
copyin	New restrictions; cannot hold basic locks or read/write locks	copyin
copyout	New restrictions; cannot hold basic locks or read/write locks	copyout
delay	New restrictions; cannot hold basic locks or read/write locks	delay
dma_pageio	New restrictions; cannot hold basic locks or read/write locks	dma_pageio
enableok	New restrictions; stream cannot be frozen	enableok
flushband	New restrictions; stream cannot be frozen	flushband
flushq	New restrictions; stream cannot be frozen	flushq

Table B-1: Release 4 to Release 4 Multi-Processor Migration (continued)

Release 4 DDI/DKI	Comments	Release 4 Multi-Processor DDI/DKI
geteblk	New restrictions; cannot hold basic locks or read/write locks	geteblk
getq	New restrictions; stream cannot be frozen	getq
getrbuf	New restrictions; cannot hold basic locks or read/write locks if *flag* is **KM_SLEEP**	getrbuf
hat_getkpfnum	Replaced	kvtoppid
hat_getppfnum	Replaced	phystoppid
insq	New restrictions; stream must be frozen	insq
kmem_alloc	New restrictions; cannot hold basic locks or read/write locks if *flag* is **KM_SLEEP**	kmem_alloc
kmem_zalloc	New restrictions; cannot hold basic locks or read/write locks if *flag* is **KM_SLEEP**	kmem_zalloc
ngeteblk	New restrictions; cannot hold basic locks or read/write locks	ngeteblk
noenable	New restrictions; stream cannot be frozen	noenable
physiock	New restrictions; cannot hold basic locks or read/write locks	physiock
physmap	New restrictions; cannot hold basic locks or read/write locks if *flags* is **KM_SLEEP**	physmap
psignal	Replaced	proc_signal
pullupmsg	Replaced	msgpullup
putbq	New restrictions; stream cannot be frozen	putbq
putctl	New restrictions; use **putnextctl(q, type)** instead of **putctl(q->q_next, type)**; cannot hold locks; stream cannot be frozen	putctl
putctl1	New restrictions; use **putnextctl1(q, type, param)** instead of **putctl1(q->q_next, type, param)**; cannot hold locks; stream cannot be frozen	putctl1

Table B-1: Release 4 to Release 4 Multi-Processor Migration (continued)

Release 4 DDI/DKI	Comments	Release 4 Multi-Processor DDI/DKI
putnext	New restrictions; cannot hold locks; stream cannot be frozen	putnext
putq	New restrictions; stream cannot be frozen	putq
qenable	New restrictions; stream cannot be frozen	qenable
qreply	New restrictions; cannot hold locks; stream cannot be frozen	qreply
qsize	New restrictions; stream cannot be frozen	qsize
RD	Extended. Accepts both read and write queue pointers	RD
rminit	Replaced	rmallocmap
rmsetwant	Replaced	rmalloc_wait
rmvq	New restrictions; stream must be frozen	rmvq
SAMESTR	New restrictions; argument cannot reference **q_next**; stream cannot be frozen	SAMESTR
sleep	Replaced	SV_WAIT_SIG
spl	Replaced; **spl0, spl1, spl4, spl5, spl6, spl7** functions eliminated; **splbase, spltimeout, spldisk** added	spl
strqget	New restrictions; stream must be frozen	strqget
strqset	New restrictions; stream must be frozen	strqset
timeout	Replaced	itimeout
uiomove	New restrictions; cannot hold basic locks or read/write locks if *uio_segflg* is **UIO_USERSPACE**	uiomove
unbufcall	Interface changed and new restrictions; argument type changed from **int** to **toid_t**; cannot hold locks	unbufcall
untimeout	Interface changed and new restrictions; argument type changed from **int** to **toid_t**; cannot hold locks	untimeout

DDI/DKI Reference Manual

Table B-1: Release 4 to Release 4 Multi-Processor Migration (continued)

Release 4 DDI/DKI	Comments	Release 4 Multi-Processor DDI/DKI
ureadc	New restrictions; cannot hold basic locks or read/write locks if uio_segflg is UIO_USERSPACE	ureadc
uwritec	New restrictions; cannot hold basic locks or read/write locks if uio_segflg is UIO_USERSPACE	uwritec
wakeup	Replaced	SV_BROADCAST
WR	Extended. Accepts both read and write queue pointers	WR

Additions to the DDI/DKI in Release 4 Multi-Processor

Many new routines and one data structure have been added to the DDI/DKI for Release 4 Multi-Processor. Many of the additions are locks to enable drivers to be multithreaded. Use of some of these routines is described in the *Integrated Software Development Guide,* in the chapter on device drivers.

The table below lists all the new routines and data structures in the Release 4 Multi-Processor DDI/DKI, along with their section numbers and a brief description.

Table B-2: Additions to the DDI/DKI in Release 4 Multi-Processor

Routine	Section	Description
LOCK	D3DK	acquire a basic lock
LOCK_ALLOC	D3DK	allocate and initialize a basic lock
LOCK_DEALLOC	D3DK	deallocate an instance of a basic lock
RW_ALLOC	D3DK	allocate and initialize a read/write lock

Table B-2: Additions to the DDI/DKI in Release 4 Multi-Processor (continued)

Routine	Section	Description
RW_DEALLOC	D3DK	deallocate an instance of a read/write lock
RW_RDLOCK	D3DK	acquire a read/write lock in read mode
RW_TRYRDLOCK	D3DK	try to acquire a read/write lock in read mode
RW_TRYWRLOCK	D3DK	try to acquire a read/write lock in write mode
RW_UNLOCK	D3DK	release a read/write lock
RW_WRLOCK	D3DK	acquire a read/write lock in write mode
SLEEP_ALLOC	D3DK	allocate and initialize a sleep lock
SLEEP_DEALLOC	D3DK	deallocate an instance of a sleep lock
SLEEP_LOCK	D3DK	acquire a sleep lock
SLEEP_LOCKAVAIL	D3DK	query whether a sleep lock is available
SLEEP_LOCKOWNED	D3DK	query whether a sleep lock is held by the caller
SLEEP_LOCK_SIG	D3DK	acquire a sleep lock
SLEEP_TRYLOCK	D3DK	try to acquire a sleep lock
SLEEP_UNLOCK	D3DK	release a sleep lock
SV_ALLOC	D3DK	allocate and initialize a synchronization variable
SV_BROADCAST	D3DK	wake up all processes sleeping on a synchronization variable
SV_DEALLOC	D3DK	deallocate an instance of a synchronization variable
SV_SIGNAL	D3DK	wake up one process sleeping on a synchronization variable
SV_WAIT	D3DK	sleep on a synchronization variable
SV_WAIT_SIG	D3DK	sleep on a synchronization variable
TRYLOCK	D3DK	try to acquire a basic lock
UNLOCK	D3DK	release a basic lock
bcanputnext	D3DK	test for flow control in a specified priority band
bioerror	D3DK	manipulate error field within a buffer header
canputnext	D3DK	test for flow control in a stream
dtimeout	D3DK	execute a function on a specified processor,

Table B-2: Additions to the DDI/DKI in Release 4 Multi-Processor (continued)

Routine	Section	Description
		after a specified length of time
freezestr	D3DK	freeze the state of a stream
getnextpg	D3DK	get next page pointer
itimeout	D3DK	execute a function after a specified length of time
kvtoppid	D3DK	get physical page ID for kernel virtual address
msgpullup	D3DK	concatenate bytes in a message
pcmsg	D3DK	test whether a message is a priority control message
phalloc	D3DK	allocate and initialize a pollhead structure
phfree	D3DK	free a pollhead structure
phystoppid	D3DK	get physical page ID for physical address
pptophys	D3DK	convert page pointer to physical address
proc_ref	D3DK	obtain a reference to a process for signaling
proc_signal	D3DK	send a signal to a process
proc_unref	D3DK	release a reference to a process
put	D3DK	call a put procedure
putnextctl	D3DK	send a control message to a queue
putnextctl1	D3DK	send a control message with a one byte parameter to a queue
qprocsoff	D3DK	disable put and service routines
qprocson	D3DK	enable put and service routines
rmalloc_wait	D3DK	allocate space from a private space management map
rmallocmap	D3DK	allocate and initialize a private space management map
rmfreemap	D3DK	free a private space management map
unfreezestr	D3DK	unfreeze the state of a stream
lkinfo	D4DK	lock information structure

C Appendix C: Multibus II DDI Extensions

C. MULTIBUS II DDI EXTENSIONS

Appendix C: Multibus II DDI Extensions

This section includes the DDI-only functions that apply to Multibus II bus architectures. These functions are grouped into two functional areas: those that apply to the Multibus II Interconnect Space and those that apply to the Multibus II Transport–Kernel Interface. For further information, see the *INTEL System V/386 Multibus II Transport Protocol Specification and Designer's Guide*.

NAME

ics_agent_cmp – checks for certain board types in the designated slot

SYNOPSIS

```
#include <sys/ics.h>
int
ics_agent_cmp (table, slot)
char *table[];
int slot;
```

ARGUMENTS

table   A null -terminated list of board names.

slot   The slot id of the board.

DESCRIPTION

A map of the backplane is built at boot time. This routine checks whether a given slot contains a certain type of board.

table is an array of strings that names the types of boards to check for in the slots. *table* is terminated by a NULL pointer.

RETURN VALUE

If the board in the *slot* is one of the types that was checked for, then ics_agent_cmp returns a zero; otherwise a non-zero value is returned.

LEVEL

Base or Interrupt

NAME

ics_find _rec – reads the interconnect register of the board in the specified slot.

SYNOPSIS

```
#include <sys/ics.h>
int ics_find_rec (slot, recordid)
unsigned short slot;
unsigned char recordid;
```

ARGUMENTS

slot   the slot number of the board that will be searched

recordid   the record ID of the searched-for record

DESCRIPTION

ics_find_rec finds a specific record in the interconnect space of a board.

RETURN VALUE

If the searched-for record is found, its starting register number is returned. Otherwise, -1 is returned.

LEVEL

Base or Interrupt

SEE ALSO

ics_read(D3D), ics_write(D3D)

NAME

ics_hostid – returns the host id field of the HOST ID record in this board's interconnect space

SYNOPSIS

```
#include <sys/ics.h>
int ics_hostid()
```

DESCRIPTION

ics_hostid returns the host id field of the HOST ID record of this board's interconnect space.

RETURN VALUE

The host ID of the board

LEVEL

Base or Interrupt

NAME

ics_rdwr – reads or writes a specified number of interconnect space registers from a given cardslot ID

SYNOPSIS

```
#include <sys/ics.h>
void ics_rdwr (cmd, addr)
int cmd;
struct ics_rw_struct *addr;
```

ARGUMENTS

cmd   Either **ICS_READ_ICS** or **ICS_WRITE_ICS**.

addr   A pointer to the description of the buffers to be used for the transfer.

DESCRIPTION

The **ics_rdwr** routine reads or writes a specified number of interconnect space registers from a given cardslot ID.

In both interconnect space and in memory, *addr* is a pointer to the description of the buffers to be used for the transfer. *addr* contains fields for length and addresses.

RETURN VALUE

None

LEVEL

Base or Interrupt

SEE ALSO

ics_read(D3D), ics_write(D3D)

NAME

ics_read – reads the interconnect register of the board in the specified slot.

SYNOPSIS

```
#include <sys/ics.h>
int ics_read (slot, register)
unsigned short slot;
unsigned short register;
```

ARGUMENTS

slot　　　　　The slot id of the board.

register　　　The register number of the board's interconnect space record.

DESCRIPTION

ics_read reads the interconnect register of the board in the slot designated by the slot parameter and returns the value read.

RETURN VALUE

If there is no board in the specified slot, or if the register number specified does not exist in the interconnect space of the board, the returned value is undefined. Thus, to determine if a board is present in a slot, the vendor ID registers in the interconnect space should be used. Zero (0) in the vendor ID register is defined to indicate the absence of a board.

LEVEL

Base or Interrupt

SEE ALSO

ics_rdwr(D3D), ics_write(D3D)

NAME

ics_write – writes a value into the specified register of the board in the specified slot.

SYNOPSIS

```
#include <sys/ics.h>
int ics_write (slot, register, value)
unsigned short slot;
unsigned short register;
unsigned char value;
```

ARGUMENTS

slot   The slot id of the board.
register   The register number of the board's interconnect space record.
value   The value to be written into the specified register

DESCRIPTION

ics_write writes *value* into register number register of the board in slot number slot. If no board is in the designated slot, the results are undefined.

RETURN VALUE

If the write is successful, 0 is returned. If the register number specified does not exist in the interconnect space of the board, **EINVAL** is returned.

LEVEL

Base or Interrupt

SEE ALSO

ics_read(D3D), ics_rdwr(D3D)

NAME

mps_AMPcancel – cancels an ongoing rsvp transaction

SYNOPSIS

```
#include <sys/mps.h>
long mps_AMPcancel(chan, socid, tid)
long chan;
mb2socid_t socid;
unsigned char tid;
```

ARGUMENTS

chan Channel number received from a previous **mps_open_chan**.

socid Identifies the socket id of the socket that initiated the transaction.

tid Identifies the transaction id for the transaction to be canceled.

DESCRIPTION

mps_AMPcancel is used to cancel an ongoing rsvp transaction. This is an asynchronous operation. **mps_AMPcancel** can be used to cancel transactions initiated by another agent.

mps_AMPcancel can also be used to cancel transactions initiated by the local host. In this case, the corresponding completion message of the locally initiated transaction is returned to the user.

RETURN VALUE

When **mps_AMPcancel** is successful, 0 (zero) is returned. If *chan* or *tid* are invalid, **mps_AMPcancel** fails and -1 is returned.

LEVEL

Base or Interrupt

SEE ALSO

mps_open_chan(D3D)

NAME

mps_AMPreceive_frag – receives solicited data in fragments when buffer space is not available at the receiving agent

SYNOPSIS

```
#include <sys/mps.h>
long mps_AMPreceive_frag(chan, mbp, socid, tid, ibuf)
long chan;
mps_msgbuf_t *mbp;
mb2socid_t socid;
unsigned char tid;
struct dma_buf *ibuf;
```

ARGUMENTS

chan   Channel number received from a previous **mps_open_chan**.

mbp   Points to a message buffer.

socid   Identifies socket id of the socket which initiated the transaction.

tid   Identifies the transaction corresponding to this **mps_AMPreceive_frag**. It is obtained from the request message.

ibuf   Specifies the data buffer to receive incoming data. Indication of completion of transfer is sent to *intr* via a message.

DESCRIPTION

mps_AMPreceive_frag is used when an agent sending solicited data requests buffer space that is not available at the receiving agent. After the Buffer Reject message is sent, the receiving agent can use **mps_AMPreceive_frag** to receive the solicited data in fragments depending on the available buffer space in the receiving agent. See the *Multibus II Transport Protocol Specification and Designer's Guide* for additional information.

The **mps_AMPreceive_frag** routine queues up the message to initiate the transfer, sets up table entries to receive data messages, and returns immediately. This routine is asynchronous in operation.

Applications must ensure that **mps_AMPreceive_frag** is repeatedly used the correct number of times with the correct fragment buffer length to transfer an entire request.

RETURN VALUE

If no error is detected, 0 (zero) is returned. When an error is detected, −1 is returned.

LEVEL

Base or Interrupt

SEE ALSO

mps_open_chan(D3D)

NAME

mps_AMPreceive – receives solicited data that corresponds to an outstanding buffer request

SYNOPSIS

```
long mps_AMPreceive(chan, dsocid, omsg, ibuf)
long chan;
mb2socid_t dsocid;
mps_msgbuf_t *omsg;
struct dma_buf *ibuf;
```

ARGUMENTS

chan   Channel number received from a previous **mps_open_chan**.
dsocid Destination socket id from which the solicited data is received.
omsg   Points to a message buffer with a buffer grant message created using **mps_mk_bgrant**.
ibuf   Describes the input data buffer.

DESCRIPTION

The **mps_AMPreceive** routine is used to receive solicited data that corresponds to an outstanding buffer request. This routine is asynchronous in operation. Solicited data is received in the input data buffer.

RETURN VALUE

If no error is detected, 0 (zero) is returned. If an error is detected, −1 is returned.

LEVEL

Base or Interrupt

SEE ALSO

mps_open_chan(D3D), mps_mk_bgrant(D3D)

NAME
mps_AMPsend_rsvp – queues request messages for transmission and sets up table entries for reply messages

SYNOPSIS
```
#include <sys/mps.h>
long mps_AMPsend_rsvp(chan, omsg, obuf, ibuf)
long chan;
mps_msgbuf_t *omsg;
struct dma_buf *obuf, *ibuf;
```

ARGUMENTS
chan	Channel number received from a previous mps_open_ chan.
omsg	Points to a message buffer containing message to be sent.
obuf	Specifies a data buffer for data to be sent.
ibuf	Specifies a data buffer to receive replies.

DESCRIPTION
mps_AMPsend_rsvp queues up request messages for transmission and sets up table entries for reception of reply messages when they arrive. This routine is asynchronous in operation.

When *obuf* is NULL, the request message is assumed to be an unsolicited message. In this case mps_mk_unsol (with a non-zero *tid* obtained by a call to mps_get_tid) should be used to build the message in *omsg*. When *obuf* is not NULL, request message is assumed to be a solicited message and *obuf* points to the data. In this case mps_mk_unsol (with a non-zero *tid* obtained by a call to mps_get_tid) should be used to build the message in *omsg*.

When *obuf* is not NULL, the request message is assumed to be a solicited message and *obuf* points to the solicited data. In this case, mps_mk_sol (with a non-zero tid obtained by a call to mps_get_tid) should be used to build the message in *omsg*. If *ibuf* is NULL, the reply message is expected to be an unsolicited message.

RETURN VALUE
mps_AMPsend_rsvp returns 0 (zero) if no error is detected; otherwise, −1 is returned.

LEVEL
Base or Interrupt

SEE ALSO
mps_open_chan(D3D), mps_mk_sol(D3D), mps_mk_unsol(D3D), mps_get_tid(D3D)

NAME

mps_AMPsend_data – sends solicited data that is not part of any request-response transaction

SYNOPSIS

```
#include <sys/mps.h>
long mps_AMPsend_data(chan, omsg, obuf)
long chan;
mps_msgbuf_t *omsg;
struct dma_buf *obuf;
```

ARGUMENTS

chan 　Channel number received from a previous **mps_open_chan**.

omsg 　Points to a message buffer containing an unsolicited message used to initiate the data transfer. This message should be constructed using **mps_mk_sol** with a transaction id of 0 (zero).

obuf 　Specifies the data buffer for the data that is to be sent.

DESCRIPTION

mps_AMPsend_data is asynchronous in operation. This routine is used for solicited data transmission that is not part of any request-response transaction.

RETURN VALUE

If no error is detected, 0 (zero) is returned. When an error is detected, −1 is returned.

SEE ALSO

mps_open_chan(D3D), mps_mk_sol(D3D)

NAME

mps_AMPsend_reply – replies to a received request that is part of a request-response transaction

SYNOPSIS

```
#include <sys/mps.h>
long mps_AMPsend_reply(chan, omsg, obuf)
long chan;
mps_msgbuf_t *omsg;
struct dma_buf *obuf;
```

ARGUMENTS

chan   Channel number received from a previous **mps_open_chan**.

omsg   Points to a message buffer containing the message to be sent. The message in *omsg* should be constructed using **mps_mk_solrply** or **mps_mk_unsolrply** (depending on whether *obuf* is NULL or not) with the EOT flag set appropriately.

obuf   Points to a data buffer containing data to be sent. When *obuf* is NULL, the reply message is assumed to be an unsolicited message. When *obuf* is not NULL, the reply message is assumed to be a solicited message. A completion indication is sent via a message to the appropriate **intr** routine.

DESCRIPTION

mps_AMPsend_reply is used to send a reply in response to a received request that is part of a request-response transaction. The **mps_AMPsend_reply** routine is asynchronous in operation. **mps_AMPsend_reply** returns immediately, queuing up to send the reply. Be sure to use the *tid* from the corresponding received request.

mps_AMPsend_reply can be used to send a reply as a number of solicited fragments. The message buffer in the last reply fragment should have the *EOT* flag set to 1.

RETURN VALUE

If no error is detected, 0 (zero) is returned; otherwise −1 is returned.

LEVEL

Base or Interrupt

SEE ALSO

mps_mk_solrply(D3D), mps_mk_unsolrply(D3D), mps_open_chan(D3D)

NAME

mps_AMPsend – sends unsolicited messages that are not part of any request-response transaction

SYNOPSIS

```
#include <sys/mps.h>
long mps_AMPsend(chan, mbp)
long chan;
mps_msgbuf_t *mbp;
```

ARGUMENTS

chan   Channel number obtained from a previous **mps_open_chan** call.

mbp   Points to a message buffer obtained from the message handler. This message buffer contains the message to be sent. The user is expected to have built the message in *mbp* using **mps_mk_unsol**, **mps_mk_breject**, or **mps_mk_brdcst** with a zero *tid*.

DESCRIPTION

The **mps_AMPsend** routine is used for unsolicited data transmission that is not part of any request-response transaction. This routine is synchronous in operation. After a message buffer has been handed over to the message handler for transmission, it is assumed to be allocated to the message handler and the sender should not try to access that message buffer.

RETURN VALUE

When no error is detected, 0 (zero) is returned. If an error is encountered, −1 is returned.

LEVEL

Base or Interrupt

SEE ALSO

mps_open_chan(D3D), **mps_mk_unsol**(D3D), **mps_mk_brdcst**(D3D), **mps_mk_breject**(D3D)

NAME

mps_close_chan – closes a previously opened channel

SYNOPSIS

```
#include <sys/mps.h>
long mps_close_chan (chan)
long chan;
```

ARGUMENTS

chan   Specifies the channel to be closed.

DESCRIPTION

This routine is used to close a previously opened channel. To close a channel a device driver must identify the channel.

The **mps_close_chan** routine is synchronous in operation. **mps_close_chan** fails if a transaction is in progress on the specified channel.

RETURN VALUE

When **mps_close_chan** succeeds it returns 0 (zero). When **mps_close_chan** fails, it returns −1 and the channel is not closed.

LEVEL

Base or Interrupt

SEE ALSO

mps_open_chan(D3D)

NAME

    mps_free_dmabuf – frees a list of data buffer descriptors.

SYNOPSIS

    #include <sys/mps.h>
    void mps_free_dmabuf(*dbp*)
    struct dma_buf *dbp;

ARGUMENTS

    dbp   the head of the list to be freed.

DESCRIPTION

    The **mps_free_dmabuf** function frees a list of data buffer descriptors allocated from a previous call to **mps_get_dmabuf**

RETURN VALUE

    None

LEVEL

    Base or Interrupt

SEE ALSO

    mps_get_dmabuf(D3D)

NAME

mps_free_msgbuf – puts a buffer back into the free memory pool

SYNOPSIS

```
#include <sys/mps.h>
void mps_free_msgbuf(mbp)
mps_msgbuf_t *mbp;
```

ARGUMENTS

mbp   the message buffer to be returned to the free memory pool.

DESCRIPTION

In this function, *mbp* points to a message buffer. The buffer is put back in the free memory pool. Note that **mps_free_msgbuf** accepts a pointer to a single message buffer, not a list of message buffers to be freed.

RETURN VALUE

None

LEVEL

Base or Interrupt

SEE ALSO

mps_get_msgbuf(D3D)

NAME

    `mps_free_tid` – frees a previously allocated transaction id.

SYNOPSIS

    `#include <sys/mps.h>`
    `int mps_free_tid(`*chan*`, ` *tid*`)`
    `long chan;`
    `unsigned char tid;`

ARGUMENTS

    chan   a channel number obtained from a previous call to **mps_open_chan**.
    tid   specifies the transaction id to free.

DESCRIPTION

    The **mps_free_tid** function frees a previously allocated transaction id for the associated port id.

RETURN VALUE

    The function returns 0 (zero) if no error is encountered; otherwise −1 is returned.

LEVEL

    Base or Interrupt

SEE ALSO

    mps_open_chan(D3D), **mps_get_tid**(D3D)

NAME

mps_get_dmabuf – returns a pointer to a list of data buffer descriptors.

SYNOPSIS

```
#include <sys/mps.h>
struct dma_buf *mps_get_dmabuf(count, flag)
unsigned int    count;
int flag;
```

ARGUMENTS

count   the number of dma buffer descriptors required.

flag   determines whether the routine sleeps while waiting for resources. Valid values are **DMA_SLEEP** or **DMA_NOSLEEP**.

DESCRIPTION

The **mps_get_dmabuf** function returns a pointer to a linked list of (*count* number of) data buffer descriptors. The list is terminated by NULL in the *db_next* field of the data buffer.

RETURN VALUE

If *count* number of data buffer descriptors cannot be allocated, and *flag* = **DMA_NOSLEEP**, a NULL descriptor is returned. Otherwise, if *flag* = **DMA_SLEEP**, the routine blocks until *count* data buffer descriptors can be allocated.

LEVEL

Base or Interrupt with DMA_NOSLEEP

SEE ALSO

mps_free_dmabuf(D3D)

NAME

mps_get_msgbuf – allocates a message buffer.

SYNOPSIS

```
#include <sys/mps.h>
mps_msgbuf_t *mps_get_msgbuf(flag)
int flag;
```

ARGUMENTS

flag   Determines whether or not this routine sleeps while waiting for responses. Valid values are **KM_SLEEP** and **KM_NOSLEEP**.

DESCRIPTION

This routine allocates a message buffer. If no free message buffers are available, and *flag* = **KM_NOSLEEP**, the system returns a NULL. Otherwise, if *flag* = **KM_SLEEP**, this routine blocks until a message buffer becomes available. The returned buffer can be used to construct a message to be sent out.

RETURN VALUE

Returns a message buffer if successful, a NULL if unsuccessful.

LEVEL

Base or Interrupt with **KM_NOSLEEP**.

SEE ALSO

mps_free_msgbuf(D3D)

NAME

mps_get_reply_len – get data length for a solicited reply.

SYNOPSIS

```
#include <sys/mps.h>
long mps_get_reply_len(socid, tid)
mb2socid_t      socid;
unsigned char   tid;
```

ARGUMENTS

socid   The source socid for the solicited reply

tid   the transaction id of the solicited reply

DESCRIPTION

This function should be invoked when an rsvp completes with an unsolicited message, instead of with a a solicited message; that is, when the flags field of the final message buffer is MPS_MG_UNSOL. In this case, the **mps_get_reply_len** function returns the length of the data for the solicited reply associated with the rsvp when it is called after the transaction completes.

RETURN VALUE

A successful operation returns the length of the data. If an error occurs, 0 is returned as the data length.

LEVEL

Base or Interrupt

NAME

mps_get_soldata – copies user data from the message buffer.

SYNOPSIS

```
#include <sys/mps.h>
void mps_get_soldata(mbp, dptr, count)
mps_msgbuf_t          mbp;
unsigned char         *dptr;
unsigned long         count;
```

ARGUMENTS

mbp   pointer to message buffer

dptr   pointer to user data

count   number of bytes to transfer (Max 16)

DESCRIPTION

The **mps_get_soldata** function copies count bytes of data from the message buffer *mbp* to *dptr*. It is used to retrieve user data from a buffer request message. A maximum of 16 bytes of user data can be copied.

RETURN VALUE

None

LEVEL

Base or Interrupt

SEE ALSO

mps_get_unsoldata(D3D)

NAME

    `mps_get_tid` – allocates transaction ids.

SYNOPSIS

    `#include <sys/mps.h>`
    `unsigned char mps_get_tid(`*chan*`)`
    `long chan;`

ARGUMENTS

    chan   a channel number obtained from a previous call to `mps_open_chan`.

DESCRIPTION

    The `mps_get_tid` function is used by users of the message handler to allocate transaction ids.

RETURN VALUE

    If no free transaction ids are available for the associated port id, or when *chan* is an invalid channel number, 0 (zero) is returned; otherwise the allocated transaction id is returned.

LEVEL

    Base or Interrupt

SEE ALSO

    `mps_open_chan`(D3D), `mps_free_tid`(D3D)

NAME

mps_get_unsoldata – copies user data from the message buffer.

SYNOPSIS

```
#include <sys/mps.h>
void mps_get_unsoldata(mbp, dptr, count)
mps_msgbuf_t          mbp;
unsigned char         *dptr;
unsigned long         count;
```

ARGUMENTS

mbp   pointer to message buffer

dptr   pointer to user data

count number of bytes to transfer (Max 20)

DESCRIPTION

The **mps_get_unsoldata** function copies count bytes of data from the message buffer *mbp* to *dptr*. It is used to retrieve user data from an unsolicited message. A maximum of 20 bytes of user data can be copied.

RETURN VALUE

None

LEVEL

Base or Interrupt

SEE ALSO

mps_get_soldata(D3D)

NAME

mps_mk_bgrant – construct a buffer grant in response to a buffer request.

SYNOPSIS

```
#include <sys/mps.h>
void mps_mk_bgrant(mbp, dsocid, lid, count)
mps_msgbuf_t        mbp;
mb2socid_t          dscocid;
unsigned char       lid;
unsigned long       count;
```

ARGUMENTS

mbp	pointer to message buffer
dsocid	32-bit destination socket id (host id:port id)
lid	liaison id
count	number of bytes to transfer

DESCRIPTION

The **mps_mk_bgrant** function is used to construct a buffer grant in response to a buffer request. Arguments to this function are not checked for valid values.

RETURN VALUE

None

LEVEL

Base or Interrupt

SEE ALSO

mps_mk_unsolrply(D3D)

NAME

mps_mk_brdcst – constructs a broadcast message to be sent.

SYNOPSIS

```
#include <sys/mps.h>
void mps_mk_brdcst(mbp, dpid, dptr, count)
mps_msgbuf_t        *mbp;
unsigned short          dpid;
unsigned char       *dptr;
unsigned long       count;
```

ARGUMENTS

mbp   pointer to message buffer

dpid   16-bit destination port id

dptr   pointer to user data to be sent with the message

count   number of bytes of user data to be sent with message (Max 20)

DESCRIPTION

The mps_mk_brdcst function takes a pointer to a message buffer and constructs a broadcast message to be sent. The message is constructed from the values passed as arguments. Arguments to this function are not checked for valid values.

RETURN VALUE

None

LEVEL

Base or Interrupt

NAME

mps_mk_breject – construct a buffer reject in response to a buffer request.

SYNOPSIS

```
#include <sys/mps.h>
void mps_mk_breject(mbp, dsocid, lid)
mps_msgbuf_t          mbp;
mb2socid_t            dscocid;
unsigned char         lid;
```

ARGUMENTS

mbp   pointer to message buffer

dsocid   32-bit destination socket id (host id:port id)

lid   liaison id

DESCRIPTION

The **mps_mk_breject** function is used to construct a buffer reject in response to a buffer request. Arguments to this function are not checked for valid values.

RETURN VALUE

None

LEVEL

Base or Interrupt

NAME

mps_mk_sol – constructs a message to be sent to initiate a solicited data transfer.

SYNOPSIS

```
#include <sys/mps.h>
void mps_mk_sol(mbp, dsocid, tid, dptr, count)
mps_msgbuf_t          mbp;
mb2socid_t            dsocid;
unsigned char         tid;
unsigned char         *dptr;
unsigned long         count;
```

ARGUMENTS

mbp   pointer to message buffer

dsocid   32-bit destination socket id (host id:port id)

tid   8-bit transaction id

dptr   pointer to user data to be sent with the message

count   number of bytes of user data to be sent with the message (Max 16)

DESCRIPTION

The **mps_mk_sol** function takes a pointer to a message buffer and constructs a message to be sent to initiate a solicited data transfer. The message is constructed using values supplied as arguments. If the solicited data transfer is not part of a request-response transaction, *tid* should be set to 0 (zero). Arguments to this function are not checked for valid values.

RETURN VALUE

None

LEVEL

Base or Interrupt

SEE ALSO

mps_mk_unsol(D3D)

NAME

mps_mk_solrply – constructs a message to be sent to initiate a solicited data reply.

SYNOPSIS

```
#include <sys/mps.h>
void mps_mk_solrply(mbp, dsocid, tid, dptr, count, eotflag)
mps_msgbuf_t        mbp;
mb2socid_t          dscocid;
unsigned char       tid;
unsigned char       *dptr;
unsigned long       count;
unsigned char       eotflag;
```

ARGUMENTS

mbp	pointer to message buffer
dsocid	32-bit destination socket id (host id:port id)
tid	8-bit transaction id
dptr	pointer to user data to be sent with the message
count	number of bytes of user data to be sent with the message (Max 16)
eotflag	1 to indicate end of transaction; otherwise, 0 (zero)

DESCRIPTION

The **mps_mk_solrply** function takes a pointer to a message buffer and constructs a message to be sent to initiate a solicited data reply. The message is constructed using values supplied as arguments. Arguments to this function are not checked for valid values.

RETURN VALUE

None

LEVEL

Base or Interrupt

SEE ALSO

mps_mk_unsolrply(D3D)

NAME
  mps_mk_unsol – constructs an unsolicited message to be sent.

SYNOPSIS
```
#include <sys/mps.h>
void mps_mk_unsol(mbp, dsocid, tid, dptr, count)
mps_msgbuf_t          *mbp;
mb2socid_t            dscocid;
unsigned char         tid;
unsigned char         *dptr;
unsigned long         count;
```

ARGUMENTS
  mbp   pointer to message buffer

  dsocid 32-bit destination socket id (host id:port id)

  tid   8-bit transaction id

  dptr   pointer to user data to be sent with the message

  count number of bytes of user data to be sent with message (Max 20)

DESCRIPTION
  The **mps_mk_unsol** function takes a pointer to a message buffer and constructs an unsolicited message to be sent. The message is constructed from the values passed as arguments. Arguments to this function are not checked for valid values. When this message is not part of a request-response transaction, *tid* should be set to 0 (zero).

RETURN VALUE
  None

LEVEL
  Base or Interrupt

SEE ALSO
  mps_mk_sol(D3D)

NAME

mps_mk_unsolrply – constructs a unsolicited reply message to be sent.

SYNOPSIS

```
#include <sys/mps.h>
void mps_mk_unsolrply(mbp, dsocid, tid, dptr, count)
mps_msgbuf_t        mbp;
mb2socid_t          dscocid;
unsigned char       tid;
unsigned char       *dptr;
unsigned long       count;
```

ARGUMENTS

mbp	pointer to message buffer
dsocid	32-bit destination socket id (host id:port id)
tid	8-bit transaction id
dptr	pointer to user data to be sent with the message
count	number of bytes of user data to be sent with the message (Max 20)

DESCRIPTION

The **mps_mk_unsolrply** function takes a pointer to a message buffer and constructs a unsolicited reply message to be sent. The message is constructed using values supplied as arguments. Arguments to this function are not checked for valid values.

RETURN VALUE

None

LEVEL

Base or Interrupt

SEE ALSO

mps_mk_solrply(D3D)

NAME

mps_msg: mps_msg_getsrcmid, mps_msg_getmsgtyp, mps_msg_getbrlen, mps_msg_getreqid, mps_msg_getlsnid, mps_msg_getsrcpid, mps_msg_gettrnsid, mps_msg_getudp, mps_msg_iscancel, mps_msg_iseot, mps_msg_iserror, mps_msg_iscompletion, mps_msg_isreq – macros used to decode message handler message

SYNOPSIS

#include <sys/mps.h>

DESCRIPTION

These macros are used to decode messages from the message handler. Each macro takes as its argument a pointer to the message buffer to be decoded. The following is a description of each macro and its return value.

MACRO	RETURN VALUE
mps_msg_getsrcmid get source message id	8-bit unsigned
mps_msg_getmsgtyp get message type	MG_UNSOL, MG_BRDCST, MG_BREQ, MG_BREJ
mps_msg_getbrlen data length in a buf request msg	32-bit
mps_msg_getreqid get request id	8-bit unsigned
mps_msg_getlsnid get liaison id	8-bit unsigned
mps_msg_getsrcpid get source port id	16-bit unsigned
mps_msg_gettrnsid get transaction id	8-bit unsigned
mps_msg_getudp get user data portion of msg buf	32-bit char pointer
mps_msg_iscancel is this a cancel message?	1 if cancel message, otherwise 0 (zero)
mps_msg_iseot is this an EOT message?	1 if end of transaction, otherwise 0 (zero)
mps_msg_iserror is this an error message?	1 if error message, otherwise 0 (zero)
mps_msg_iscompletion is this a completion message?	1 if completion message, otherwise 0 (zero)
mps_msg_isreq is this a request phase message?	1 if request phase, otherwise 0 (zero)

RETURN VALUE
        Listed above.
LEVEL
        Base or Interrupt

NAME

mps_open_chan – opens a channel

SYNOPSIS

```
#include <sys/mps.h>
long mps_open_chan (portid, intr, priolev)
unsigned short portid;
(void) (*intr() );
unsigned short priolev;
```

ARGUMENTS

portid   Port ID of a local port.

intr   Pointer to a function that is invoked for every incoming unsolicited message for the port specified by *portid*. A pointer to the message buffer containing the incoming message buffer is passed to intr as an argument. If *intr* is NULL, all incoming unsolicited messages are discarded and all incoming request messages belonging to a request-response transaction result in a transaction cancel being sent to the originating socket. If the message handler encounters an error on a message transmission, the function pointed to by *intr* is invoked with the erroneous message as an argument. If *intr* is NULL, all error messages are ignored.

priolev   Specifies the priority level at which the *intr* routines are executed. *priolev* should be set to **MPS_SRLPRIO** for serial I/O drivers, **MPS_BLKPRIO** for block I/O drivers, and **MPS_NRMPRIO** for all other uses of the message handler. These are the only valid values allowed for *priolev*.

DESCRIPTION

A call to **mps_open_chan** is required before any message operations can be done on a port. **mps_open_chan** is synchronous in operation. To open a channel a device driver must identify three parameters: a port, an interrupt handler routine, and an interrupt priority level, as described above.

Message buffers passed to *intr* routines are assumed to be allocated to the handler for that port. It is the responsibility of the *intr* routines to free the message buffers it receives from the message handler.

RETURN VALUE

When **mps_open_chan** is successful, a channel number is returned that is to be used in requests for message services. When **mps_open_chan** fails, -1 is returned.

LEVEL

Base or Interrupt

SEE ALSO

mps_close_chan(D3D)